ARTHUR J. RAY

Indians in the Fur Trade: their role as trappers, hunters, and middlemen in the lands southwest of Hudson Bay

1660-1870

UNIVERSITY OF TORONTO PRESS

Toronto and Buffalo

© University of Toronto Press 1974
Toronto and Buffalo
Printed in Canada
Reprinted 1976, 1983, 1988, 1991

ISBN 0-8020-2118-2 (cloth)
ISBN 0-8020-6226-1 (paper)

Canadian Cataloguing in Publication Data
Ray, Arthur J., 1941–
  Indians in the fur trade
  Bibliography: p.
  Includes index.
  ISBN 0-8020-2118-2 (bound)   ISBN 0-8020-6226-1 (pbk.)
  1. Indians of North America – Canada, Western –
  Economic conditions. 2. Fur trade – Canada,
  Western – History. I. Title.
  E78.C2R39 1974   380.1'439   C75-001103-3

INDIANS IN THE FUR TRADE

To Carolyn

Contents

ILLUSTRATIONS / ix

PREFACE / xi

1
Trade rivalries, inter-tribal warfare, and migration / 3

2
Land and life in the western interior before 1763 / 27

3
Traders and middlemen / 51

4
Arms, brandy, beads, and sundries / 72

5
Migrations, epidemics, and population changes, 1763–1821 / 94

6
The destruction of fur and game animals / 117

7
New economic opportunities / 125

viii Contents

8
Economic dependency and the fur trade: contrasting trends / 137

9
Land and life: a changing mosaic / 166

10
The changing demographic picture after 1821 / 182

11
Declining opportunities in a changing fur trade / 195

12
End of a way of life / 217

BIBLIOGRAPHY / 232

INDEX / 243

Illustrations

1 Cultural geography of Northern Ontario and Manitoba to 1690 / 5
2 Physiography / 7
3 A section from the map 'Tabula Novae Franciae,' by Father du Creux, 1660 / 8
4 A section from Jean-Baptiste Franquelin's map, 'Partie de l'Amerique septentrionalle, 1699' / 9
5 A section from P. Coronelli's map, 'Partie occidentale du Canada ou de la Nouvelle France, 1688' / 10
6 Canoe routes of the western interior of Canada / 15
7 A section from Joseph La France's map, 'New Map of Part of North America, 1739–1742,' / 17
8 Distribution of Indians trading at York Factory, 1714–17 / 20
9 Tribal distributions, ca. 1765 / 22
10 Distribution of vegetation / 28
11 Range limits of important game species / 29
12 Distribution of wild rice / 30
13 The yearly cycle of the bison in the parkland–grassland area / 33
14 Break-up and freeze-up dates / 42
15 Parkland exploitation cycles / 47
16 Volume of furs traded at York Factory, Fort Albany, and Fort Churchill / 52
17 The western fur trade, ca. 1700–20 / 54
18 The western fur trade, ca. 1750 / 56
19 York Factory trade receipts / 58

20 Origin of canoe traffic at York Factory, 1756–61 / 62

21 Hudson's Bay Company fur trade / 64

22 York Factory trade in guns and gun powder, 1689–1780 / 74

23 York Factory trade in ammunition, 1689–1780 / 76

24 Composition of the gun trade at Fort Albany and York Factory / 77

25 York Factory trade in blankets and beads, 1719–80 / 80

26 York Factory trade in yard goods, 1719–80 / 82

27 York Factory trade in hatchets and kettles, 1719–80 / 83

28 York Factory trade in knives, ice chisels, and files, 1719–80 / 84

29 York Factory trade in luxury goods, 1719–80 / 86

30 Distribution of the Assiniboine in 1808 according to Alexander Henry the Younger / 95

31 Distribution of the Assiniboine, ca. 1821 / 97

32 Distribution of the Cree, 1790–1821 / 100

33 Tribal distributions in 1821 / 101

34 A section from Alexander Henry the Elder's map, 'The North West Parts of America,' 1775 / 103

35 Smallpox epidemic of 1780–1 / 107

36 Fur trading districts of the Hudson's Bay Company / 109

37 Analysis of Peter Fidler's estimate of population for the Red River area in 1815 / 112

38 Fur trading posts, 1763–1821 / 127

39 Fur trade provision supply network in the early nineteenth century / 129

40 Mean daily January temperatures / 160

41 Vegetation cross-sections / 176

42 Tribal distributions in 1860 / 184

43 Distribution of the Western Cree, 1857–60 / 186

44 Smallpox epidemic, 1837–8 / 189

45 Trading posts, 1821–70 / 201

46 Indian land cessions, 1871–7 / 229

Preface

The fur trade was the most pervasive force influencing the economic and political development of Western Canada between 1660 and 1870. During this period it operated as an integrating force between Indians and Europeans. To be successfully prosecuted, the fur trade required the cooperation of both parties. In the broadest sense, it was a partnership for the exploitation of resources. Although it was not an equal partnership, nor one in which the same group always held the upper hand, at no time before 1870 would it have served the interests of one party to destroy the other since by doing so the aggressors would have been deprived of their supplies of goods, or furs and provisions. It is not surprising therefore that peace prevailed between Indians and Europeans in the western interior of Canada prior to 1870.

Yet, although it was a time of peaceful relations between settlers, traders, and Indians, it was a time of cultural change for the Indians. The various Indian groups were continually adjusting to the transformations of their environmental and cultural surroundings which were underway. This book deals with some of the adaptive responses that were made by the Indians living in the central and southern portions of Manitoba and Saskatchewan. Attention is focused on the ways in which different Indian groups perceived and responded to the varying opportunities which the fur trade offered to them. In particular, detailed consideration is given to the different roles that key Indian groups played in the fur trade and to the implications that this role differentiation had for tribal migration, inter-tribal relations, material culture changes, and ecological adaptations. With respect to the latter, the implications that the progressive deterioration of the resource base had for culture change are also discussed.

I would like to thank professors C.A. Bishop of the State University of New York, Oswego, D. W. Moodie of the University of Manitoba, John Warkentin and Conrade E. Heidenreich of York University, and David Baerreis, James Stoltman, and William M. Denevan of the University of Wisconsin, for the valuable assistance which they gave me while I was conducting the research for this manuscript. Their comments on the preliminary draft were also greatly appreciated. I would like to extend special thanks to Professor Andrew H. Clark for the encouragement which he gave me from the inception of this project to its final completion; his numerous suggestions and criticisms have been extremely helpful. The author is, of course, responsible for this study.

I would like to thank the Hudson's Bay Company for giving me permission to consult and quote from their microfilm collection on deposit in the Public Archives of Canada, Ottawa. Without their kind cooperation it would not have been possible to carry this project through to completion. The assistance of the friendly and helpful staff at the Public Archives of Canada is also greatly appreciated.

I would like to thank the Graduate School and Department of Geography of the University of Wisconsin for the grants which they made available to me to help defray travel and research expenses incurred during the early phases of this project. The financial assistance which the York University Minor Research Grants Committee provided for later research into material culture change and the Canada Council provided for historical population study are also greatly appreciated.

Finally, the author would like to thank Ms. H. Guzewska and the staff of the cartographic laboratory of York University for drafting the final diagrams, figures, and maps, and York University's Secretarial Services for typing the manuscript.

This book has been published with the help of a grant from the Social Science Research Council of Canada, using funds provided by the Canada Council.

York University
August 1973

INDIANS IN THE FUR TRADE

1

Trade rivalries, inter-tribal warfare, and migration

Throughout most of the historical period, the Siouan-speaking Assiniboine and the Algonquian-speaking Western Cree Indians were the principal inhabitants of central and southern Manitoba and Saskatchewan, and they figured prominently in the fur trade of the Canadian West. Yet, archaeological and historical data indicate that these two groups were probably late immigrants to the area.

In northern Minnesota and the adjacent portions of Manitoba and Ontario, archaeologists have identified three proto-historic foci which they have termed Blackduck, Manitoba, and Selkirk.[1] The first two of these assemblages are culturally synonymous and have been tentatively associated with the proto-historic Assiniboine, albeit with some dispute.[2] The Selkirk material, on the other hand, is generally thought to be of Cree origin.[3] Figure 1 shows the distribution of Blackduck sites. It reveals that the greatest density of sites occurs in the territory lying between the northwest shore of Lake Superior and the lower Red River–southern Winnipeg River area. The oldest sites, some dating back to ca. 1200 AD, are found in this country. Farther to the northwest, the sites are fewer in number and of a more recent date, with the Tailrace Bay site on the lower Saskatchewan River and the MacBride site on Southern Indian Lake containing historic trade goods.[4]

The western and southern limits of the distribution of Selkirk sites correspond, as expected, with the northern and northeastern margin of the area outlined above, with a considerable mixture of Blackduck and Selkirk materials occurring in border sections, such as along the southwestern margins of the laurentian shield. Of considerable importance, the stratigraphic sequences of many of the boreal and mixed-forest sites of Manitoba show that beginning about 1400 the Selkirk material replaces the underlying Blackduck culture, suggesting that a westward push of population out of the shield may have begun long before the disturbing influences of the European intrusion into the continent were felt. In the grassland area, the Selkirk culture did not appear for another 150 years, becoming first evident at Pelican Lake, northeast of Turtle Mountain, by 1550 (Figure 2). However, in this environment the Selkirk culture never replaced the Blackduck cultural assemblage.[5]

On the basis of this archaeological data it would appear that, just prior to contact, the Assiniboine occupied the boundary-waters area between Minnesota and Ontario as well as a large portion of south-central Manitoba. Their neighbours to the north and east were the Cree with whom they had a considerable amount of contact, judging from the mixture of Cree and Blackduck material in many of the late archaeological sites.

INITIAL EUROPEAN CONTACTS

The first documentary references to the Assiniboine appear in the Jesuit *Relations* of 1640;[6] however, no specific information is given regarding their location or their relationship to their close relatives, the Yankton Sioux, from whom they separated some time during the very early historic period. The timing and reason for this break are difficult to determine. David Thompson reported in 1797: 'From their own accounts [Assiniboine], some forty or fifty years ago a feud broke out, and several were killed and wounded on both sides; about five hundred Tents separated from the main body, and took up their hunting grounds on the Red River and the Plains stretching northwestward along the right bank of the Saskatchewan River to within 300 miles of the Mountains.'[7] If this story is correct, the separation occurred sometime between 1747 and 1757; but the story seems to have been an old one and roughly equivalent versions were related to the Europeans earlier and appear in journals less well known than Thompson's. For instance, M. de la Chauvignerie's 1736 enumeration of the Indians of Canada indicated that the Assiniboine 'vie with the Sioux from whom they formerly sprung.'[8] An earlier memoir, that of M. le Chevalier de Beaurain written in 1702 and dealing with Louisiana, suggested on the basis of Indian information that the splitting of the two groups had occurred after the Hudson's Bay Company was established on Hudson Bay in 1670. According to this version of the story, the company provided the Cree with access to a plentiful supply of arms,

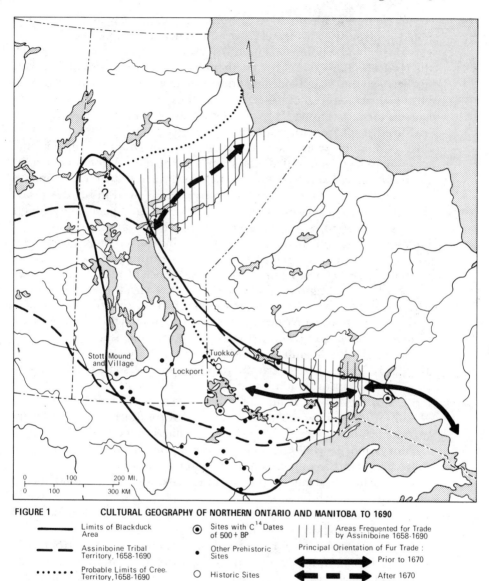

FIGURE 1   **CULTURAL GEOGRAPHY OF NORTHERN ONTARIO AND MANITOBA TO 1690**

——— Limits of Blackduck Area	⊙ Sites with C¹⁴ Dates of 500 + BP	‖‖‖ Areas Frequented for Trade by Assiniboine 1658-1690
– – – Assiniboine Tribal Territory, 1658-1690	• Other Prehistoric Sites	Principal Orientation of Fur Trade :
•••••• Probable Limits of Cree Territory,1658-1690	○ Historic Sites	⟵⟶ Prior to 1670 ⟵ ⟶ After 1670

making them formidable foes to their Siouan enemies. The Assiniboine were said to have sued for peace with the Cree and as a consequence became the enemies of the rest of the Sioux.[9]

Although this last account of the breakaway seems quite plausible, the

Assiniboine were identified as a distinct group as early as 1640, as was noted previously. This is nearly a hundred years before the date suggested by David Thompson and thirty years before the establishment of the Hudson's Bay Company. Whether or not open hostilities had broken out between the Assiniboine and other Siouan groups by 1640 will probably remain a mystery, but it is certain that the division had occurred by the late seventeenth century. Perhaps for a time prior to 1670 the Assiniboine had lived in peace with other Siouan bands to the south and yet had differed enough from them, either in terms of culture or geographic location, to be recognized as a separate tribe by their Algonquian neighbours. Or, more likely, the Assiniboine may have develped trade contacts with other Algonquian groups and consequently lived in relative peace with them. As hostilities intensified between Algonquian and Siouan groups after 1670, when the English fur trade began to push into the interior, the Assiniboine then may very well have allied themselves to the Cree, as the Indians suggested, because of the growing military superiority that the latter group gained as a consequence of their more reliable supply of goods (English rather than French). Such a theory may explain why the Indians attributed the outbreak of the Assiniboine-Sioux hostilities to the English intrusion in the Bay, even though the tribe appeared as an identifiable group before the English were established.

Although the Assiniboine are mentioned in the Jesuit *Relations* of 1640, it is not until 1658 that the *Relations* provide some specific, albeit fragmentary, information regarding the tribe's location: 'thirty-five leagues or thereabout from Lake Alimibeg [Lake Nipigon] is called the Nation of the Assinipoualak or "Warriors of the Rock."'[10] Considering that the league was a rough time-distance measurement (the amount of territory canoeists could travel in an hour, approximately three miles), it follows from this account that the Assiniboine lived some one or two days' travel, or a hundred miles to the west of Lake Nipigon. This would put the eastern limit of their territory somewhere in the vicinity of the Pigeon and Kamanistiquia rivers on the northwest shore of Lake Superior and Sturgeon Lake in northern Ontario.[11]

Supporting evidence for this conclusion can be found in cartographic record. In 1660, Father François du Creux drafted a map entitled 'Tabula Novae Franciae,' which included the region north of Lake Superior (Figure 3). De Creux's map is the first French map that shows Lac Alembegyeci [Lake Nipigon] and three connecting rivers, the Assinipoualacus, the Kilistonum, and the Eitayikytchidyanus to the north of Lake Superior. The map was based on a report filed by Father Gabriel Druillettes in

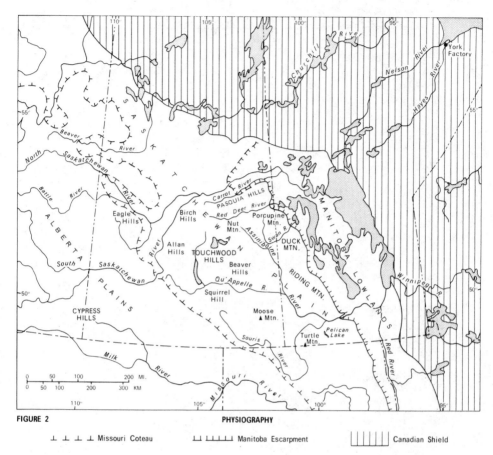

FIGURE 2   PHYSIOGRAPHY

⊥ ⊥ ⊥ ⊥ Missouri Coteau   ⊔ ⊔⊔⊔⊔ Manitoba Escarpment |||||| Canadian Shield

Sources: Atlases of Manitoba, Saskatchewan and Alberta.

1657–8, which dealt with the different canoe routes that led from Canada down to Hudson Bay. Druillettes had obtained this information from Radisson and Grosseilliers, and it originally included a map that has since been lost.[12] The Eitayikytchidyanus River on the du Creux map represented the Ogoki-Albany river route to James Bay and the Kilistonum River was the present Nipigon River.[13]

The identity of the Assinipoualacus River [Assiniboine] is more difficult to establish with certainty. A strong case can be made that this river was a confused rendering of either the Pigeon River canoe route to the northwest or perhaps the English River route. The former seems the

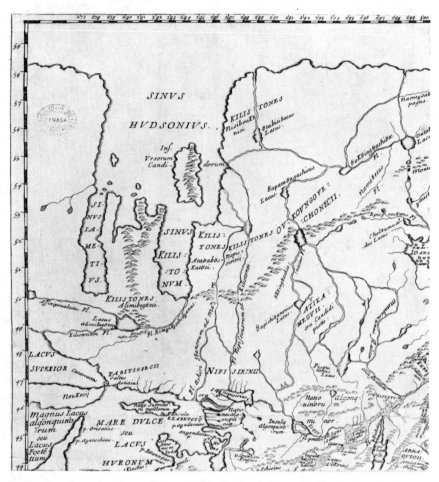

FIGURE 3   A section from the map 'Tabula Novae Franciae' by Father du Creux,
1660 (copy in Public Archives of Canada)

most likely since the Pigeon River was shown as the River Assinipoualacus
on later French maps such as those of Franquelin and Coronelli (Figures 4
and 5).[14] The river was probably given this name because it was one of the
key routes which led to the Assiniboine country, and the Assiniboine were
said to live along its course. The mistaken connection of this river to Lake
Nipigon on the du Creux map was undoubtedly due to the fact that the
Assiniboine travelled to the latter lake via the Pigeon River, Lake

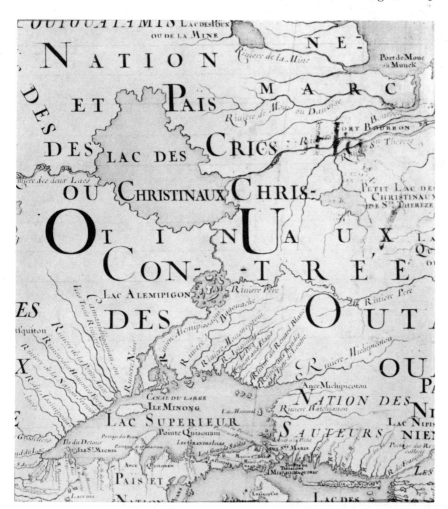

FIGURE 4   A section from Jean-Baptiste Franquelin's map, 'Partie de l'Amérique septentrionalle, 1699' (copy in Public Archives of Canada)

Superior, and the Nipigon River. From Lake Nipigon, they could also reach James Bay via the Ogoki-Albany river system. It was not until Father Allouez visited the Nipigon River in 1667 that the French obtained a first-hand account of the geography of the northwestern shore of Lake Superior. On the basis of Allouez's information and that gathered by Father Dablon the Jesuits were able to establish a clear picture of the

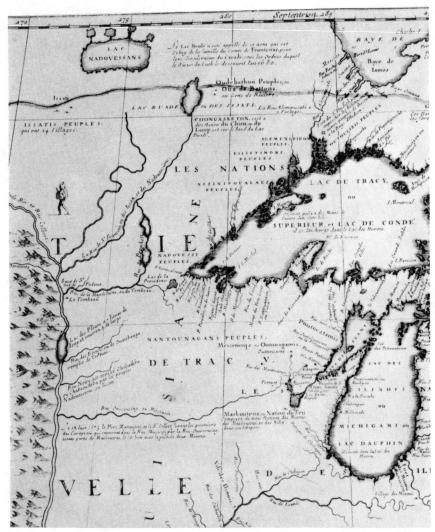

FIGURE 5 A section from P. Coronelli's map, 'Partie occidentale du Canada ou de la Nouvelle France, 1688' (copy in Public Archives of Canada)

distribution of the above waterways, as is evident on the Jesuit map of Lake Superior produced in 1670–1. Thereafter, the Assinipoualacus River is shown flowing into Lake Superior (Figures 4 and 5).[15]

Thus, du Creux's map of 1660 and the Jesuit *Relations* of 1657–8 indicate that the Assiniboine lived some three days or one hundred miles to the west of Lake Nipigon, probably along the lower Pigeon River. Furthermore, they were frequent visitors to the northwestern shore of Lake Superior and to Lake Nipigon.

The first direct French contact with the Assiniboine was made in this same general area in 1678, when Daniel Greysolon, Sieur du Lhut, met them there and attempted to arrange peace between them and their Siouan relatives to the south. Six years later, in 1684, he built a post on Lake Nipigon in order to trade with the Assiniboine and their Cree allies and thereby divert them from the English posts that had been established on Hudson Bay.[16] In 1685, Governor Jacques René de Brisaye, Marquis de Denonville, stressed the need to intensify these efforts since he was aware that the Assiniboine were one of the primary supplies of furs to other Algonquian groups who were tied into the Ottawa-Indian-French trading system.[17] According to another memoir of Denonville, written two years later in 1687, du Lhut's efforts at Lake Nipigon were successful and he traded with more than 1500 Indians.[18] Thus, du Lhut's choice of Lake Nipigon as a location for a post was strategically sound, partly because it lay on one of the major canoe routes which the Assiniboine and Cree groups used to travel down to the Bay, and partly because it was a key trade contact area between the Assiniboine and eastern Algonquian groups.

All of these contacts with the Assiniboine were made along the eastern margins of their territory and, consequently, provided no precise information regarding their locations inland from Lake Superior. Indeed, such information is very fragmentary and consists of only a few observations which were made by Father Louis Hennepin, Jacques de Noyon, and Henry Kelsey. Yet, because they were all made within a ten-year period they do provide us with a reasonably good idea of the extent of the area that the group occupied at that time. In 1680, Father Hennepin was living in captivity among the Sioux near Mille Lacs Lake, Minnesota, and while there he reported that Indian visitors arrived from the West, and told him that 'the Nation of the Assenipoulacus ... lie North East of the Issati [Eastern Sioux] ... not above six or seven Days' Journey from us.'[19] This description would locate the Assiniboine in the vicinity of Rainy Lake. About eight years later, in 1688, Jacques de Noyon travelled from Kaministikwa to Lake of the Woods and met the Assiniboine and Cree in the vicinity of Rainy Lake. He reported that the latter lake was called 'Lac des Cristinaux,' and Lake of the Woods 'Lac des Assiniboils.'[20] The Assiniboine were still resident in the area of Rainy Lake as late as 1696 and a letter, dated 10 October 1731, from Beauharnois and the Intendant Giles Hocquart stated that the Lake of the Woods was still called 'Lac des Assiniboins' but cautioned against assuming that it was the only lake around which this tribe lived.[21]

Beyond the northern Ontario region, the only information regarding the western margin of the Assiniboine territory is the observations made by Henry Kelsey on his expedition from York Factory to the Touchwood Hills region of Saskatchewan in 1690–1. His journal makes it clear that the Assiniboine occupied the land along the Carrot River and southward as far as the Touchwood Hills (Figure 2.).[22] This probably marked the western limits of their territory since the Gros Ventre held the upper Qu'Appelle valley and the lower South Saskatchewan River at that time.[23] In short, the documentary evidence indicates that in the late seventeenth century the tribal territory of the Assiniboine reached from the vicinity of Rainy Lake on the southeast to central Saskatchewan on the northwest. In addition to occupying this vast territory, they were frequent visitors to the Lake Superior and Lake Nipigon areas as well as to northeastern Manitoba where they traded at York Factory after 1670 (Figure 2). According to Radisson, over four hundred Assiniboine came to the latter post in 1684.[24] The post was reached by the Churchill, Nelson, and Hayes rivers.

The information regarding the location of the Western Cree during this early period is even more sketchy than that for the Assiniboine. The Jesuit *Relations* of 1658 suggest that the tribe was centred in the region between James Bay and Lake Nipigon. The westernmost Cree tribal group which the Jesuits identified at that time were the Alimbegouek (Nipigon), who lived around Lake Nipigon.[25] Thirty years later, in 1688, Jacques de Noyon encountered them as far to the southwest as Rainy Lake, while to the northwest Kelsey's journals indicate that their territory included all of the forest region between the lower Nelson River and the lower Saskatchewan River.[26] In brief, the initial contacts with the westernmost Cree groups suggest that they bordered on the Assiniboine territories throughout northern Ontario and Manitoba. Of considerable significance, the record also shows that the two groups were living together rather peacefully.

THE EARLY HUDSON'S BAY COMPANY TRADE PERIOD

Prior to the establishment of the Hudson's Bay Company in 1670, the Assiniboine and Western Cree had been linked to the Ottawa-Indian-French trading network. As has been noted, they were said to be among the most important suppliers of furs to that network during the middle of the seventeenth century. Under these circumstances, it seems reasonable to suppose that the general effect of the fur trade on the distribution of these two groups would have been to draw them toward the east, particularly to the Lake Nipigon region. There, the Assiniboine and Western Cree trappers exchanged their furs for goods that Indian middlemen brought from the East.

The construction of posts on Hudson Bay after 1670 favoured a more northwesterly movement of the Assiniboine and their Cree allies, especially after the 1680s when these two groups began to take over the role of middlemen in a trade that was increasingly oriented toward York Factory – the most important post on the Bay. The assumption of this new role was facilitated in large part by the fact that their early historic occupation of the lower Nelson River basin placed them in a strategically advantageous position to control the trade of the largest and probably most densely populated river system that drained into Hudson Bay. As Figure 6 shows, nearly all of the major canoe routes leading to York Factory pass through central Manitoba and converge on Split Lake. Any inland group coming to trade thus had to pass through Assiniboine and Cree territory.

The large steady supply of arms and ammunition which the Assiniboine and Cree were able to obtain at York Factory permitted them to exploit this initial locational advantage. At an early date they began sending major trading expeditions to York Factory. In 1684 the French reported that 300 canoes went to the Bay to trade and most of them were manned by Assiniboine and Cree. Based on James Isham's later observations, the total number of men involved would have been approximately 750.[27] The total number of guns that were being traded at that time was probably about 420 a year, judging from the volume of sales between 1689 and 1694 when nearly the same number of canoes were coming to the post.[28] Considering that tribal populations in this territory averaged three to six times the total number of adult males, it would appear that as many as 400 firearms a year per population of 3400 were distributed – one for every seven persons.[29]

The rate at which the number of serviceable firearms increased is more difficult to estimate, but it was undoubtedly much less. The length of time an Indian could use a firearm was short in the late seventeenth century because the guns were of poor quality and because the Indians lacked the technological capabilities to maintain or repair them. Assuming that the average life of a gun was three years, the total number of usable weapons which would have been available to the Indians trading at York

Factory in any one year would have been approximately 340, or nearly one gun for every four persons.[30] Being well-armed, the Assiniboine and Cree had a decided military advantage over their neighbours, the Dakota Sioux to the south, the Gros Ventres and Blackfoot to the southwest, and the Chipewyan to the north who lacked this direct and steady source of supply.

As noted earlier, the oral traditions of the Indians suggest that the arming of the Cree and Assiniboine was responsible for the severing of relations between the Assiniboine and the Dakota Sioux. Whether or not this was the case, the historical record clearly indicates that the Assiniboine and Cree were allied against the Dakota Sioux and that warfare between them was almost incessant throughout the period from 1670 to 1870. Initially, the French attempted to arrange peace between the two groups, du Lhut's efforts of 1678 on the northwest shores of Lake Superior being among the first, but they failed. In 1717, Zacharie Robute de la Noue built a small post on Rainy Lake, and he reported that through warfare the Sioux had taken control over most of the Rainy Lake – Lake of the Woods area and were raiding as far northeast as Kaministikwia.[31] Their occupancy was temporary, however, since the Cree and Ojibwa held the area at the time La Vérendrye penetrated the Northwest in the 1730s.

Although they had initially attempted to bring peace to this area, the French subsequently tried to exploit the situation in the hope of disrupting the Hudson's Bay Company trade at York Factory. They used the Dakota Sioux to attack the flanks of the Hudson's Bay Company trade network in a manner similar to the way in which the English had used the Iroquois against the French in the East. By the late 1720s, the raids of the Sioux were having a serious effect on the trade at York Factory; for example, it was reported in the Post Journal of 1729 that:

the said Senipoetts [Assiniboine] are gone to Churchill this Summer to trade which we are glad to hear of the Same we being informed the 1st this Summer that the ... Poetts [Sioux] had Destroyed most of our Senipoetts by the Instigation of the french[.] It is much to be wished for that our masters Could prevent the frenches constant Encouraging the Above Said poetts going to warr with most of the Indians that Resorts to this place. Likewise with those that goes to Albany Fort[.] we have Been In formed by most of the upland Indians this Summer that 8 French wood Runners went to warrs Last Summer with the poetts against our Sinepoetts with a design to Destroy them or force them to trade with them.[32]

It appears that the raids of the Sioux reached their maximum northward

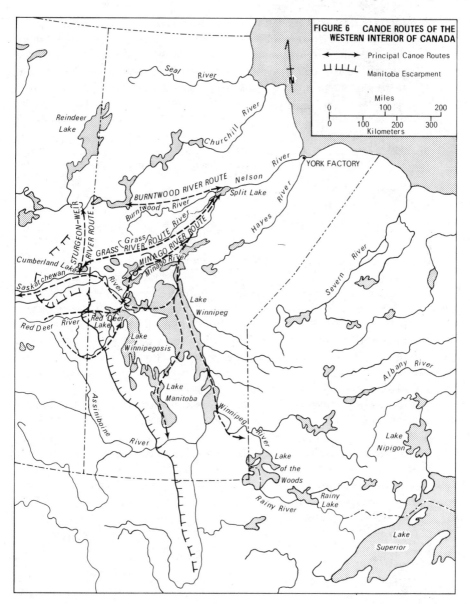

FIGURE 6   CANOE ROUTES OF THE WESTERN INTERIOR OF CANADA

penetration in 1728, judging from another entry in the York Factory Journal dated 12 June 1729: 'I understand by severall of our home Indians [Cree] that last summer the poetts went to warrs with our

Senipoetts and drove our Senipoetts As farr as the Head of the Churchill River.'[33] With these turbulent conditions along their southern frontier and an increasing involvement in the Hudson's Bay Company trade, the Assiniboine began a more rapid movement toward the Northwest. By the 1730s, they had abandoned the southeastern portion of their early historic homelands along the Rainy River east of Lake of the Woods. This relocation of their population was indicated by information which La Vérendrye received from a band of Indians who had visited Lake Winnipeg in 1730 and in the course of their voyage, had encountered many Assiniboine living along the Winnipeg River.[34] Also, as late as 1731, the Lake of the Woods was still referred to as Lake of the Assiniboine;[35] however, when La Vérendrye actually reached the lake in 1733, he encountered few Assiniboine. During his first year's residence on the lake, he commented, 'We are with the Cree and near the Assiniboin. None of them has yet come to the Fort as they have in some way been made afraid of us.'[36] This fear, in all probability, was caused by the recent alliances the French had had with the Sioux. What La Vérendrye meant by 'near' is unclear, but the inference is that no Assiniboine were living on the lake at that time and his only contact with the group was limited to occasional trading parties. Furthermore, when he made his journey to the Missouri River in 1739 he did not encounter any of their villages until reaching the Portage La Prairie area of Manitoba to the south of Lake Manitoba (Figure 2). This has led some scholars to infer that the tribe had abandoned all of eastern Manitoba by the 1730s.[37]

Other evidence from La Vérendrye, as well as from Arthur Dobbs and James Isham, suggests quite a different conclusion. For instance, in 1737 La Vérendrye travelled overland from Lake of the Woods to Fort Maurepas, then located on the lower Red River, where he met with a group of Cree and Assiniboine to discuss the building of additional posts. In the course of the conversations an Assiniboine chief told him that if he would build a post at the forks of the Red River (the confluence of the Red and Assiniboine rivers) his tribe would establish a permanent village there to support it. Clearly the tribe still considered this land to be part of its territory. Indeed, the Assiniboine claimed it was their 'own proper territory.'[38]

Furthermore, as late as 1740 at least one band of Assiniboine lived to the east of Lake Winnipeg. This information was derived by Arthur Dobbs from Joseph La France who had travelled from Lake Superior to York Factory on Hudson Bay via Lake Winnipeg between 1739 and 1742. According to La France, the Eagle-Eyed Indians lived on the eastern side of Lake Winnipeg in the vicinity of Poplar River (Figure 7). Of impor-

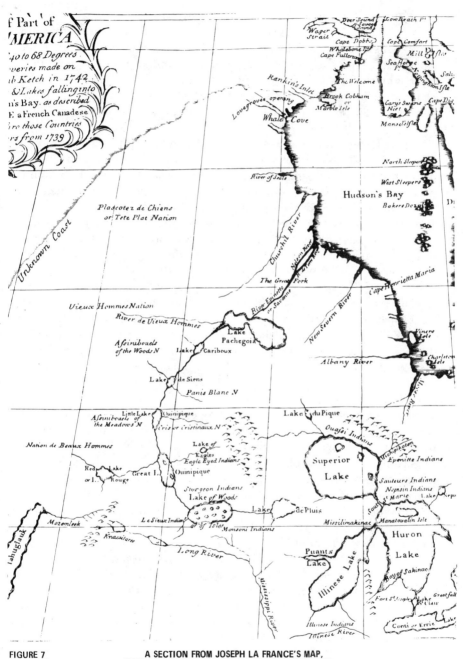

FIGURE 7

**A SECTION FROM JOSEPH LA FRANCE'S MAP,
"NEW MAP OF PART OF NORTH AMERICA, 1739-1742**

tance, Nicholas Jérémie, the man in charge of the fort during the twenty years of French control between 1694 and 1714, informed him that this band belonged to the Assiniboine tribe since they spoke the same language.[39] James Isham concurred in this identification.[40] Apparently, the Eagle-Eyed Assiniboine had occupied this area for some time before 1742, since the York Factory account books of 1718 indicate that a gift was given to a leading Indian chief from this band who was said to have come from that general vicinity.[41]

When La Vérendrye moved into the boundary-waters area between Minnesota and Ontario in the 1730s, he initiated a change in French policy and tried once more to bring about peace between the warring parties in that quarter; but he achieved no more success than his seventeenth-century French predecessor had. Hostilities had continued and the Assiniboine and the Cree were now joined by certain bands of the Ojibwa who participated in their raids into Siouan country. The failure to bring this turmoil to an end led Charles de la Boische Beauharnois, governor of New France, to complain in 1742 that:

The chief in question [La Colle, a Monsoni war chief from Rainy Lake] with tribes from Nipigon, Kaministikwia, Tecamamiouen [Rainy Lake], the Monsoni, Cree and Assiniboin are all to fall on them [Sioux] and create all the carnage they can; they are absolutely resolved to destroy them in spite of all that can be done to prevent them. This chief ... told him last spring that the Sioux were only good to eat, and that he wanted, for his part, to kill enough of them to feed his village.[42]

Though there is little evidence that any cannibalism was practised (the chief merely intended to demonstrate his resolve to continue the war), the statement does give some indication of the intensity of the hostilities. Regarding the conduct of the war, it appears that the War Road River of northern Minnesota was the usual route of attack. In La Vérendrye's time the Monsoni and Cree usually travelled up the river where they met the Assiniboine in the prairies. These raiding parties into Siouan territories were sufficient to thwart Sioux attempts to expand northward, but did not enable the Assiniboine to secure a solid foothold in southeastern Manitoba, and the upper Red River valley above the forks remained a no-man's-land.[43] The situation in southwestern Manitoba was different as the area was more distant from the homeland of the Dakota Sioux and the Assiniboine were able to hold that region. Further eastward, the Sioux were pushed out of the Rainy River area and the Cree, along with the Ojibwa, resumed control.

Tribal locations and movements to the north and west in central Manitoba and Saskatchewan are more difficult to piece together for this early period because of the more limited nature of the historical records. Nicholas Jérémie's account of his experience at Fort Bourbon (York Factory) between 1694 and 1714 and three maps which were drawn from it provide us with some of the earliest documentation of the northern limits of the Assiniboine and Cree territory in the early eighteenth century. This evidence indicates that the Woodland Assiniboine and Cree jointly held the land between the lower Saskatchewan and upper Nelson rivers and the middle Churchill River between Southern Indian Lake and Reindeer Lake.[44] Between the time the English regained control of York Factory, in 1714, and 1720, when the Hudson's Bay Company was able to re-establish its trade, the Cree and Assiniboine had apparently begun pushing their trapping and trading area rapidly to the west in the forested country between the Churchill and Saskatchewan rivers. The York Factory journals between 1714 and 1720 indicate that the territory of the Woodland Assiniboine and Cree reached as far as the head of the Churchill River.[45] The Cree also held the lands to the southeast of Lake Athabasca.

This territorial expansion was accompanied with a great deal of bloodshed, expecially along the northern and southwestern frontiers. For instance, James Knight, who was in charge of York Factory, said the Indians told him that as many as 6000 men had been killed along the Cree-Chipewyan border. Most of these losses had been borne by the Chipewyans, which Knight said would not have been the case had they been armed earlier.[46] However, the Woodland Assiniboine and Cree did not go unscathed in these conflicts, and their dependence on arms and ammunition sometimes worked to their disadvantage. This was especially true from 1694–1714, while the French held York Factory. It appears that the French ships did not arrive with the same regularity as the English ships did when the Hudson's Bay Company was in control of the trade. Consequently, the more acculturated groups like the Woodland Assiniboine and their Cree neighbours often found themselves in short supply of ammunition and thus vulnerable to attack. Knight stated that they suffered heavy losses as a result. For instance, in 1716, he reported:

the wars has allmost ruin'd this Country it being so thin Peopled at the best. there has been all those Indians as they Call em Sinnepoets Destroyd so that of about 60 Canos as us'd to Come Yearly there is not Above 6 familys left wch they told me this Reason for it that they had lost the Use of there Bows and Arrows by having

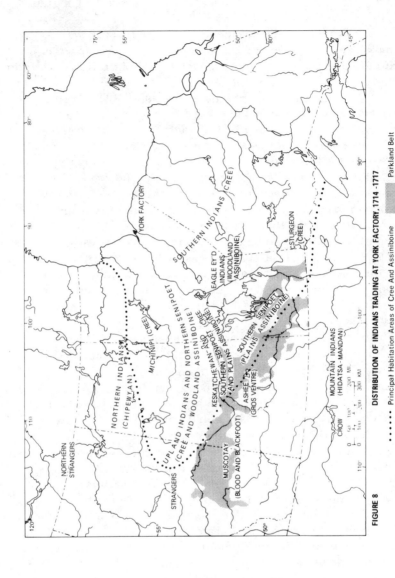

FIGURE 8 DISTRIBUTION OF INDIANS TRADING AT YORK FACTORY, 1714-1717

•••••• Principal Habitation Areas of Cree And Assiniboine   ▨ Parkland Belt

Source: PAC HBC B 239/a/1-5

Guns so long Amongst them and when they were disappointed of Powder Shott wch was Often by the Ships not coming there Enemies found They had no guns to Defend themselves wth made warr Upon them & Destry'd above 100 Tents Men, Women and children.[47]

The next summer, in 1717, he revised his estimate of their losses, saying they had numbered 200 tents of whom only five or six were left. He considered this to be a great loss to the company since they were said to be amongst 'the best beavour Indians as Comes to trade with us.'[48]

Most of the losses the Assiniboine suffered appear to have been inflicted by the Muscotay Indians, or Indians from the Buffalo Plains between the north and south branches of the Saskatchewan River. These Indians would probably have been the Blood and Blackfoot. Other groups living farther to the west, perhaps Sarcee and Beaver Indians, were also at war with the Assiniboine since the York Factory journals state that hostilities existed with four or five groups to the west and southwest.[49]

The southern boundaries of the Assiniboine territory in Saskatchewan do not appear to have changed very much between the time of Kelsey's visit to the region in 1690 and 1720. The Touchwood Hills still marked the limits of their territory in 1720, and they lived mostly to the north and east of that area. Immediately to the west, and perhaps also occupying part of the Touchwood Hills with the Assiniboine, were the Ashkee, or Plains Indians as they were called. According to the York Factory account book of 1718–19, a leading chief from that tribe came to the post to receive gifts. He was said to have come from 'about the Mountain Near Redd Deer River.'[50] Since the Ashkee Indians were from the grassland region, the chief must have come from the Nut Mountain or Touchwood Hills area near the upper headwaters of the Red Deer River (see Figure 2). Porcupine Mountain and the Pasquia Hills of the Lower Red Deer River region can be ruled out because they lie well within the forest zone. Presumably, therefore, the Ashkee Indians were the Gros Ventre since they were not considered to be a band of either Cree or Assinboine.

Figure 8 shows the distribution of the Assiniboine and Cree in about 1720, as well as the relative locations of the various other Indian tribes with whom they were in contact. After 1720, the Assiniboine expansion seems to have occurred primarily in a west-northwesterly direction, through the parkland corridor. When Anthony Henday made his inland trip from York Factory to eastern Alberta in 1755, he encountered many groups of Assiniboine in the parkland zone until he reached Sounding Creek, Alberta, at a longitude of approximately 111 degrees west. It is

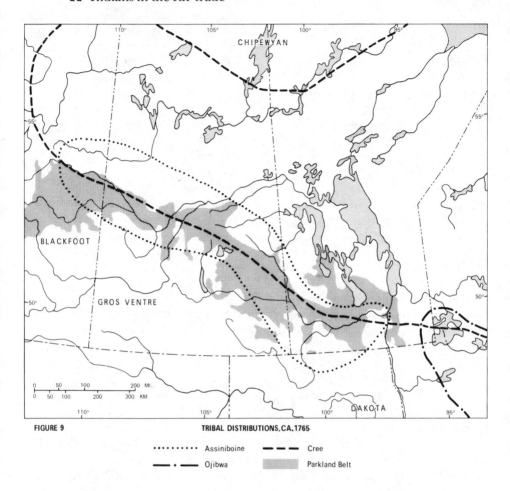

FIGURE 9   **TRIBAL DISTRIBUTIONS, CA.1765**

············ Assiniboine   — — — Cree

—·—·— Ojibwa   ▨ Parkland Belt

unclear whether their movement into this section was more peaceful than
the earlier westward push of the woodland Assiniboine in the bordering
forests had been. When Henday visited the area, he saw the Assiniboine
camping and travelling with the Gros Ventre and Blackfoot on numerous occasions, and the area seemed to be quite tranquil. Meanwhile, the
principal expansion of Cree territory appears to have taken place between
Reindeer Lake and Lake Athabasca. This frontier was pushed back until
1760 when they concluded a peace with the Beaver and Slave Indians.[51]
East of Reindeer Lake, the northward expansion of the Cree ebbed about
1720. The opening of Fort Churchill in 1717 made it possible for Indians

living in this area to arm themselves, and the Cree no longer had any military advantage over them. This probably explains why the expansion of the latter group was halted in northern Manitoba almost forty years before it ended in northwestern Saskatchewan and Alberta.

By 1763 the distribution of Indian tribes had changed radically from that of 1690 (Figure 9). After having initially been drawn eastward as trappers into the French-Ottawa trading system before 1670, the Assiniboine and Cree began moving rapidly in a northwesterly direction after 1670 as they became involved in the Hudson's Bay Company trade. Using the arms they obtained at the Bay, they quickly assumed the role of middlemen in the evolving trade network and expanded their trading areas with force. By 1720, the bulk of that expansion appears to have been completed and a somewhat more peaceful period began as inter-tribal trading patterns became well established. These relationships will be discussed below.

NOTES

1 A focus may be defined as a class of archaeological materials which in the finest analysis of detail shows particular characteristics thought to correspond roughly with the local tribe in ethnology. McKern, 'The Midwestern Taxonomic Method as an Aid to Archaeological Cultural Study,' 308. Readers should note that the bibliography supplements the author/short title references in the notes.

2 L.A. Wilford first associated this complex with the Assiniboine in 1941; see, 'A Tentative Classification of the Protohistoric Cultures of Minnesota.' Later work by C. Vickers lent support to Wilford's conclusions: 'Burial Traits of the Headwaters Lakes Aspect in Manitoba,' and 'The Historic Approach and the Headwaters Lakes Aspect.' Subsequently G.E. Evans challenged that view, arguing instead for an identity with the Cree: 'Prehistoric Blackduck–Historic Assiniboine: A Reassessment.' Most recently, in a series of articles J.V. Wright has posited an association with the Ojibwa: 'Cree Culture History in the Southern Indian Lake Region.' In this article Wright makes his most forceful argument for an Ojibwa authorship.

3 McNeish, 'An Introduction to the Archaeology of Southeastern Manitoba,' 51–3

4 Mayer-Oakes, 'Archeological Investigation in the Grand Rapids, Manitoba Reservoir, 1961–1962,' 352–3 and Wright, 'Cree Culture History in the Southern Indian Lake Region,' 3–9

5 For a discussion of the above stratigraphic sequences see Mayer-Oakes, 'Prehistoric Human Populations of the Glacial Lake Agassiz Region.'
6 Thwaites, *Jesuit Relations*, 18:231
7 Glover, *David Thompson's Narrative, 1784–1812*, 164
8 O'Callaghan, *Documents Relative to the Colonial History of the State of New York*, 1055
9 Margry, *Découvertes et Etablissements des Français*, 'Extrait du Mémoire de M. Le Chevalier de Beaurain Sur la Louisiane,' 6:82–3. In a letter from Hudson Bay dated 1694 Father Marest provided an even earlier account of the story. When discussing the Assiniboine he wrote, 'The language of the Assiniboines is very different from that of the Crees. It is the same as that of the Sioux among whom my brother has made two journeys. It is even contended that the Assiniboines are a Sioux nation long separated from the parent nation and making war on it continually ever since. The Crees and Assiniboines are allies. They have the same enemies and carry on the same wars. Some Assiniboines speak Cree and some Crees Assiniboine.' Tyrrell, *Documents Relating to the Early History of Hudson Bay*, 123
10 Thwaites, *Jesuit Relations*, 44:249
11 Heidenreich, 'The Historical Geography of Huronia during the First Half of the 17th Century,' 460–1. The Assiniboine travelled to Lake Nipigon via the Rainy River, Pigeon River, Lake Superior, and Nipigon River. See also, Heidenreich, *Huronia*, 23.
12 Crouse, *Contributions of the Canadian Jesuits to the Geographic Knowledge of New France*, 143–4
13 Ibid., 154
14 Ibid., 137–8
15 By La Vérendrye's time (the 1720s) this river became known as La Pluie (Rainy River).
16 Margry, *Découvertes et Etablissements des Français*, 'Extrait d'une Lettre de Grey selon Du Lhut à M. de la Barre, escrit au dessous du Portage Teiagon, le 10 sept 1684,' 50–1. Du Lhut's post was built on the northeast. It is shown on H. Jaillot's map 'Le Canada Ou Partie De La Nouvelle France, 1696.' Copy in Public Archives of Canada
17 O'Callaghan, *Documents*, 'Memoir on the Present State of Canada and the measures to be adopted for the Safety of the Country, 12 nov. 1685,' 9:286. An earlier memoir, dated 13 November 1681 and written to the minister by M. Duchesnau, pointed out that the Ottawa obtained most of their furs from the Cree, Assiniboine, and Sioux ('Memoir of Du Chesneau on Irregular Trade in Canada' in ibid., 160–1)
18 Ibid., M. de Denonville to M. de Seignelay, Ville Marie, 25 Aug. 1687, 343

19 *A New Discovery of A Vast Country in America 1679–1681*, 266–7
20 Burpee, *Journals and Letters of La Vérendrye*, 6–7, and Ruggles, 'The Historical Geography and Cartography of the Canadian West,' 297
21 Burpee, *Journals and Letters of La Vérendrye*, 86
22 Rich, *The Fur Trade*, 70–5. It is problematical whether or not the 'Mountain Poets' which Kelsey met near the Touchwood Hills were Gros Ventre as Rich suggests. They may have been a band of Assiniboine since the Gros Ventre appear to have been referred to as the Ashkee Indians in the early years at York Factory, as will be discussed subsequently.
23 Ray, 'Indian Exploitation of the Forest-Grassland Transition Zone of Western Canada, 1650–1860' 47–58
24 Adams, *The Explorations of Pierre Esprit Radisson*, 227
25 Thwaites, *Jesuit Relations*, 44:247, 325
26 Burpee, *Journals and Letters of La Vérendrye*, 6–7, and Ruggles, 'The Historical Geography and Cartography of the Canadian West,' 327. Kelsey travelled through Cree territory until he reached 'Dering's Point' which is generally thought to have been located on the lower Saskatchewan River in the vicinity of The Pas, Manitoba. Shortly after passing beyond 'Dering's Point' he indicated that he was entering the territory of the Assiniboine. Rich, *The Fur Trade*, 73
27 In 1743 James Isham stated that 250 canoes came to trade manned by 550 men, or about two and one-half men per canoe since some carried two and others three men, 'Observations on Hudson's Bay, 1743,' PAC HBC E 2/1
28 York Factory Account Books, 1688–9 and 1693–4, PAC HBC B 239/d/1–5
29 Wissler, 'Population Changes among the Northern Plains Indians,' 6
30 The figure of 840 was obtained by adding to the annual trade total of one year two-thirds that amount for the previous year and another one-third for the last year, that is, 420 + 280 + 140 = 840.
31 Ruggles, 'The Historical Geography and Cartography of the Canadian West,' 309–10
32 York Factory Journals, 1728–9, PAC HBC B 239/a/11, p. 18–19
33 Ibid., 18
34 Burpee, *Journals and Letters of La Vérendrye*, 45
35 Beauharnois and Hocquart writing from Quebec City said Lake of the Woods and Lake of the Assiniboine were the same lake, but cautioned against assuming that this lake was the only one around which the tribe lived. They were said to extend as far as Lake Winnipeg, ibid., 86–7
36 Ibid., 96
37 Hlady, 'Indian Migrations in Manitoba and the West,' 32–3
38 Burpee, *Journals and Letters of La Vérendrye*, 250–1. Also, at the time of the conference some Assiniboine were camped at the forks, 240–4

39 Dobbs, *An Account of the Countries Adjoining to Hudson's Bay in the Northwest Part of America*, 24, 35. The band was said to have been given this name because many eagles were reported to be found in their territory.
40 Rich, *James Isham's Observations and Notes, 1743–1749*, 118
41 PAC HBC B 239/d/10, p. 2
42 Burpee, *Journals and Letters of La Vérendrye*, 384
43 Ibid., 186; and Hickerson, 'Genesis of A Trading Post Band,' 295
44 Ray, 'Early French Mapping of Western Interior of Canada'
45 PAC HBC B 239/a/1–5
46 York Factory Journals, 1715–16, PAC HBC B 239/a/2, p. 28
47 Ibid., 22
48 York Factory Journals, 1716–17, PAC HBC B 239/a/3, p. 34
49 Ibid.
50 PAC HBC B 239/d/10, p. 3
51 Burpee, 'Journal of a Journey Performed by Anthony Hendry,' 327, 330–4, and 340. Henday had long been identified in the literature of the fur trade as Hendry. Hlady, 'Indian Migrations in Manitoba and the West,' 28–9

2

Land and life in the western interior before 1763

The territory occupied by the Assiniboine and Western Cree during the seventeenth and eighteenth centuries was diverse in its bio-geography. It included three distinctly different types of habitat – the woodland, parkland, and grassland zones – each of which offered a different array of resources to the Indians (Figure 10). Most significant was the difference in the abundance of food resources between the woodlands and the grasslands. Only two large game species were found in the forests, the woodland caribou and the moose (Figure 11). Although historical data suggest that the population densities of these two animals, particularly that of the woodland caribou, were much greater in the early eighteenth century than they are at present, especially in the shield region between Lake Winnipeg and Hudson Bay, they were nevertheless modest in comparison to those of the parkland and grassland sections.[1] Small game, on the other hand, was relatively abundant and included the valuable species of marten, fisher, lynx, otter, mink, muskrat, and beaver. These animals were prized not only for their furs, but often for food as well. Beaver and muskrat were significant sources of food, and cub beaver was considered to be a delicacy by many Indians.[2] Besides game, fish were an important resource in the wooded areas, especially in the sedimentary rock zones fringing the shield (Figure 2). Waterfowl were abundant in season throughout the region, and wild rice was plentiful in the forested area to the southeast along the Winnipeg and Rainy rivers (Figure 12).

In considerable contrast to the modest game resource of the forest region, that of the grasslands was richer in both the total number of large

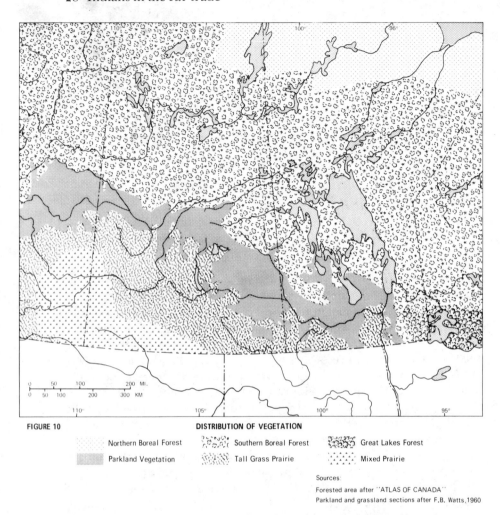

FIGURE 10   DISTRIBUTION OF VEGETATION

Northern Boreal Forest   Southern Boreal Forest   Great Lakes Forest

Parkland Vegetation   Tall Grass Prairie   Mixed Prairie

Sources:
Forested area after "ATLAS OF CANADA"
Parkland and grassland sections after F.B. Watts,1960

game animals and in species variety. Pronghorn antelope, mule deer, wapiti or red deer, and bison were all present (Figure 11). However, small game were rather limited, being found in only the wooded river valleys and uplands such as Turtle Mountain and Moose Mountain (Figure 2).

The transitional parkland belt provided the Indian with most of the resources of both the forest and grasslands. All of the game animals were present with the exception of woodland caribou. Fish were plentiful and the waters of the Assiniboine, Red, and Saskatchewan rivers were ex-

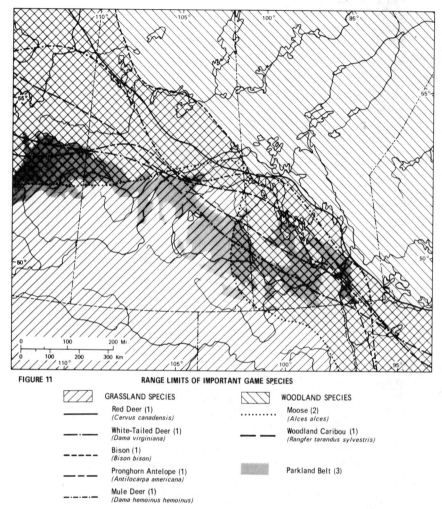

FIGURE 11   RANGE LIMITS OF IMPORTANT GAME SPECIES

GRASSLAND SPECIES   WOODLAND SPECIES

Red Deer (1)
(Cervus canadensis)

White-Tailed Deer (1)
(Dama virginiana)

Bison (1)
(Bison bison)

Pronghorn Antelope (1)
(Antilocarpa americana)

Mule Deer (1)
(Dama hemoinus hemoinus)

Moose (2)
(Alces alces)

Woodland Caribou (1)
(Rangfer tarandus sylvestris)

Parkland Belt (3)

Sources: E.T. Seton,1909 (1) E.R. Hall & K. Kelson, 1959 (2) F.B. Watts, 1960 (3)

ploited in prehistoric as well as historic times. Similarly there was a considerable overlapping of vegetation, although wild rice was limited to the southeastern parklands where it was never abundant (Figure 12).

Besides the spatial variations in resources, there were temporal variations of two types: irregular and regular or seasonal. Irregular fluctuations of resources were brought about by diseases and short-term

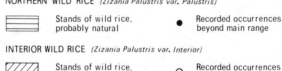

FIGURE 12   **DISTRIBUTION OF WILD RICE**

NORTHERN WILD RICE *(Zizania Palustris var. Palustris)*

| | Stands of wild rice, probably natural | ● | Recorded occurrences beyond main range |

INTERIOR WILD RICE *(Zizania Palustris var. Interior)*

| | Stands of wild rice, probably natural | ○ | Recorded occurrences beyond main range |

Source: William G. Dore, "Wild Rice" PLANT RESEARCH INSTITUTE PUBLICATION 1393,
RESEARCH BRANCH, CANADA DEPARTMENT OF AGRICULTURE, OTTAWA 1969

changes in climate. Of the two, the latter appears to have been the more important. In the forest and parkland zones periodic changes in rainfall often had a considerable effect on small game populations, particularly muskrat. This animal lived along the shallow margins of lakes and rivers and was very sensitive to water-level fluctuations. High-water conditions drowned many of the young muskrat, while low-water levels often meant that the animals froze to death during the winter. Also, according to

Governor George Simpson of the Hudson's Bay Company, muskrat were more susceptible to disease during dry periods because of stagnating water conditions when epidemics killed them by the thousands.[3] Tulerimia bacteria in particular often reached high levels of concentration in stagnant water and the resulting epidemics usually took a heavy toll. With a return to more humid weather their numbers recovered in about three years. These cyclic variations of muskrat were particularly important in eastern Saskatchewan and southern Manitoba. The numerous and extensive bodies of shallow water in this region provided a habitat for the animal that was ideal, though unreliable due to frequent droughts.

In addition to its effect on animal populations, the variation in moisture conditions also strongly influenced the very important resource of wild rice. Once again, high- or low-water levels would seriously reduce the yield, and, consequently, the harvest was unreliable. A poor return could be expected one out of every four years.

Seasonal changes had a more predictable effect on the availability of food supplies. Significantly, the cyclic variations of the forest, parkland, and grassland habitats did not parallel each other, but rather, tended to be complementary. For example, the summer season, particularly the late spring–early summer and later summer–early autumn, were times of relative food abundance in the woodlands when the fishing was good and waterfowl was plentiful. Food supplies were spatially concentrated around lakes and along rivers at that time. In the winter months, the situation was quite different. By mid-October most of the waterfowl abandoned the area and the fisheries fell off as temperatures plummeted and fish sought out deeper waters. December, January, and February were often grim months for the Indians, and the threat of starvation was always present. Large game animals could be taken, but they were widely scattered, since many sections of the boreal forests could not support sizeable game populations. These lean conditions did not improve until the arrival of spring.

The parkland food cycle exhibited some of the characteristics of the forest cycle, but there were some basic differences. During the summer months fish and waterfowl were plentiful, although the former were taken primarily in the spring when the sturgeon were running in the rivers. The fall fishing season was of limited importance compared to that of the forest region. Even though large game was present in the area all summer, the most important animal, the bison, migrated toward the open grassland during the summer and was not abundant. With the onset of winter the situation changed and increasingly harsh weather conditions led the animals to seek shelter. The bison moved into the parklands in greater numbers, grazing in small prairies during mild spells and taking refuge in wooded sections during periods of severe weather. Consequently, food was plentiful in the winter season when it was becoming scarce in the adjacent forest. Indeed, contrary to what one would expect, mild winters in the parklands produced hardships, since the bison remained in the open grasslands and game was scarce.

The grassland food cycle closely parallelled that of the forests. Summer was a time of plenty as the bison massed in large herds during the rutting season (Figure 13). In the winter, the circumstances changed considerably. Under average or severe weather conditions the bison scattered in search of shelter. Other game responded in a similar fashion since they could not survive on the open grasslands in the face of the chilling winter winds. At these times it would have been difficult for any Indians to remain in that environment, and there is little evidence that many did.

In short, during the long winters, the parkland zone must have been the most suitable for occupation on the basis of the availability of food and shelter. During the warmer months of the year, regional variations in food resources would have existed, but were probably less significant. Food was relatively easily obtained in all three zones at that time.

The Assiniboine and Western Cree economies revolved around hunting and gathering activities. Archaeological and historical data show that these two groups used a limited variety of tools to exploit their environment and that the seasonal food-gathering activities and correlated patterns of movement which they followed were closely adjusted to these three food cycles.

The materials which comprised the Manitoba or Blackduck and Selkirk foci are quite similar and indicate that chipped and ground stone, bone, and ceramics were the principal resources used in the manufacture of tools and utensils prior to European contact. Undoubtedly wood was also extensively employed, although little of it has been recovered from archaeological sites due to problems of preservation. In both foci small projectile points, such as the 'eastern triangular point' are common, suggesting the use of the bow and arrow. Bone was used to fashion barbed points, needles, awls, and a variety of other tools. Ceramic pots were constructed by both tribes, and impressions on them indicate that fabrics and nets were made of woven rawhide thongs and strings. The nets were probably used for fishing, since polished stone sinkers have also been found.

FIGURE 13

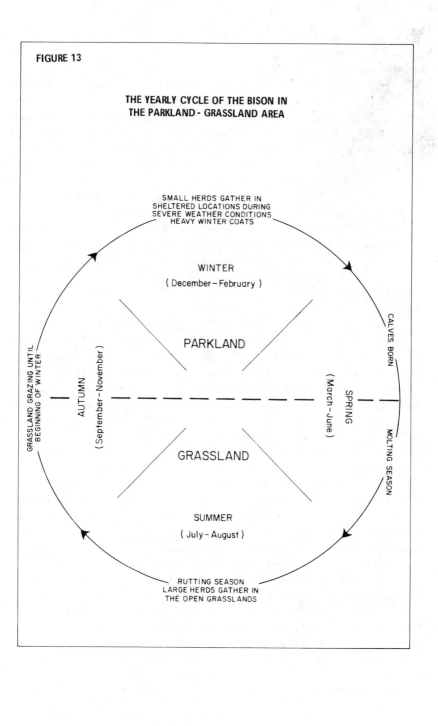

THE YEARLY CYCLE OF THE BISON IN
THE PARKLAND - GRASSLAND AREA

SMALL HERDS GATHER IN
SHELTERED LOCATIONS DURING
SEVERE WEATHER CONDITIONS
HEAVY WINTER COATS

WINTER
(December – February)

PARKLAND

CALVES BORN

SPRING
(March – June)

MOLTING SEASON

GRASSLAND GRAZING UNTIL
BEGINNING OF WINTER

AUTUMN
(September – November)

GRASSLAND

SUMMER
(July – August)

RUTTING SEASON
LARGE HERDS GATHER IN
THE OPEN GRASSLANDS

The differences between the two archaeological assemblages are primarily ones of detail, not of basic tool types. For example, one of the major contrasts between the two foci is related to the pottery decorations, with the Selkirk focus being noted for its 'Winnipeg Fabric Impressed Ware' and to a lesser extent 'Cementary Point Corded Ware' while 'Manitoba Corded Ware' is characteristic of the Manitoba focus site. Likewise, there are slight dissimilarities in the inventories of small points with 'Plains Side-Notched' being more common at Manitoba focus sites and 'Prairie Side-Notched' and 'Selkirk Side-Notched' at Selkirk focus sites. In addition to these essentially stylistic differences, there are a few artifacts that are largely limited to one or the other of the two cultural assemblages. Beaver-tooth gouges, ground and polished steatite tubes (probably used for smoking), and conch-shell beads occur at Manitoba focus sites, whereas scapula hoes or shovels for use in digging storage pits, and bone celts are more common at Selkirk focus sites. Nonetheless these tools make up a small portion of the total inventories.[4]

Significantly, the sites of both foci are generally extensive in terms of their surface area but lack deep layers of accumulation. Furthermore, although each focus has a great deal of internal consistency, there are marked variations between individual sites in terms of the relative abundance of certain types of tools, floral and faunal remains that are found. Most of the woodland sites of the Selkirk focus are located along lakes and rivers, with the faunal remains consisting chiefly of fish bones and clam shells, indicating that they were fishing camps, while at Pelican Lake in the grasslands the abundance of bones suggest that hunting was the major activity.[5] Similar variations have been recorded among the Manitoba focus sites. Levels 5 and 6 at Lockport on the Red River and level 2 at the Tuokko site on the Winnipeg River (the Manitoba focus levels of these multi-component sites) show a predominance of fish bones over animal bones though the latter were important too (Figure 1). Increasing in frequency in the upper levels were bird bones and small projectile points hinting at a growing use of these resources beginning in the late prehistoric period. As both sites are located on rivers, it is assumed that they served as fishing camps, with some hunting carried on as well.

The Stott Mound and Village site near Brandon, Manitoba, was of more recent habitation, ca. 1670, and it differed from the above two sites in a number of significant respects (Figure 1). The faunal remains were predominantly bison bones – 99 per cent of the total. In addition, dog, wolf, bear, deer, beaver, red deer, coyote, lynx, skunk, snowshoe rabbit, squirrel, and other rodent bones were present. Fish bones, turtle shells, bird bones, and clam shells were found as well. Evidence nearby shows that bison were slain by driving them over a precipice. Other game was apparently taken with bow and arrow or through the use of a variety of traps. The tool inventory of the site reflected the economic orientation of the people who occupied it, and the items which were used in game hunting, butchering, and the preparing of skins predominate.[6]

In brief, it appears that the internal differences in the proto-historic cultures of southern Manitoba are due to the economic specialization that had taken place among Indian groups. Investigations of most sites have revealed that in nearly every instance the local environment was intensively exploited. Often a heavy dependence was placed on a single resource, such as bison or fish, which was seasonal in character. In some cases, such as at the Stott site, repeated occupation occurred as indicated by the presence of fire pits above, in, and below the accumulation of bison bones.[7] Therefore, it is likely that in the late prehistoric period the Assiniboine and Cree travelled in migratory bands the size of which depended upon the season and local resources. Furthermore, it seems reasonable to assume that through these movements many bands exploited two or three of the major environmental zones on a seasonal basis.[8]

The earliest historical observations of the life ways of the Assiniboine and Cree are those made by the Jesuits on the basis of information they had received from tribal groups having trading contacts with northern Ontario and southern Manitoba. One of the earliest of these commentaries is found in the *Relation* for the year 1669–70. In discussing the location of the Assiniboine the author (anonymous) stated that they lived to the westward of 'St. Esprit [Duluth] ... fifteen or twenty days journey ... on a Lake where they gather wild oats, and fish a very plenty.'[9] Father Gabriel Marest's later writings point out that the Cree also exploited these resources on a seasonal basis. When making notes about the tribes that traded at Fort Bourbon (York Factory) Marest said of the Assiniboine and their Cree allies:

They are always wanderers and vagabonds, living by hunting and fishing. Nevertheless, in the summer they assemble near the Lakes, where they remain two or three months; and afterward they go to gather wild oats, of which they lay in a store.

The Savages who are nearest to this point [Swampy Cree] live only by hunting; they continually range the woods, without stopping in any place, either in winter or summer, unless they have good sport; but in that case they build cabins on the spot and remain therein until they no longer have anything to eat.'[10]

Besides describing the practice of living along lakes and rivers to hunt and fish during the warmer months, the above observation is of added interest in that it suggests that in this respect those Cree living in the outer regions of the forest differed sharply from those residing closer to the Bay. Marest thought enough of this difference to speculate that the Assiniboine and their Cree neighbours would be easier to Christianize since their concentration in relatively large groups for prolonged periods of time at fixed locations would enable missionaries to teach them more effectively. Other groups, such as the Swampy Cree, were widely scattered and constantly on the move, making the priest's job very difficult.

Under the leadership of La Vérendrye, the French penetrated into the southeastern margins of the Nelson River drainage basin in the 1730s. This establishment of direct European contact with the Assiniboine and Cree provided information about the activities and movements of the two groups throughout the year rather than for just the summer months, as was the case previously. It also gives us some insights into their attitudes toward their differing environmental surroundings. For example, shortly after La Vérendrye established his post on Lake of the Woods in 1732, he learned that the Cree living along the southern margins of Lake Winnipeg regarded the boreal forest as a 'sterile country,' particularly those portions closest to the Bay.[11] It was said to be especially difficult to subsist in those lands during the winter. Indeed, because of the latter problem, La Vérendrye was unsuccessful in his first attempt to establish a post on the lower Winnipeg River. In 1732 he had instructed his nephew Christophe de la Jemeraye to build a house down the river toward Lake Winnipeg, but Jemeraye failed because his men and their Indian guides refused to winter there, fearing that they would starve to death.[12]

La Vérendrye's subsequent encounters and discussions with the Cree indicate that, rather than winter on the Shield, many of the tribal bands moved to the parklands or lived in the outer fringes of the forest. In these settings they had access to the bison of the parkland and the relatively sizeable moose population of the forest. To illustrate, in 1737 La Vérendrye walked overland from Fort St Charles on Lake of the Woods to Fort Maurepas then located on the lower Red River. The trip was undertaken in February and he would have travelled through portions of the Great Lake Forest, the outer edges of the boreal forest, and the parkland belt. After reaching his destination he summarized his journey as follows: 'It took me eighteen days to get to Fort Maurepas. Nearly every day I came to lodges of savages, who wished me "bon voyage" and offered me provisions that I had no need for, as the men who were with me killed two or three moose every day.'[13] Judging from the frequency with which he claimed to have encountered Indian hunters and their lodges, it would appear that the lands to the southwest of the Shield were relatively heavily populated in winter. Presumably this was related to the abundance of game there.

Regarding his conversations with the Indians at Fort Maurepas, La Vérendrye remarked:

The chiefs complimented me. The season was so advanced that the Cree were in a hurry to leave for their hunting: they had been waiting for me for a long time. We had settled upon the fourth of March as the date of the council, because time was required to notify two villages of the Assiniboin situated at the great fork of the Red River ...

In this interval ... I have employed this time in obtaining information about Lake Winnipeg, the rivers that fall into it and the tribes dwelling on its shores; also respecting another great lake to the west called Brother of Winnipeg ... surrounded by wooded mountains extending from the north to the southwest, and abounding in martens and lynxes; it is the hunting ground of the Cree and Assiniboin.[14]

The anxiety of the Cree to leave in order to hunt is significant in that La Vérendrye had reported earlier that they, as well as the Assiniboine camped at the post, were obtaining buffalo meat daily from their men in the parklands.[15] It is unlikely therefore that game would have been the object of this hunt, since they had plentiful supplies of the latter already. Rather, the tribe probably intended to make a late winter fur hunt in the Riding Mountain–Porcupine Mountain region, an area that had been specifically designated as rich in marten and lynx.

In the spring and early summer, many of the same bands gathered on the shores of Lake Winnipeg and other water bodies in the area to fish; and in middle and later summer they hunted bison in the open grasslands after these animals had become fattened on summer pastures. Often the summer hunt in the grasslands took the group as far as the Missouri River where they traded with the Mandan. Descriptions of these activities again come from the Journals of the Jesuits and La Vérendrye. For example, when discussing his plans for the summer of 1736, Father Aulneau said: 'It is on the shores of this last lake [Lake Winnipeg], about one hundred and fifty leagues from here [Lake of the Woods], that I purpose passing a part of the summer with the Assiniboels, who occupy all of the land to the south of it.'[16] Aulneau does not specify which part of the summer the tribe would be camped on the lake, but it is reasonable to assume that it would have been during the late spring and early summer when fishing was at its peak.

La Vérendrye's account of his 1737 council with the Indians at Fort Maurepas lends support to the above conclusion. In his report he wrote: 'I inquired of the Assiniboin where they meant to spend the summer; and they said that on returning from the war they would go to the country of the Kouathéattes [Mandan] to buy Indian corn and beans ... They promised to bring all these things [items which La Vérendrye had requested] at the fall of the leaves to Fort Maurepas.'[17] Considering that the Assiniboine commonly raided Siouan territory in the spring, it is probable that the warriors established their families in fishing camps where they could obtain subsistence during their absence. To make the return trip to the Mandan villages, these men would have had to return for their families by the middle of July, since later references by La Vérendrye indicated that it took the various bands two to three months to make the return trip. By leaving in July they would have been able to return to Fort Maurepas by the 'fall of the leaves' as promised.

The lengthy trading expeditions to the Mandan villages were undertaken annually by the Assiniboine bands living in southern Manitoba. La Vérendrye's journals suggest that the expeditions set out most frequently in the summer, as in the above instance, but some bands appear to have made the trip in late fall or early winter. For instance, after detailing his plans for the summer of 1736 Father Aulneau added: 'Sometime about the feast of all saints [November 1], if it be the will of our good Lord, I intend, with as many of the french as are willing to encounter the same dangers, to join the Assiniboels, who start every year, just as soon as the streams are frozen over, for the country of the kaotiouak, or Autelsipounes to procure their supply of indian corn.'[18]

Although the French repeatedly stressed that agricultural produce was one of the prime objects of these undertakings, it would be incorrect to view them simply as trading ventures. Unlike the trading parties that were sent to the Bay in which only the men took part, those that headed south for the Mandan villages included men, women, and children, the old, and the disabled.[19] Consequently, they moved very slowly on foot, hunting as they proceeded to provide for their daily food requirements while en route and to build up a surplus of meat for consumption while visiting the Mandan. According to La Vérendrye, the surplus was necessary because the Mandan were said to eat their corn plain, 'having for the most part neither meat nor fat.'[20] In brief, the Assiniboine seasonally exploited the grassland environment in the process of carrying out these expeditions. It was for this reason that they were of such long duration. Bands that departed from the Portage la Prairie area of Manitoba took over a month and a half to reach the Missouri River Valley, when La Vérendrye claimed that the same distance could have easily been covered in twenty days at most.[21]

European contact with the lands to the west of the Manitoba escarpment was established much earlier than with the southern Manitoba lowlands. As noted previously, Henry Kelsey left York Factory in 1690 and spent two years inland reaching as far southwest as the Touchwood Hills of Saskatchewan. During his two years in the interior Kelsey undertook two separate trips, both of which were begun at 'Dering's Point,' probably near The Pas, Manitoba, which the Englishman said was in the territory of the Wood Assiniboine. Unfortunately Kelsey did not leave a detailed account of his first journey. Rather, he summarized it in the form of a brief rhymed verse. Nonetheless, enough information is contained in it to indicate that the Wood Assiniboine band which he followed left 'Dering's Point' in July, headed to the southwest, and spent the winter in the parkland where they lived off the bison herds. The band returned to 'Dering's Point' the next summer.[22] If 'Dering's Point' was actually located at The Pas, the Assiniboine would have been returning each summer to one of the best fishing locations of the lower Saskatchewan River. There the men could have left their families while they made the long trading voyage down to the Bay by canoe to trade with the English. This was the common practice of later Cree inhabitants, as will be described.

Kelsey's journal for his second expedition to the parklands provides much more information about the daily activities of his Indian companions, but covers only the period from 15 July to 12 September 1691. During this time, the Assiniboine travelled along the forest's edge until late August. Sometime about 22 July they headed into the parklands and began hunting bison. Kelsey described the method the tribe used to take these animals:

we pitched [he and his Assiniboine companions] into the barren ground it being very/dry heathy land and no water here & there a small pond ... could not see ye woods on y other side ... This instant y Indians going a hunting kill'd/great store of buffillo/now y manner of their hunting/these beasts on y barren ground is when they see a great/parcel of them together they surround them w men w down/they gather themselves into a smaller compass keeping / y beasts still in y middle and so shooting ym till they / break out at some place or other and get away.[23]

This is the first description of the use of the 'surround' in the parkland area and the techniques employed were quite similar to those observed by La Vérendrye on his 1739 trip to the Mandan in company of an Assinoboine band.[24] Kelsey reported that the tribe also trapped a great many beaver in the shallow ponds found in the wooded 'Islands' of the parkland area.[25]

Although Kelsey did not provide enough information for one to draw firm conclusions regarding the Assiniboine economy in the late seventeenth century, he does provide clues which make it possible to draw some inferences about the Indians' seasonal exploitation habits. During the early part of the summer the bands that traded at the Hudson's Bay Company camped at 'Dering's Point' and other suitable fishing sites while the men travelled back and forth from York Factory. The remainder of the year, late summer through early spring, was spent in the parklands. In the latter zone bison was the chief food resource and Kelsey's observations make it clear that the Assiniboine had devised a suitable means of carrying out mass hunts without the use of the horse, precipices, or firearms, all items that are commonly given prominent attention in discussion of buffalo hunting practices.[26]

Nearly seventy years after Henry Kelsey's travels, Joseph Smith and Joseph Waggoner left York Factory on three separate occasions and headed for the territory of southwestern Manitoba and adjacent Saskatchewan, lands that lie immediately to the east and southeast of those visited by Kelsey. Unlike the latter's accounts, the unpublished journals of Smith and Waggoner contain a wealth of detail about the seasonal activities of the Indian groups who accompanied them. The first of their three voyages was begun on 23 August 1756. Smith indicated that he was being escorted by a band of Sturgeon Indians (Cree) who had invited the Hudson's Bay Company to send men inland to winter in their homeland.

The group proceeded southwesterly by canoe until 18 October when shoal waters forced them to abandon their craft. By this time they had passed over the north end of Lake Winnipeg and were on the Saskatchewan River somewhere to the east of Cedar Lake. The lake was reached on the 31st of the month and the band stopped there for eight days, camping at an abandoned French post. When the group began to move again, it set a more southwesterly course. A short while later Smith reported: 'We came to a Lake very Large on three days Journey from the french house [the one located on Cedar Lake], SW Course see'd plenty of Islands, and a Great many Moose on them, in the Evening Came to the hills very Lofty [undoubtedly the Manitoba escarpment] with plenty of moose.'[27] The hilly area described above was not reached until 11 November. Most of the autumn season had therefore been spent in the region between Cedar Lake and the Manitoba escarpment. During that time the Sturgeon Cree moved slowly, often stopping for prolonged periods, and subsisted largely on northern pike and moose.

After crossing the escarpment, Smith's party continued in a southwesterly direction, passing through a wooded country, much of which was said to have been burned. From the 1st through the 5th of December the group stopped to kill 'buffeloo,' the first such reference to the animal, while from the 6th to the 18th they were on the move again journeying mostly through wooded lands. On 18 December Smith wrote: 'This day [18th] Came to a herd of Beasts there we Lay by for 3 weeks. 19th to y 9th of Janry., 1757 Lay by killing buffeloo, no Beaver got at Yet no houses to be Seen, as for wolves they will not take the trap.'[28] The band did not begin moving until 7 February when they altered their former course and began heading north-northeasterly over land said to be covered with 'burnt woods.'[29] On 19 February they reached a hill of 'Green woods' (coniferous forest) where five moose were killed. Thereafter moose was the only large game species which was taken.

On 3 March the group arrived at the river (Swan River) where they intended to make their canoes. They camped there for two months staying until 5 May, or long after the snow had melted and the river opened. The later break-up dates for the rivers near the Bay undoubtedly favoured this delayed departure (Figure 14). By leaving during the first week in May they would have arrived at York Factory shortly after the ice had melted on the lower Hayes and Nelson rivers. On the first day of the return canoe trip Smith remarked: 'Sett out and padled down the River NE course. The shores were flatt on both Sides and burnt woods; there were Waskesews going in droves, we killed a great many very good living for we had nothing but Rahigan [dried meat] and fatt.'[30] This was the first reference to waterfowl, clearly a welcome addition to the daily diet of the group.

In the following year the two Englishmen left once again for the lands of the Sturgeon Cree, but this time they proceeded by the Lake Winnipegosis–Lake Manitoba route.[31] Roughly the same cycle of activities was recorded, with the exception that the Cree band arrived in the parklands

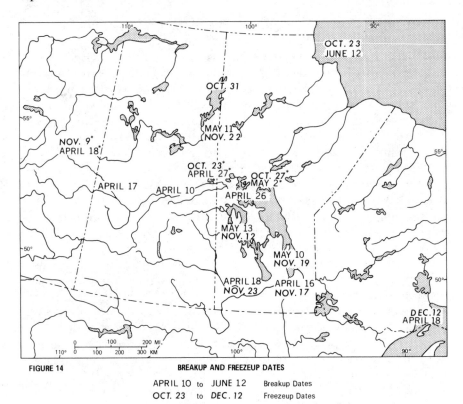

FIGURE 14   BREAKUP AND FREEZEUP DATES

APRIL 10 to JUNE 12   Breakup Dates
OCT. 23 to DEC. 12   Freezeup Dates

* A.J.W. Catchpole et al., "Content Analysis" Professional Geographer, 22 (5),   p.256.

Source: Canada Department of Transport, Cir - 3156

nearly a month earlier than in the previous year. On 1 November they came to an Assiniboine camp in southwestern Manitoba. Smith described the encounter as follows: 'November the 1 tuesedy we lea by and wandey the 2 we moved and want wbn and camt to twenty teantes of the Sineapoits [Assiniboine] and there was a pownd as the[y] maed to kill the boffles in and that day wandey ther was 67 came in at onse.'[32] This was one of the earliest references to the use of the fenced enclosure or 'pound' and the hunting of bison in southern Manitoba. His party remained at the Assiniboine camp for nearly a month, during which time another eighty-six bison were taken. On 24 December the Cree departed from the pound to trap furs and for the next month they drifted rather aimlessly in the parklands. Toward the end of February, on the 27th, Smith noted in his journal that there were few Indians because they had all gone to make their canoes.[33]

The last of Smith's three voyages was undertaken in 1763–4. The exact route which was followed is uncertain, but judging from his descriptions of the physical geography and the Indian groups he met, it is likely he visited the same general area that he had visited on the preceding two occasions. Throughout the autumn season his Indian companions hunted in the wooded sections of the parklands. The observations below are typical of the journal entries which were made during that period.

September 8, 1763: Whe Laft our canous and moved and want sw whe pick by the rever. Tied to kill baver/in Land bornt wods as four as I could see by the rever Lied asp ... [September 15, 1763] Whe moved and want SbW wind nne burnt woods. at the rever lied Asp with pine, plaenty of bavers of sorts.[34]

Smith's commentary continues on in a similar fashion until the end of October. Beaver were being taken in the river bottom forest through which they were passing and moose were providing them with adequate stocks of food. As late as 27 October, the band had not killed any bison. It was on that day that Smith wrote, 'the Iden plaenty vitels but no bofeler as yet.'[35]

On 26 October the band headed out into the open grasslands moving in a southwesterly direction. Eight days later they killed their first bison, taking six of the animals, and they began setting their traps for fox and wolves. In the months of November and December they continued heading to the southwest, stopping frequently to set their traps and hunt bison. The Assiniboine were encountered for the first time on 18 January and they were met frequently thereafter. On 20 March, Smith and his fellow travellers reached the point where they intended to make their canoes. Nearly 2 months were spent at that location and the craft were not launched until 14 May. After paddling downstream for ten days he recorded: 'Whe Lea by for ther whe Laft the fameleys and ther cam 8 canous mour of the Sinepoits then ther was all mst 200 canus.'[36] Thus, the families were left in a fishing camp in the late spring and early summer while the men made their trading expedition to York Factory, a practice common among the Assiniboine inhabitants of the area seventy-five years earlier.

Three years after Smith made the above trip, William Pink set out from York Factory and journeyed up the Saskatchewan River as far as the area of the present city of Prince Albert, Saskatchewan.[37] Like his predecessors he was accompanied by a group of Indians who traded regularly with the Hudson's Bay Company. Initially the body of Indians was rather large, but as they proceeded westwards bands split off to go to their winter hunting lands. Significantly, they all turned southward, moving up the minor tributaries of the Saskatchewan River. The band with which Pink remained travelled by canoe in a west-northwest direction until 7 October when they abandoned their canoes and for the next month walked overland, reaching the prairies on 8 December. There the group immediately began hunting bison and trapping fox and wolf. Two days later the Indians divided into two groups of equal size; Pink followed the one that headed to the southwest to an aspen grove where they stopped for four days to make snowshoe frames and sleds. Between 20 and 22 December another group of Indians, numbering some twenty families, joined Pink's party and they camped for fourteen days while they strung their snowshoes. During the same period, the band that had separated from his group returned. For the remainder of December and the month of January the Indians stayed in the parklands.

On 31 January Pink indicated that all of the Indians who traded at York Factory were beginning to move toward their canoe building grounds. His own group reached the river on which they intended to make their canoes on 8 February and travelled along it on foot until the 28th of the month. In the course of this trip several men were dispatched to fetch meat and hides that had been cached in the fall. Three days after they arrived, 3 March 1767, they made a four-day trip to the south to obtain birch bark from a large ridge of birch trees, probably in the Birch Hills of Saskatchewan (Figure 2). For the next two months the group camped on the river while they built their canoes, fished, shot waterfowl and trapped fur animals. The canoes were ready on 14 May and the Indians departed for the Bay.[38] In short, the routine that Pink outlined for the trading bands of central Saskatchewan was quite similar to that recorded by Smith and Waggoner for areas to the east and southeast.

Although all of the above observations were limited to groups that had direct trading contacts with the Hudson's Bay Company posts, there is evidence to indicate that seasonal movement back and forth between the parklands and the forests was common to other groups as well. For example, in August of 1774 Matthew Cocking, an employee of the Hudson's Bay Company, was camped at the mouth of the Red Deer River where he was meeting with the Indians. While there he obtained a good deal of information about the physical geography and resources of the Saskatchewan River Valley. Although having some doubts about its veracity, he believed that this information could be valuable to Samuel Hearne who had been sent by the company inland in the same year to establish Cumberland House on Cumberland Lake. Therefore, on 16 August 1774, he wrote a letter to Hearne saying:

The Indians I am with say that Elk and other Beasts are but scarce at the Lake Your Leader intended to take you to, particularly in the Winter; and the Natives will leave you there and proceed to the Barren Land [the prairies]. Basquis [the Pas] in their opinion would be [a] Better Place Being a great place of rendevous of the Natives in the Summer, and where they are more likely some of them to stay [during the winter] and provide for you than where you are; But that even at Basquis Provision is likely to be scarce at times; and that the best places for the Provision are here or else a great distance above you near the Barren Ground, where Buffelo Flesh may be easily brought. They pretend to advise that you send some of Your men to the Barren Land along with the Natives [?] that you will certainly be distressed for want of Provisions in the Winter, the Barren Land being too far distant to have any quantity from thence to you.[39]

Of great importance, the Indians thus indicated that even at The Pas, one of the best fishing spots in the lower Saskatchewan River, conditions were difficult in the winter, and most of the tribal groups abandoned the area at that time. The accuracy of the comments about the Cumberland Lake district were subsequently borne out by Hearne's and Cocking's experiences there. Hearne and his men nearly starved during their first winter on the lake in 1774–5, and Cocking, who succeeded Hearne there the following year, was forced to send two men to the parklands with the Indians in January so that the stocks of food on hand at the post would last until the spring break-up when relief could be expected.[40] Also, in the winter of 1775–6 Alexander Henry the Elder travelled overland from Beaver Lake, located to the north of Cumberland Lake, to Fort des Prairies, situated on the Saskatchewan River just below the forks. Henry set out on 1 January, and in the course of his journey, most of which was through the boreal forest, did not encounter any Indian bands. Furthermore, he and his two travelling companions nearly starved to death en route. His hardships stand in marked contrast to the experiences that La Vérendrye had on his winter trip through the forest margins of southern Manitoba in 1737.[41] From the above it is clear that there was a general winter movement of Indian populations out of the forests of Saskatchewan into the parklands. Beginning in the spring many of them began to move back into the forests to set up their fishing camps.

The accounts of both the French and English for the period from 1690 to 1765 suggest that there were two cycles of exploitation that were characteristic of tribal groups living in central and southern Manitoba and Saskatchewan (Figure 15). One of these was based in the forests and parklands and was most common among the Cree and certain bands of the Assiniboine who maintained direct contacts with the Hudson's Bay Company posts. This cycle was one in which the tribal bands spent the warmer months of the year in the forests. At that time the men made their trading expeditions to the Bay while their families fished and hunted along the shores of lakes and rivers in the forest land beyond the Shield. In late August, September, and October they hunted in the wooded areas adjacent to the prairies, taking moose and trapping beaver. From November to March they moved into the parkland belt proper where they often lived with the Assiniboine, hunting bison and trapping wolves and fox. In March, April, and May they reassembled along lakes and rivers to build their canoes, trap furs, fish, and hunt waterfowl.

In contrast to this scheduling of activity by Woodland-Parkland Indians, there was another cycle having a grassland-parkland orientation which was typical of the Assiniboine groups who had only indirect contact with Hudson Bay through Cree or Assiniboine middlemen, or, in other cases, who traded principally with the French (Figure 15). These bands commonly resorted to the parklands in the winter season to seek shelter, hunt bison, and trap wolves. In the spring they often set up fishing weirs along the principal rivers of the parklands, such as the Assiniboine, to take sturgeon. At this time, and often extending into early summer, raiding parties were sent into Siouan and Gros Ventre territory. In middle and late summer, the tribal populations shifted to the open grasslands to prey on the large bison herds. Toward the end of the summer and into autumn, even into early winter in some instances, the trading trip was made to the Mandan villages to obtain Indian corn. Upon completion of these expeditions the two groups returned to the parklands, except those who wintered in the scattered outliers of the forest zone, such as in Turtle Mountain. It was through these overlapping economic systems, outlined in Figure 11, that the tribes of the grasslands, forests, and parklands came into contact with each other. These economic contacts encouraged an inter-regional exchange of ideas. Through these exchanges, the various bands learned to cope with the different habitat zones that characterized the regional landscape. The Cree, for example, learned the technique of constructing and using the buffalo pound from the Assiniboine. The ability to exploit all of these zones gave these groups a great deal of

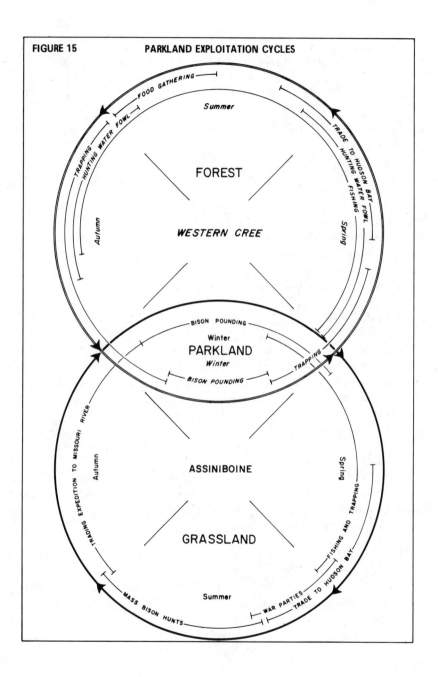

FIGURE 15   PARKLAND EXPLOITATION CYCLES

FOOD GATHERING

TRAPPING HUNTING WATER FOWL

Summer

TRADE TO HUDSON BAY HUNTING WATER FOWL FISHING

FOREST

Autumn

WESTERN CREE

Spring

BISON POUNDING

Winter

PARKLAND

Winter

TRAPPING

BISON POUNDING

TRADING EXPEDITION TO MISSOURI RIVER

Autumn

ASSINIBOINE

Spring

FISHING AND TRAPPING

GRASSLAND

MASS BISON HUNTS

Summer

WAR PARTIES TRADE TO HUDSON BAY

ecological flexibility. This flexibility permitted them to make rapid adjustments to changing economic conditions in the late eighteenth century, as will be elaborated subsequently, and it facilitated rapid inter-regional migration.

NOTES

1 For example, Nicolas Jérémie reported that there were large herds of Caribou inland from Fort Bourbon (York Factory) during the early eighteenth century. Douglas and Wallace, *Twenty Years of York Factory, 1694–1714*, 22

2 Governor George Simpson, York Factory, to the Governor and Committee in London, 31 July 1822, PAC HBC D 4/85, p. 17

3 Governor George Simpson, York Factory, to the Governor and Committee in London, 10 August 1824, PAC HBC D 4/87, p. 46

4 Mayer-Oakes, *Life, Land and Water*, 369–72

5 MacNeish, 'An Introduction to the Archaeology of Southeastern Manitoba, 67–71

6 MacNeish, 'The Stott Mound and Village Near Brandon Manitoba,' 20–59

7 Ibid., 50

8 It is somewhat surprising that this facet of the cultural history of the region has received so little attention. In a brief article the author discussed the historical evidence for such movements: Ray, 'Indian Adaptations to the Forest-Grassland Boundary of Manitoba and Saskatchewan, 1650–1821.' Mayer-Oakes suggests that these movements probably occurred in the prehistoric period also; see, Mayer-Oakes, *Archeological Investigations in the Grand Rapids Manitoba Reservoir, 1961–62*, 372–3.

9 Thwaites, *Jesuit Relations*, 54: 193

10 Ibid., 66: 107–9. This letter was written in 1694. It is included in Tyrrell, *Documents Relating to the Early History of Hudson Bay*, 105–41. The English translation of Tyrrell differs slightly from that of Thwaites.

11 Burpee, *Journals and Letters of La Vérendrye*, 127

12 Ibid., 95

13 Ibid., 243

14 Ibid., 243–4

15 Ibid., 240

16 Thwaites, *Jesuit Relations*, 68: 291–3

17 Burpee, *Journals and Letters of La Vérendrye*, 253–4

18 Thwaites, *Jesuit Relations*, 68: 293

19 Burpee, *Journals and Letters of La Vérendrye*, 517

20 Ibid., 315

21 Ibid., 312
22 Doughty and Martin, *Kelsey Papers*, 1–4
23 Ibid., 13
24 Burpee, *Journals and Letters of La Vérendrye*, 317
25 Doughty and Martin, *Kelsey Papers*, 13
26 Horses did not spread into the parklands of Saskatchewan until much later. Kelsey indicated that the Assiniboine still made bows and arrows which they used for hunting. Ibid., 1–4
27 York Factory Journals, 1757, PAC HBC B 239/a/43, pp. 9–10
28 Ibid., 12
29 According to E.E. Rich, Smith and Waggoner's party had travelled from Cedar Lake to the Assiniboine River. They would have been in the latter area in January and early February. In the middle of the latter month they headed northward to the Swan River area where they subsequently built their canoes. See, Rich, *The Fur Trade*, 127–9
30 York Factory Journal, 1757, PAC HBC B 239/a/43, p. 14. Considering the context of the reference it would appear that 'Waskesews' were a variety of water fowl, since he said they went in droves and his party shot them while paddling their canoes. What is puzzling is the fact that red deer were called 'Warkesews.' This suggests the possibility that the waskesews were herds of red deer; however, this seems unlikely because the lower Saskatchewan River area was outside of the primary range of this animal.
31 Rich, *The Fur Trade*, 127–9. The Location of the Sturgeon Indians in western Manitoba in the 1760s is of considerable interest in that in 1740, some sixteen years earlier, Joseph La France informed Dobbs that the group was living on the shores of Lake of the Woods. According to La France the tribe was so named 'from the great Number of Sturgeons they take in this Lake, which is the greatest Part of their Provisions,' *Report From the Committee Appointed to Enquire Into the State and Condition of the Countries Adjoining to Hudson's Bay and of the Trade Carried on There*, Appendix 11, p. 244. Smith's and La France's accounts thus indicate that the group had moved some 125 to 175 miles to the west-northwest in sixteen years – a rate of about ten miles a year. Furthermore, when La France's account of their subsistence is compared to that of Smith's, one can gain some idea of the rapidity with which some groups were able to alter their economic orientations to fit new environmental situations.
32 York Factory Journals, 1758, PAC HBC B 239/a/45, p. 3
33 Ibid., 4
34 York Factory Journal, 1764, PAC HBC B 239/a/52, pp. 6–7
35 Ibid., 9
36 Ibid., 20

37 See, Tyrrell, *The Journals of Samuel Hearne and Phillip Turnor Between the Years 1774 and 1792*, 6

38 Pink's journal is included in the York Factory Journals of 1766–7, PAC HBC B 239/a/56, pp. 2–21.

39 York Factory Journal, 1774–5, PAC HBC B 239/a/72, p. 9. Cocking doubted the account because the Indians he was camped with wanted the company to build the post closer to their homelands, that is, farther down the Saskatchewan River.

40 For a more extended discussion of the winter provision problems at Cumberland House see Ray, 'Indian Exploitation of the Forest-Grassland Transition Zone of Western Canada, 1650–1860,' 33–6.

41 Henry, *Travels and Adventures in Canada and the Indian Territories Between the Years 1760 and 1776*, 267–74

3
Traders and middlemen

During the early years of the fur trade in western Canada, competition between the English and the French was largely centred on Hudson Bay, and certain key posts such as York Factory changed hands several times. This period of instability ended in 1713 with the signing of the Treaty of Utrecht which gave the English permanent control of the Bay. As the English fur trade was re-established in the postwar years under the direction of the Hudson's Bay Company, two posts quickly emerged as the leading centres of trade for the western interior of Canada – York Factory and Fort Albany. Of the two, York Factory was more important in terms of its volume of trade (Figure 16) and the size of its hinterland (Figure 17). Before 1717 its trading area included the whole of Manitoba and Saskatchewan. The hinterland of Fort Albany, on the other hand, reached only to the lands lying just to the east of Lake Winnipeg during this period. In 1717, the Hudson's Bay Company opened Fort Prince of Wales (later called Fort Churchill) on the lower Churchill River, and this post siphoned off part of the trade at York Factory. However, as Figure 16 shows, the new post never rivaled York Factory as a trading centre, and it drew in the trade of relatively few Indian groups living to the south of the Churchill River basin. The few who did come were chiefly Woodland Assiniboine and Cree groups who inhabited the North Saskatchewan River region.

Having been blocked from the Bay, the French redoubled their efforts to cut the Hudson's Bay Company off from its hinterland. Although this effort had begun as early as 1680 when Du Lhut built his post on Lake

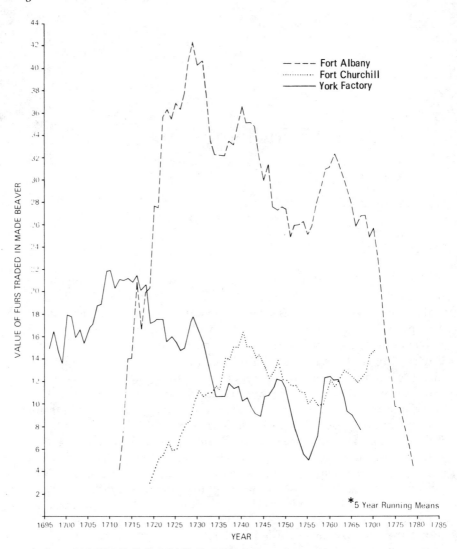

FIGURE 16   VOLUME OF FURS TRADED AT YORK FACTORY, FORT ALBANY AND FORT CHURCHILL

Nipigon to intercept the Assiniboine and Cree on their way to Fort Albany, it had had little effect on the English trade except at the latter post. Beginning in the 1730s, however, the French began to penetrate into the hinterland of York Factory, as La Vérendrye built a string of posts at strategic points in southern Manitoba and Saskatchewan (Figure 18), and these posts began to draw off a portion of York Factory's trade. Figure 19 shows that the volumes of furs and of goods traded were increasing until the early 1730s; thereafter they began an erratic decline reaching their lowest levels in the 1750s when competition was sharpest; and in the late 1750s they began to rise again as the French were forced to withdraw. The values for the *overplus*, which will be explained below, are even more sensitive to changing levels of competition and exhibit the same trends.

While the French and English vied with each other for the trade of the Indians inhabiting the Western Interior, the various Indian groups competed with each other for control of the carrying trade to and from the European posts, particularly that of York Factory.

Unfortunately, very little information is available regarding this aspect of the trade at York Factory until 1714, when the Hudson's Bay Company regained control of the post for the last time. Thereafter, the record becomes increasingly voluminous. James Knight was placed in command of the post in 1714, and he began a concerted effort to re-establish company contacts with the Indians in the interior. In the summer of 1715, 172 canoes came down to the post manned by Misshenipee, Sturgeon, Stone, Upland, Muscotay, Mountain, and Strange Indians.

The first four of these groups were regular visitors at the post and can be readily identified. The Misshenipee, also listed as the Misshenepih and Michinipi, were Cree bands who came from the upper Churchill River region between Reindeer Lake and the Athabasca River.[1] The Sturgeon Indians were another band of Cree who lived in southeastern Manitoba where they were met by La Vérendrye in the 1730s.[2] The Stone Indians were Assiniboine, and were also identified as the Northern Sinepoetts (Woodland Assiniboine) and Southern Sinepoetts (Parkland-Grassland Assiniboine) – and Sinepoets is one of many variant spellings. The Upland Indians included both Assiniboine and Cree, particularly the Woodland Assiniboine and Cree bands living to the west of York Factory between the Saskatchewan and Churchill rivers. The term Southern Indians was also applied to the Cree coming from that quarter, but more often to those coming from southern Manitoba and northern Ontario. Immediately upon the resumption of trade by the Hudson's Bay Company, these four groups accounted for most of the canoes coming down to York Factory.

The other trading parties that arrived at the post were fewer in number and generally came from much greater distances.[3] One of these

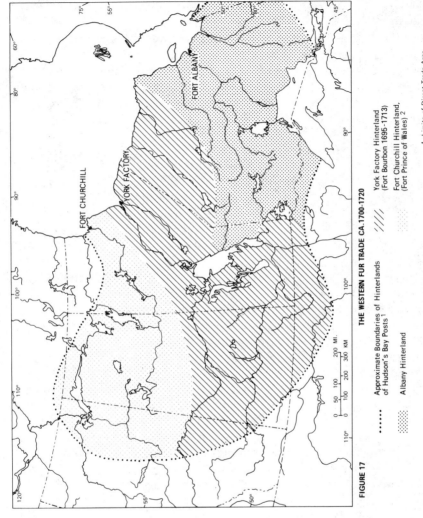

FIGURE 17

THE WESTERN FUR TRADE CA.1700-1720

······ Approximate Boundaries of Hinterlands
        of Hudson's Bay Posts [1]

⋮⋮⋮⋮ Albany Hinterland

⁄⁄⁄⁄ York Factory Hinterland
      (Fort Bourbon 1695-1713)

⋮⋮⋮⋮ Fort Churchill Hinterland,
      (Fort Prince of Wales) [2]

1. Limits of Direct Trade Area
2. Part of York Factory Hinterland Until 1717

FORT CHURCHILL

YORK FACTORY

FORT ALBANY

groups were the Muscotay (as noted earlier, Muscotay was a geographic term referring in this instance to the grasslands between the forks of the Saskatchewan River).[4] The ethnic identity of the Muscotay will, therefore, never be known precisely, but they were, in all probability, either Blood, Blackfoot, or perhaps Gros Ventre, although the latter seems unlikely in this instance since the term Ashkee Indians seems to have been applied to the Gros Ventre at that time.[5] All of the above tribes were known to have traded at the post in later years. For instance, as late as 1758 James Isham, then in charge of York Factory, wrote to Ferdinand Jacobs at Fort Churchill and informed him that five canoes of 'Bloody Indians (or Mithcoo Ethenue) [his parentheses] came down to trade.'[6] Significantly, he added, 'none of the tribe has been here since 1733.'[7] This remark clearly implies that some of the Blood had the practice of coming down to the Bay during the early decades of the eighteenth century. Similarly, in 1757, the 'Earchithinues' came to York Factory in company with a large party of Assiniboine and Cree from the Saskatchewan River area.[8] The term 'Earchithinue' and its more commonly used variant, 'Archithinue,' was a Cree word that was applied to the Blackfoot and the Gros Ventre.[9] Precise ethnic identification is therefore not possible, but both groups came from the same general region – the Muscotay Plains.

Of all of the Indians who came to York Factory in 1715, the Mountain Indians were said to have travelled the greatest distance. Knight reported that it took them thirty-nine days to make the trip downstream and three months to return. In 1715, thirty canoes of these Indians arrived at the post. Included in the trading party was an old chief who informed Knight that he had been at Fort Albany sixteen years earlier. In an effort to obtain as much information as he could regarding the Mountain Indian country, Knight held long discussions with this chief as well as with two Upland Indian leaders in the following year. The latter had apparently been to the region. According to Knight:

both agreed in one thing they Say the Country is very Mountainious and of [such] a Prodigious height ... they can not see the capp without it be Clear Weather [.][T]hey tell me their is abundance of Natives and ... Sev'll Nations of them and their grows a great deal of Indian Corn Plumbs Hazle Nutts and they have not much Beavor, but abundance of Moose, Buffolo, Wascashus [red deer] and Small Furrs ... all them Mountain Indians Garnish themselves with a White Mettle ... they [also] have a Yellow Mettle Amongst them.[10]

Although this description contains elements of exaggeration and pure

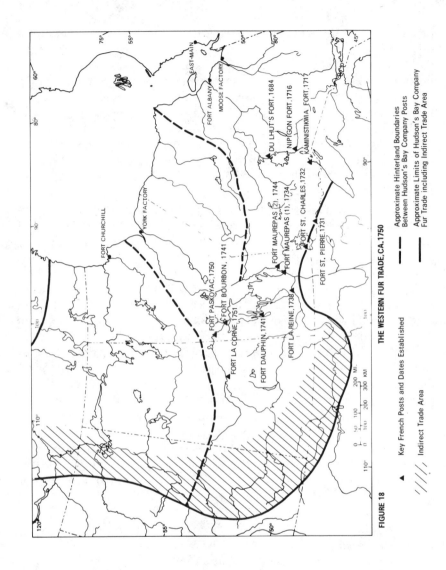

FIGURE 18   **THE WESTERN FUR TRADE, CA. 1750**

▲   Key French Posts and Dates Established

//////   Indirect Trade Area

— — —   Approximate Hinterland Boundaries Between Hudson's Bay Company Posts

———   Approximate Limits of Hudson's Bay Company Fur Trade Including Indirect Trade Area

fabrication to please the English traders, such as the allusions to silver and gold, it is significant that reference is made to agriculture, bison, red deer, and mountainous terrain. The only region that could have included this combination of elements is the plains region stretching from the Upper Missouri River to the Rocky Mountains. The Mountain Indians were therefore either Mandan or Hidatsa, and the scraps of information in Knight's journal suggest that the term may have been applied indiscriminately to both groups. For instance, the Mountain Indians were said to live next to the Crow with whom they were at war. When the Mountain Indians arrived at York Factory in 1716, they brought some Crow slaves along with them. In order to extend his trade to the latter tribe, Knight attempted to use these slaves to conclude a peace between the Crow and Mountain Indians. Thus, he wrote that the Mountain Indians returned home with a 'leading Indian his Brother & Wife wch I had Employ'd to go Amongst ye Cocauchee or Crow Indians wch was a Slave Woman of yt Country yt had Undertaken to go into her Country again with her husband and a great many more Indians and make a peace and bring me down a great deal of the Yellow Mettle wch she told me, it was so plenty.'[11]

Considering that it is generally believed that the Crow separated from the Hidatsa sometime during the early eighteenth century due to a feud, it seems likely that the Mountain Indians to whom Knight was referring were Hidatsa.[12] However, in 1721, the Mandan arrived at York Factory to trade. Henry Kelsey was then in charge of the post and referred to them as the Mai-tain-ai-thi-nish.[13] It is distinctly possible therefore, that Knight's early use of the term Mountain Indian was a corruption of this word. However, the Mandan did not live next to the Crow. For these reasons, it seems likely that the name was applied rather loosely to both the Mandan and Hidatsa at different times at York Factory.

The 'Strange' Indians who arrived at York Factory between 1715 and 1720 are difficult to identify since this term was generally applied to newcomers at the post. In all probability they came from the far west, and they may have been Sarsi Indians. Journal entries in later years suggest that this group did, in fact, visit the post. In 1728–9, 1729–30, 1730–1, and 1740–1, a group variously called the Shussuanna, Shusuanna, Su Hannah, and Susuhannah came to York Factory, usually in company with the Assiniboine and Western Cree (then listed as Keskatchewan Indians).[14] Although they cannot be identified positively, considering that they came from the Saskatchewan region but were not listed as either a band of Assiniboine or Cree according to Andrew Graham, a trader at York

Figure 19

YORK FACTORY TRADE RECEIPTS

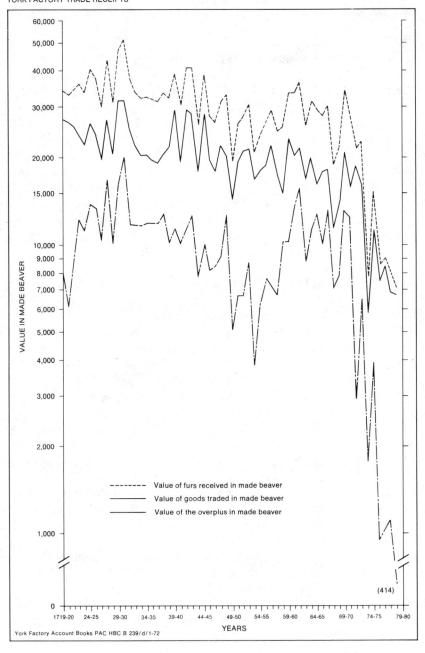

York Factory Account Books PAC HBC B 239/d/1-72

Factory, they may well have been the Sarsi.[15] Graham reported that this tribe was known as the Sussou in the late eighteenth century.[16]

In addition to the various Indian trade parties who arrived by canoe, the Northern Indians were also frequent visitors at York Factory before 1717. This group consisted largely of the Athabascan-speaking Chipewyan who arrived on foot in these early years.[17] Included among these parties were Northern Indian Strangers who came from beyond Lake Athabasca toward Great Slave Lake. They were said to live next to the Yellow Mettle Indians (Yellow Knives) with whom they had recently been at war.[18]

Figure 8 shows the distribution of these various Indian groups. It reveals that in the unsettled period immediately following the resumption of English control at York Factory the post was drawing Indian trading parties from a vast territory reaching from the Missouri River on the southwest to at least Great Slave Lake on the northwest. However, this pattern of trade was relatively short lived. In 1717, when Fort Churchill was opened, the latter post took over nearly all of the trade with the Chipewyan and most of that of the Michinipi Cree. A small trade was carried on with the Northern Assiniboine as well.

More importantly, through the use of force the various Assiniboine and Cree bands increasingly took over control of the inland trade of York Factory. Although Knight attempted to arrange peace treaties between the Upland Assiniboine and Cree and the Northern, Western, and Muscotay Indians in the hopes of increasing trade, his efforts largely failed. Most of the treaties that he did manage to arrange were quickly broken. Consequently, after 1720 very few of the more distant tribes appear at York Factory. For example, there are no further references to the Mountain Indians after 1721.[19]

Those that did occasionally make the voyage such as the Shussuanna, Blood, and Archithinue, always arrived in company with the Assiniboine and Cree, suggesting that perhaps they were not permitted to do so without the escort of the latter groups. Individual Cree and Assiniboine may also have travelled as envoys with these parties. For instance, one of the leading Bloody Indian Captains (Trading Leaders) who regularly visited York Factory was an Assiniboine.[20] He may have served in some essentially diplomatic fashion that enabled the Bloody Indians to pass peacefully through Assiniboine and Cree territory.

Besides the Assiniboine and Cree trading blockade, other factors tended to discourage the Plains Indians from continuing to trade directly with York Factory. By 1740 the use of horses had spread northward as far as the parkland belt in Alberta and the Missouri River in the Dakota region. This development, along with an increasingly grassland economic orientation which became characteristic of such groups as the Blood and Blackfoot, meant that many bands of these tribes no longer would have been able to make the journey to the Bay, since they abandoned the use of canoes. This may have been an additional reason why the few who continued to do so travelled with Assiniboine and Cree in the later years on their trips down to York Factory. The Assiniboine and Cree could have served as helmsmen in the Blackfoot and Blood canoes though there is no evidence that this was the case.

In addition, because the Mountain, Blood, and Archithinue had to travel such great distances, they were unable to carry enough provisions in their canoes to supply themselves on the voyage down and back from the Bay. As European traders were to learn in later years, hunting en route was difficult because of the time factor and meager nature of the forest-resource base. These problems were further aggravated by the occasionally late arrivals of the ships from England. These late arrivals delayed the departure of the Indians from the post and meant that in the cases of these distant tribes, it was impossible to return home before the arrival of winter. Consequently, they ran a considerable risk of facing starvation when undertaking their trading expeditions to York Factory. For instance, the failure of the ships to arrive on time in the summer of 1716 was said to have caused many deaths from starvation of the Mountain, Ashkee, and some of the Northern Sinepoett on their return home. Such losses were very upsetting to James Knight because he believed they could be avoided if more forethought were given to the time ships were despatched from England. When the Mountain Indians returned next summer on 10 June 1717, he took the opportunity to stress the gravity of the problem and to vent his feelings writing:

here is 22 Canoos of the Mountain Indians Come & some others as border upon them Says that most of all the Indians as went away from here so Late last fall was Starv'd & Died not being Able to gett home to their Own Country & here is not above 1/3 part of them Indians as came down here Last Year. It Grieves Me to the very heart to think how a Country is Ruin'd by a Senseless Blockhead not having thought care nor consideration.[21]

Unfortunately, the Indians were to experience similar hardships later on. In 1763, Ferdinand Jacobs sent a letter from York Factory to Moses Norton at Fort Churchill, informing him that 'the Bloody Indians were,

Some of them, Starved to Death Last year going Back which So intimidated them that I am afraid we Shall never have any more of them Come to Trade.'[22] Jacobs' fears proved to be well founded and the Blood Indians do not appear to have returned to the Bay afterwards.

It is not surprising, therefore, that in 1772 when the Hudson's Bay Company sent Mathew Cocking inland in an attempt to encourage the Archithinue Indians to bypass the Assiniboine and Cree middlemen and come down to York Factory, they refused. According to Cocking 'they said that they would be starved & were unacquainted with Canoes & mentioned the long distance.'[23] It was this combination of distance, hardships experienced in the past, and the abandonment of canoes by many inland bands that played into the hands of the Assiniboine and Cree middlemen. By playing them up, and using intimidation as necessary, they were able to hold a virtual monopoly on the trade at York Factory during most of the eighteenth century. Reflecting this, the canoe tallies that were kept at the post in 1757, 1758, 1759, and 1761, indicate that nearly all of the Indians coming to the post were either Cree or Assiniboine. The only other group that brought a significant portion of the trade were the Ojibwa who accounted for about 12 per cent of the canoe traffic. Of the Assiniboine and Cree canoes, roughly 50 per cent came from the Saskatchewan River Valley, 18 per cent from the Churchill River, and approximately 20 per cent from the area close to the Bay. The latter were the Home Guard Indians, who were later to be known as the Swampy Cree (Figure 20).[24]

In order for the vast York Factory trading system to operate smoothly, a set of complex relationships had to be worked out between the participating groups. This involved the development of a series of devices whereby the barter economy of the Indians could be tied in with the market-oriented enterprise of the Hudson's Bay Company. Throughout the seventeenth and eighteenth centuries, the Indians, especially the Assiniboine and Cree middlemen, held the upper hand in the fur trade at York Factory, and to a considerable extent they dictated the terms of trade. Thus, the company was forced to make most of the adjustments during this period.

Since the Indians lacked any concept of money, the Hudson's Bay Company was forced to devise a scheme which would allow them to keep records of their barter trade. To achieve this end, the company employed the *made beaver* (MB) as its standard unit of evaluation. It was equivalent to the value of a prime beaver skin and the prices of all trade goods, other

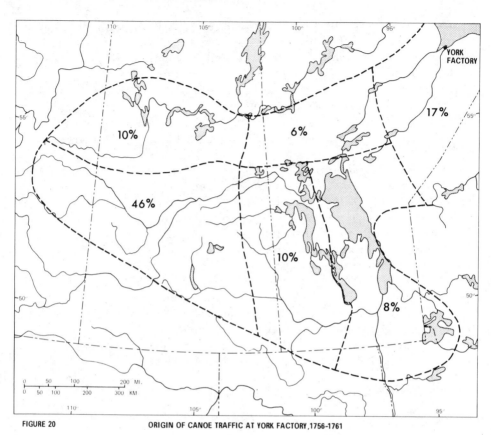

FIGURE 20   ORIGIN OF CANOE TRAFFIC AT YORK FACTORY,1756-1761

Figures indicate percentage of total canoe traffic originating in the various portions of the hinterland

Note: Figures do not total to 100% due to rounding of values to nearest whole number. Also,3
percent of traffic is unidentifiable as to area of origin.

furs, and country produce were expressed in terms of MB. As Figure 21 shows, trade goods coming from Europe were assigned these values according to the *official standard of trade*, while the furs received from the Indians were evaluated according to the *comparative standard of trade*. One of the primary problems that the company faced was that once the Indians agreed to a standard rate, they were resistant to changes. This often meant that the company was placed in a very difficult position. For example, between 1689 and 1697, while England was engaged in war with France, the prices of goods and seamen's wages were inflating rapidly. The company, therefore, wanted to raise the standard of trade to offset its rising costs. Numerous letters were sent to the Bay from London advocating this measure. Typical of these dispatches was the one that the company sent to Governor Geyer at Port Nelson (York Factory) on 13 July 1689. Regarding the standard of trade, Geyer was instructed:

to Consider the great Losses wee have of Late sustained, the many hazards wee Run through in these times of danger, Besides the extrordinary expence wee are now at in sending suplies, which Tribles the Charge of former years; from hence you may urge the natives the great difficulties wee undergoe to come to them, and that theirfore they ought now allow more beaver in Truck for our goods then heretofore, but this also is Left to your wise Conduct, for our benefitt the best you can, Carefuly avoiding any measures which may disgust them.[25]

In short, it was left to Geyer's judgment as to what should be done as long as he was careful not to alienate the Indians. The note of caution was stressed in nearly all of the letters that the company sent. An examination of the account books for York Factory in subsequent years reveals that only minor changes were made in the official standard of trade (Table 1). The same was true for the comparative standard.

Because of the relatively inflexible attitudes of the Indians towards these two standards, the company had to find some other way of adjusting prices as European market conditions and local levels of competition varied. As the letter cited above shows, the company left it up to its chief traders or factors to come up with a solution. They responded by employing their own standard, the *factor's* or *double standard* as it was called. This involved raising the values of goods above that which was stated in the official standard of trade. They did this by simply asking for more beaver per item whenever they could or, more commonly, by giving short measures to the Indians of those commodities such as cloth, powder, beads, and so forth that were measured out at the time of trade. However, the Indians also understood this system and again would not tolerate radical departures from accepted norms, though they did permit some adjustments.

Their seemingly greater tolerance for changes in the double standard was undoubtedly a consequence of the fact that they could better understand them and bargain more effectively over the amounts involved. Changes in the official standard of trade quite often would have involved changes in volumetric, linear, or weight measurements which meant little to the Indians who were more accustomed to bartering objects – in other words, discrete units. On the other hand, if a trader tried to give them

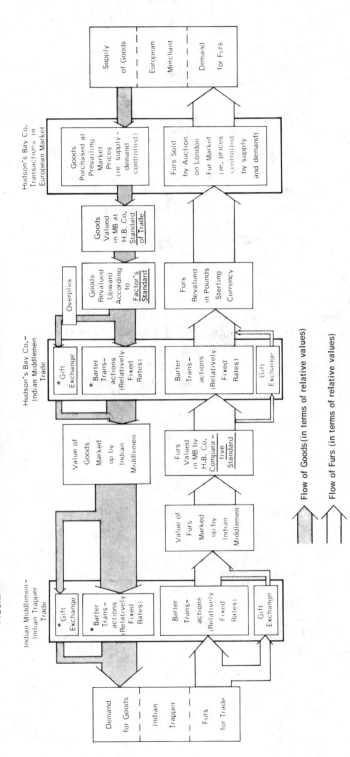

FIGURE 21   HUDSON'S BAY COMPANY FUR TRADE : ECONOMIC OPERATIONS

Flow of Goods (in terms of relative values)

Flow of Furs (in terms of relative values)

MB = Made Beaver Value

* Some goods such as tobacco and liquor immediately
consumed at these points

only one-half a horn of powder for a beaver skin after they had become accustomed to obtaining a full one, they could readily perceive the change and make an attempt to haggle over it and arrive at a compromise. In this way the Indians forced the traders to bargain within their own terms of reference. The official standard of trade thus appears to have served more as a base guideline to the traders themselves. It was essentially their minimum price or exchange level.[26]

At York Factory, as at the other posts, the traders invariably exceed this base level and the gain which they made was reported as *overplus*. They obtained this figure by subtracting the value of goods traded, in terms of the standard of trade, from the values of all the furs received priced in reference to the comparative standard. If the exchange at the post had been conducted according to these two standards, then the result would have been zero. As Figure 19 shows, this was never the case. The value of the goods traded was always less than that of the furs due to the application of the double standard. The magnitude of this difference, or the value of the overplus, depended on competitive conditions. While the Hudson's Bay Company held a monopoly in the Western Interior, the factors were able to drive hard bargains and steadily push the value of the overplus upwards. However, as the French moved into the Manitoba area and consolidated their position, they were able to offer enough opposition to force the York Factory traders to relax their standard or lose an increasingly large portion of the fur trade. The latter traders responded to this threat, and as Figure 19 shows the overplus totals began falling, reaching their lowest point during the 1750s at the height of French competition.

Much of the gain that the traders obtained by applying the double standard was re-invested in the fur trade. To a considerable extent, the traders at York Factory drew upon the overplus account to finance gifts which were given to Indians (Figure 21). These presents were given to band leaders a day or two before actual trading began. The leaders would distribute the gifts to other members of their respective bands after having made token presents of furs to the company factor. This reciprocal gift-giving ceremony was an Indian institution which served to affirm friendship. Had the company refused to participate, no trade would have taken place. In the seventeenth and eighteenth centuries, tobacco, beads, and brandy were some of the items that were given most frequently on those occasions.

Having accepted this feature of inter-tribal trade as a necessary institution, the company began to use it to attempt to arrange treaties between

TABLE 1

Hudson's Bay Company standard of trade goods (valued in terms of made beaver)

Goods	1720–1*	1742–3†	1760–1‡
Kettles	1 1/2 per lb.	1	
1 pint			
2 quart			
3 quart			16
1 gallon			18
Gun Powder	1 per 1 lb.	1 per lb.	1 per 1 lb.
Shot	1 per 4 lbs.	1 per 5 lbs.	
Duck			1 per 4 lbs.
Bristol			1 per 4 lbs.
Goose			1 per 4 lbs.
Low East Ind.			1 per 4 lbs.
High East Ind.			1 per 4 lbs.
Tobacco			
Brazil	2 per lb.	1 per lb.	1 per 3/4 lb.
English Roll	1 per lb.	1 per 1 1/2 lbs.	1 per 1 lb.
Virg. Leaf		1 per 1 1/2 lbs.	
Beads			
large	4 per lb.		
small	2 per lb.		
long white			5 per lb.
small white			4 per lb.
round, all colours			
and sizes			2 per lb.
barley corn			6 per lb.
Guns	14 each		
4 ft.		12 each	14 each
3 1/2 ft.		11 each	14 each
3 ft.		10 each	14 each
Gun worms	1 per 4	1 per 4	1 per 4
Gun flints	1 per 16	1 per 20	
Hatchets	1 per 1	1 per 2	1 per 1
Ice chisels	1 per 1	1 per 2	1 per 1
Scrapers	1 per 2	1 per 2	1 per 2
Fire Steels	1 per 4	1 per 4	
Files	1 per 1	1 per 1	1 per 1
Awl blades	1 per 8	1 per 12	1 per 8
Hawks bells	1 per 12	1 per 8	1 per 12
Twine	1 per sk.	1 per sk.	1 per 1
Net lines	1 per 1	1 per 2	1 per 1
Blankets	7 per 1	6 per 1	7 per 1

TABLE 1 (*continued*)

Hudson's Bay Company standard of trade goods (valued in terms of made beaver)

Goods	1720–1*	1742–3†	1760–1‡
Cloth			
broad	3 per yd.	2 per yd.	
corded			3 per yd.
fine			5 per yd.
flannel	1½ per yd.	1½ per yd.	1½ per yd.
duffel	2 per yd.	1½ per yd.	2 per yd.
Brandy	4 per gal.	4 per gal.	4 per gal.
Knives		1 per 8	1 per 4

* York Factory Account Books, 1720–1, PAC HBC B 239/d/11, pp. 2–3
† Dobbs, *An Account of the Countries Adjoining to Hudson's Bay*, 193–6
‡ York Factory Account Books, 1760–1, PAC HBC B 239/d/51, pp. 23–6

warring tribes in the interior and to lure groups down to the Bay. Thus, when Knight sent Upland Indian parties inland between 1715 and 1718 to settle their differences with the Northern, Western, and Muscotay Indians, he provided them with trade goods that were to be given away to demonstrate the good faith of the Upland Indians to these other groups. Goods were also given to leading Indians who were instructed to give them to other bands who were not in the habit of trading at the Bay in the hope that it would encourage them to do so. Occasionally, company employees were dispatched from the posts for the same purpose, as was Henry Kelsey. In these instances the variety of goods given away was greater than in the case of gift exchanges at the post because they were intended to show the range of goods that would be available to those bands who were willing to make the trip down to the Bay. For example, Henry Kelsey was sent inland with the following inventory of goods:

2 long eng guns, 1 blanket, 1 man's laced coate, 1 man's laced cap, 2 ice chissels, 3 hatchets, 56 flints, 1 silke sash, 2 ivory combs, 2 Leath Looking glasses, 4 gun worms, 26 lbs. powder, 71 lbs. shott, 1/4 lbs. beads, 3/4 lbs. red Lead, 4 Steeles, 16 knives, 24 bells, 1 brass kettle, w3 lb., 1 pr. scissors, 2 skeins twine, 2 nett lines, 2 scrapers, 20 lb. brazil tobacco, 2 sword blades, 1 steele tobacco box, 1 Large powder horne, 1 small ditto, 1 dagger.[27]

This consignment was to be given to the Plains Indians of Saskatchewan.

Thus, although the gift-giving ceremony was initially primarily a socio-political institution, designed to cement alliances and reaffirm friendships, under the competitive conditions of the fur trade, it increasingly served as a device that could be used to win trading loyalties of Indian bands. The Indians responded to generous gift-giving as an affirmation of good will, especially when trading rates were also relaxed.

One of the inherent weaknesses in the fur-trading system from the point of view of the survival of the Indian cultures of the west related to the fact that even though the Indian traders responded to lavish gift-giving and favourable trading terms, they did not react in the same manner as did the Europeans. As Andrew Graham and many other traders pointed out, the Indians' demand for goods during this early period, and indeed, essentially until 1821, was relatively inelastic. According to Graham, the average Indian required only 70 MB value of goods a year to satisfy his basic needs, and another 30 MB value to 'squander' at the post.[28] This inelastic demand was in part a consequence of the nomadic lifestyle of the Indian and in part a function of his limited transport capabilities, which placed constraints on the quantities of goods he could take back to his home territory. Therefore, while favourable terms and lavish gifts would bring them to trade, it did not induce them to bring more furs on a per-capita basis. In fact, the reverse was the case. With demand levels relatively fixed, a drop in the effective price for goods meant that the Indians could bring in fewer furs to obtain what they wanted. Their potential free time was thereby increased and they could spend it at the posts drinking and smoking and living what the traders called, an 'indolent life.' It was partly for this reason that the fur trade was to prove so disruptive to the Indian way of life under fiercely competitive situations of a later date. However, prior to 1763, the level of competition did not reach sufficient degrees of intensity for this combination of factors to come fully into play. Furthermore, since the Indians travelling to York Factory were on rather tight travel schedules they did not have much time to spend around the posts.

The fixed demand-level of the Indian middlemen did, however, have important implications for quantities and types of trade goods that reached other inland groups during the eighteenth century. With the Assiniboine and Cree holding a virtual monopoly on the inland trade of York Factory after 1720, their preferences for certain goods and the size of that demand largely determined the kinds and numbers of European goods that would have been available to the Mandan, Gros Ventre, Blood, Blackfoot, and Sarcee, with whom they traded. Prior to the 1750s, there is little evidence that the Assiniboine and Cree acquired many goods at York Factory specifically for trade with the latter tribes. Rather, they bartered their furs for the items that they intended to use themselves. After a year or two of usage, they then passed them on to these other groups, as used or second-hand trade goods. As Figure 21 shows, the Hudson's Bay Company traders reported that the Cree and the Assiniboine middlemen when passing them on, marked them up in price. Guns, which had been traded at York Factory for 12 MB, were said to be exchanged to the Blackfoot for 36 MB, and knives, which were bartered at the rate of 1 MB each to the Cree, were passed on by the latter to the Chipewyan for 9 MB.

The Assiniboine and Cree marked up their barter rates for a number of reasons, even though they were not motivated by the desire to make a sustained-yield profit as was the case with their European counterparts. The company traders expressed these mark-ups in terms of the official standard of trade. However, as we have seen, that did not represent the rate at which the goods were actually traded to the Assiniboine and Cree because of the use of the double standard. Therefore, part of the seemingly large middlemen mark-up was necessary to make up for this difference. In addition, the Cree and Assiniboine middlemen would have had to place some increased value on their used trade goods to allow for the quantities that were lost through breakage during the year or two they used them prior to trade. Finally, the Assiniboine and Cree traders also had to participate in reciprocal gift-giving exchanges with other Indian groups (Figure 21). Since European goods were the primary items demanded from the Assiniboine and Cree by these other bands, they would have been obliged to give some trade goods away as gifts. The furs that they obtained in return were not necessarily of equal worth. Some adjustment of values therefore would have been required by the Indian middlemen to avoid their suffering losses. As long as the Assiniboine and Cree held a monopoly, they could keep this delicately balanced system operating. Through their inland trade, they managed to obtain nearly all of the furs they required to satisfy their own demand for goods, and Graham reported that very few of them did their own trapping.

The inland penetration of the French during the 1730s and 1740s did not upset this monopoly, since they did not penetrate beyond the area held by these two tribes (Figure 18). Rather, the French merely made it unnecessary for some of the Assiniboine and Cree middlemen to make the long trek to the Bay. After they acquired their furs from the Blackfoot, Gros Ventre, Mandan, and others they could trade a part of them at the French houses located along the lower Saskatchewan River or in southern Manitoba. Thus, by 1720 a pattern of trade had emerged in which the Assiniboine and Cree middlemen were the central figures.

Being in such a position, they were able to dictate the terms of the trade to Europeans and other Indians alike. Furthermore, because of the nature of the system which evolved, they largely regulated the rate of material culture change, and to a considerable extent they also influenced its directions.

NOTES

1 York Factory Journal, 1715, PAC HBC B 239/a/1, pp. 39–52. Lake Michinipi, or Great Water Lake, appears to have been the name given to Reindeer Lake during this period. See, Ray, 'Early French Mapping of the Western Interior of Canada.' The term Michinipi was also a general one for the upper Churchill River upstream from its confluence with the Reindeer River. This is clearly shown on an unpublished map of Alexander Henry the Elder entitled 'The North West Parts of America,' dated ca. 1775 (copy in PAC, Ottawa).

2 Also, Joseph La France informed Arthur Dobbs that they were still living in the region around Lake of the Woods as late as 1740. See La France's map (Figure 7).

3 Some groups of the Northern Sinepoets were an exception. According to James Knight, some of them lived near the headwaters of the Port Nelson River (Nelson–Saskatchewan river system) and he reported that these Assiniboine had to travel some of the greatest distances of any Indian groups to reach York Factory. York Factory Journal, 1717, PAC HBC B 239/a/3, p. 58

4 Morton, *A History of the Canadian West to 1870–1871*, 246

5 According to the York Factory Account Books of 1718–19, a gift was given to an Ashkee Indian leader called Ashkee Ethinee who was said to live near the 'Mountain' near 'Redd Deer River' (probably the Touchwood Hills near the headwaters of the Red Deer River of Saskatchewan). This is roughly the area which was occupied by the Gros Ventre during the middle of the eighteenth century. It is unlikely that the Ashkee Indians were Assiniboine since the latter were usually identified as Stone, Northern, or Southern Sinepoetts at that time. York Factory Account Books, 1718–19, PAC HBC B 239/d/10, p. 3

6 York Factory Correspondence Books, 17 July 1758, PAC HBC B 239/b/16, p. 3–4

7 Ibid.

8 York Factory Journals, 1756–7, PAC HBC B 239/a/42, p. 35. This trading party included ninety-nine canoes.

9 Rich identifies the 'Archithinue' as the Blood while G. Williams contends that they were the Gros Ventre. See Rich, *The Fur Trade*, 124, and Williams, *Graham's Observations*, 202. Ewers points out that the term 'Archithinue' was a

Cree word which was applied to the Blackfoot and their Sarsi and Gros Ventre allies as well: *The Blackfeet*, 25.

10 York Factory Journal, 1716–17, PAC HBC B 239/a/2, p. 57

11 York Factory Journal, 1716–17, PAC HBC B 239/a/2, p. 58

12 Denig, *Five Indian Tribes of the Upper Missouri*, 138n. According to Ewers the earliest reference to the Crow in the literature is that of Jean Baptiste Trudeau of 1795. The Hudson's Bay Company archival reference thus precedes it by nearly eighty years. Furthermore, it suggests that the Crow-Hidatsa split may have occurred in the early eighteenth century since the two groups appear to have been at war in 1716.

13 York Factory Journal, 1720–1, PAC HBC B 239/a/6, p. 19

14 York Factory Journals, 1728–31 and 1740–1, PAC HBC B 239/a/13 and 22

15 Williams, *Graham's Observations*, 207

16 Ibid., 6-7. In addition to the Sussou he said that the Mithco (Blood) and Blackfoot lived west-southwest of York Factory 800 miles and used horses.

17 York Factory Journals, 1714–17, PAC HBC B 239/a/1-3

18 York Factory Journals, 1715–16, PAC HBC B 239/a/2, p. 28. Some of these groups took up to two years to make the trek overland to York Factory.

19 Kelsey's reference to the Mai tain ai thi nishe's visit of 26 May 1721 is the last such reference.

20 York Factory Correspondence Books, 1762, PAC HBC B 239/b/23, p. 15

21 York Factory Journals, 1716–17, PAC HBC B 239/a/3, p. 56

22 York Factory Correspondence Books, 1762-3, 25 July 1763, PAC HBC B 239/b/24

23 Burpee, 'An Adventurer From Hudson Bay.'

24 These groups of Cree were known as the Home Guard Indians because they lived near the posts and were employed by the company as hunters, guides, messengers between the posts, canoe builders, and so forth.

25 Rich, *Hudson's Bay Company Letters Outwards*, 96

26 Ibid., xlii-xlv

27 York Factory Account Books, 1689–90, PAC HBC B 239/d/2, p. 4

28 Williams, *Graham's Observations*, 263

4
Arms, brandy, beads, and sundries

York Factory was the most important single source of supply of European trade goods for the Indians of central and southern Manitoba and Saskatchewan because of its pre-eminent position in the early western fur trade and its virtual monopoly of the English trade of the Nelson River basin. By examining the trade data of the post in terms of the changing patterns of trade, it is possible to gain some insights into the types and quantities of goods which the Assiniboine and Cree were taking into the interior for their own use and that of other Indian groups.

Figures 22 and 23 show the trade in arms and ammunition. They reveal that in the late seventeenth century, gun sales were very large: 510 guns were purchased in 1691, a record year. Thereafter, there was an erratic downward trend in the numbers that were exchanged. The effects of French competition can be seen by the drop in the average trade figures beginning in 1731, and the traffic in guns for the remainder of the decade amounted to only 75 per cent of what it had been in the 1720s. Significantly, there was no equivalent rise in sales following the French retreat. In fact, during the 1760s, when the Hudson's Bay Company had little opposition in the interior, the firearms trade was less than it had been in the 1750s. Supply was not a limiting factor, even in the war years of the late 1750s and early 1760s. The record shows that only in the years from 1714 to 1717 were the stocks of arms on hand depleted. Frequently, the quantities available were more than double the demand.[1] The prices of firearms remained constant throughout the period, and consequently price increases can also be dismissed as the determining element (Table 1, p. 66).

Rather than supply shortages or increasing prices, it would appear that a declining demand may have been responsible for the continued diminution in the number of guns bought by the Indians. For instance, if firearms were used primarily as weapons in war by most of the Indians instead of for hunting purposes, the initial demand would have been quite high, since they had great shock value when first employed against unarmed groups. Tribes possessing these weapons were thereby able to exert on their less-fortunate enemies pressures that were out of proportion to the actual effectiveness of the guns.

Prior to 1774, it is likely that only the Assiniboine and Cree bands inhabiting the woodlands, especially the Home Guard Indians living close to the Bay, had incorporated firearms into their hunting practices, thereby becoming dependent upon them. In the forest where game was stalked and killed at relatively close ranges, the gun would have been more efficient than the bow and arrow. Death by the former weapon came quickly, and, therefore, the hunter did not have to track his prey for long periods waiting for it to weaken through loss of blood, as was often the case when the bow and arrow was used. Also, hunting was frequently done in brushy settings where an arrow could be easily deflected from its path, but this was less of a problem with shot. Thus, the Woodland Indians would have valued guns most highly and it was for this reason that many of the Upland Assiniboine and Cree were said to have become so accustomed to using them that they had forgotten how to use bows and arrows as early as 1716.[2]

However, for those groups living in the interior toward the parkland and grassland areas, the situation must have been quite different. These tribes accounted for well over half the total number of canoes coming to York Factory, and an examination of the composition of the gun trade at this post in comparison to that of Fort Albany (Figure 24) suggests that they also accounted for an equally large portion of the arms trade. For example, the shorter three-and-one-half-foot gun made up the bulk of the arms trade at Fort Albany. It had first been introduced into that area by the French and quickly became popular among the Woodland Indians, who then pressured the Hudson's Bay Company to begin to import them.[3] The primary advantage this new weapon offered was ease of handling. Accuracy was reduced somewhat, but this was not critical to Woodland Indians as they killed large numbers of birds with scatter shot and fired at moose and deer only at close quarters. As a result of these factors, at Fort Albany four-foot guns declined rapidly in importance after 1700 and three-and-one-half and three-foot guns accounted for most of the trade thereafter. In contrast, at York Factory, the four-foot

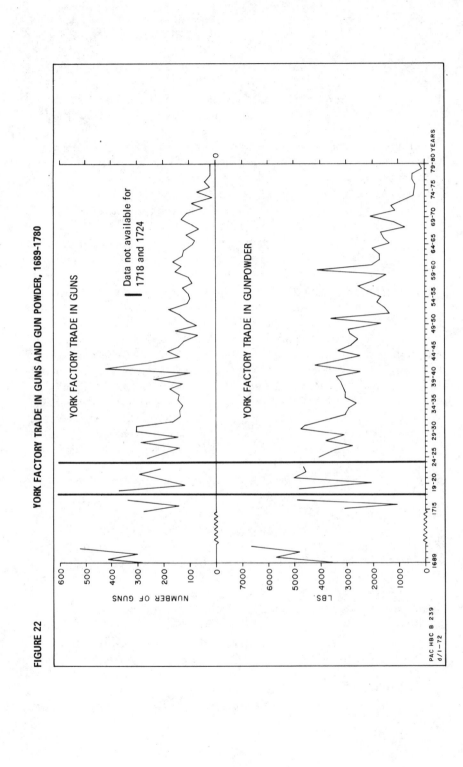

FIGURE 22

YORK FACTORY TRADE IN GUNS AND GUN POWDER, 1689-1780

PAC HBC B 239
d/1—72

gun comprised 55 to 70 per cent of the trade throughout the period. Its greater popularity was probably a reflection of the fact that the Parkland-Grassland Indians used their weapons mostly for warfare, and accuracy was undoubtedly more significant than ease of handling. This would have been particularly the case during the first half of the eighteenth century when the Assiniboine and Cree, who had few if any horses, skirmished with mounted grassland groups. Being able to strike the first blow and then retreat into woodlands would have cancelled out some of the military advantage that the horse would have given the grassland groups at that time. As soon as intensive competition cut the parkland area out of the York Factory hinterland, beginning about 1765, the trade in four-foot guns dropped off rapidly (Figure 24).

There are a number of reasons why the Parkland-Grassland Indians did not make greater use of guns in their daily hunting activities. One difficulty, which was also shared by Woodland groups during this period, related to the Indian's lack of technological knowledge or tools to repair his guns. If a gun failed, as often happened, it was useless to him until he could make the long return trip to Hudson Bay in the spring where a gunsmith or 'armourer' could effect the needed repairs. Even though the French had penetrated inland, they were not equipped to repair firearms, and York Factory remained the chief 'service centre.' There, one or several men were occupied on a full-time basis, fixing guns during the trading season. Besides having problems in obtaining service for his gun, the Indian was also hampered by the fact that the flint lock was not well suited to the extremely cold winter weather of Interior Western Canada. This was brought to light in 1743 by James Isham. In outlining what he said would be a typical trade speech of a tribal chief he wrote: 'Let us trade light guns small in the hand and well shap'd, with locks that will not freese in the winter.'[4]

The hunting techniques that the tribes in the parklands and grasslands had developed to take bison also favoured the continued use of the bow and arrow. For example, the walking surround and the fenced-enclosure or pound were most often used. In both instances, the buffalo was killed in large numbers at close range where the gun would have offered little advantage; in fact, it was inferior to the bow since it could not be fired rapidly and it might easily have stampeded the herds prematurely. This would have been a serious problem before the Indians had horses. Economic considerations should not be overlooked either. One of the reasons the Parkland Indians preferred to hunt bison was that it could easily be taken with their traditional weapons. Moose and red deer, on the

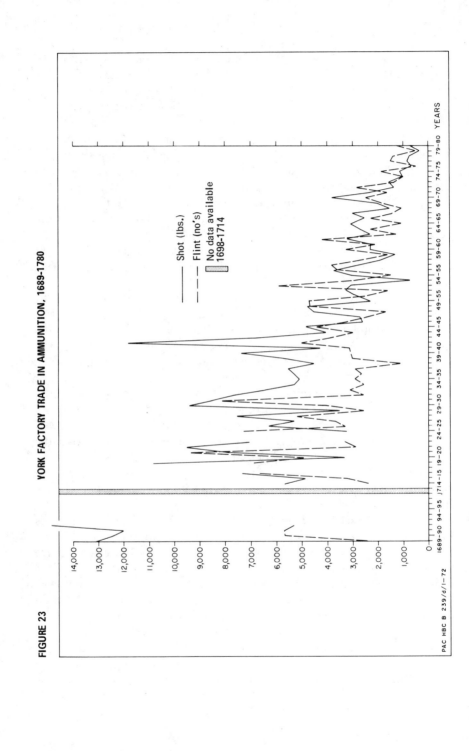

FIGURE 23

YORK FACTORY TRADE IN AMMUNITION, 1689-1780

Shot (lbs.)

Flint (no's)

No data available
1698-1714

PAC HBC B 239/d/1—72

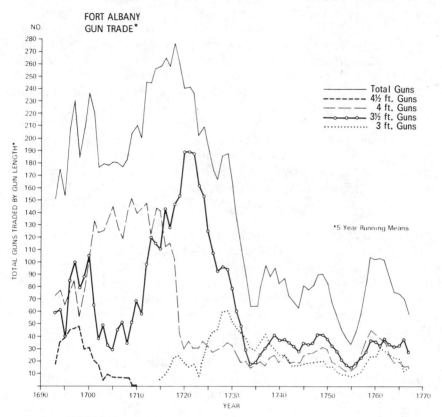

FORT ALBANY
GUN TRADE*

*5 Year Running Means

Source PAC HBC B 3/d

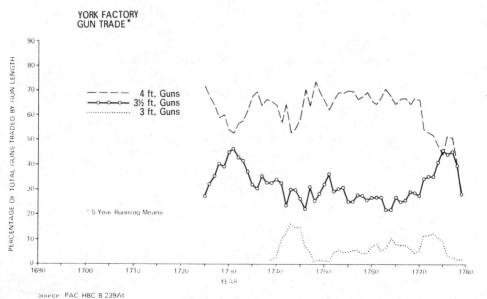

YORK FACTORY
GUN TRADE*

* 5 Year Running Means

Source PAC HBC B 239/d

other hand, were usually killed with guns for the reasons indicated earlier. An expenditure of ammunition that could not be reclaimed was consequently required. In contrast, when the bow was employed, the arrow could be retrieved, or one could be made without trade. With these considerations in mind, the Parkland hunters often neglected other game when bison herds were nearby. Anthony Henday noted this in 1754. When passing through the parklands of Saskatchewan in autumn, he observed:

I went with the young men a Buffalo hunting, all armed with Bows and Arrows: Killed seven ... So expert are the Natives, that they will take the arrows out of them when they are foaming and raging with pain ...
We saw a few Moose & Waskesew; but as the Natives seldom kill them with the Bow & Arrows they will not expend ammunition, while Buffalo are so numerous.[5]

With the largest percentage of the Indians trading at York Factory making only limited use of firearms, the initially high demand which was associated with their use in warfare would have been met fairly early. The dampening effect that this would have had on consumption levels was no doubt reinforced by the habit of the Indian middlemen of buying only enough supplies to suit their own needs. Presumably, if they had not done so, the demand for guns by their inland trading partners would have kept the volume of traffic at a higher level. Also, the strategic advantage which the Assiniboine and Cree middlemen would have maintained by holding a balance of power in their favour cannot be dismissed, even though there is little concrete evidence to indicate that it was a factor. Nonetheless, it too could have served to restrict the flow of arms beyond the area these two groups controlled. After having satisfied their initially large demands, subsequent sales of arms at York Factory would have served primarily to replace worn-out or defective guns in service and would have resulted in a lower volume in later years. It would also partly explain why the retreat of the French from the region led to only a slight rise in the traffic in guns at the post. These traders had vied most successfully for the furs of the Parkland groups and the latter tribes placed the least reliance upon European arms.

The information concerning the York Factory trade in guns, gun powder, shot, and flint corroborates the above conclusions. To illustrate, it would be reasonable to assume that if the number of usable firearms was slowly but steadily increasing among the Indian population, and if they were growing more dependent on them to obtain their daily food, then a rise in the consumption level of gunpowder and ammunition should have occurred. However, a glance at Figures 22 and 23 shows this was not the case. The volume of exchange of these trade goods exhibits the same erratic downward trend that has already been observed for guns. Once again, the French can probably be discounted as alternate suppliers as there was only a slight depression in the barter of these commodities at the Hudson Bay post in the 1750s. Furthermore, there was no major rebound in sales after the French withdrew. In brief, there is little evidence to support a commonly held view that all of the Indians became critically dependent upon firearms very soon after their introduction. This appears to have been true only of the more acculturated Woodland groups, especially the Home Guard Indians, but as the post-1774 trade at York Factory demonstrates, they were buying barely a quarter of all of the arms which were sold.

The records of Indian purchases of clothing items such as blankets and cloth indicate that the same groups were the most important buyers, and the per-capita consumption of the more distant Inland groups was low by comparison. Moreover, this disparity seems to have increased through time. As an example, during the 1720s, just prior to the French invasion of the Northwest, an average of 85 blankets were bartered each year (Figure 25). In the 1750s, the trade continued to move upwards, attaining a yearly average of 140 a year in spite of the considerable numbers of Assiniboine and Western Cree who had shifted their alliances to the French. In the late 1770s, after the virtual cessation of inland commerce at York Factory following the opening of Cumberland House in 1774, nearly 105 blankets were still being bought. This figure amounted to 75 per cent of that of the 1750s, even though the total volume of the furs taken at the post had declined by three-quarters.

The sales of cloth show roughly the same pattern as that of blankets (Figure 26). In 1690, only 212$\frac{1}{3}$ yards were purchased, but thereafter volume increased substantially, averaging 895 yards in the 1720s, 956 in the 1740s, 859 in the 1750s, and 890 in the 1760s.[6] The impact of the French competition on the traffic of this commodity was very slight. In addition, the termination of the Saskatchewan and other interior trade did produce a slump in sales, but again it was not of the magnitude that would be expected if all of the tribes were buying comparable quantities. In the 1770s, the annual cloth trade was totaling nearly five hundred yards or about 55 per cent of the preceeding fifty-year average. In other words, Indian bands that were accounting for some 20 to 30 per cent of the canoe traffic and fur pelts at the posts were purchasing more than half of all the cloth which was sold.

Ecological factors played an important role in producing this trade

FIGURE 25

YORK FACTORY TRADE IN BLANKETS AND BEADS, 1719-1780

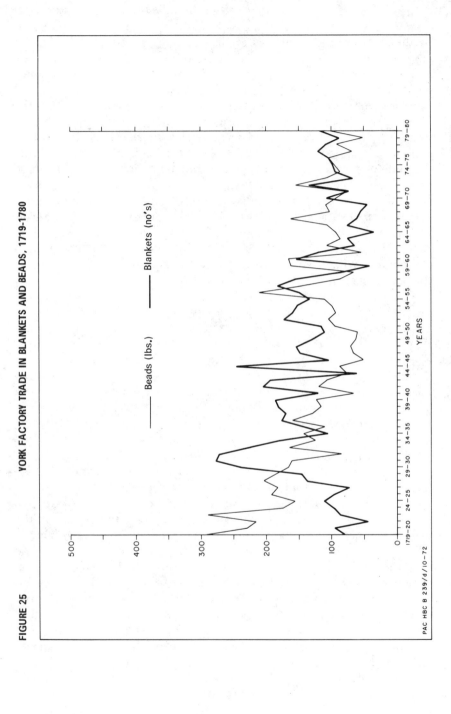

pattern. The initially limited large game resources of the boreal forest of the shield region were depleted quickly due to the early adoption of firearms. Furthermore, trapping activities diminished the populations of fur-bearing animals. The Home Guard Indians were thus finding it increasingly difficult to find enough skins and furs to make their clothing. Therefore, economic necessity as well as acculturation processes led them to turn more and more to the European clothing materials. Blankets were thrown over other garments in winter for added warmth and they were also cut up for use as socks and mitten linings. Cloth was used in a wide variety of ways, often being substituted for deer and moose skins.[7] In the parkland and grassland environments of southern Manitoba and Saskatchewan, the rather large bison and moose populations meant that the tribes did not have to be as reliant on the European fur traders. Comfort may also have been important: cool, wet weather was more common in the northeast and leather clothing would have taken long periods to dry, but European clothing dried more quickly and was more comfortable to wear. However, in the drier parkland-grassland area, this would have been less of a consideration. Here yardgoods and blankets were more on the order of luxury goods than items of necessity.

The trading pattern for metal goods appears to have been rather mixed. As Figures 27 and 28 suggest, knives, files, and hatchets were being evenly distributed throughout the different environmental zones and the effects of inland competition can be clearly seen. This is especially the case of the hatchet trade with the graph showing a pronounced slump in sales during the years from 1747 to 1756. Another marked decline began again 1773 as the pedlars from Montreal increasingly undermined the position of the York Factory traders. The above fluctuations in the volumes of exchange implies that 70 to 80 per cent of the trade in these items was going to inland groups, quantities which were roughly proportional to their population numbers. The bartering of ice chisels, used to open frozen beaver lodges, and of kettles exhibit somewhat different patterns. The trade in chisels shows an erratic downward trend which started in the early 1730s. French activities in the 1750s seem to have had only a minor effect on this trend, but the termination of York Factory's inland trade in 1774 led to an almost complete cessation of Indian purchases of this commodity. The bulk of the ice chisels thus appear to have been going to inland tribes.[8] The traffic in kettles shows no particular fluctuations upwards or downwards through time. Kettles were bulky, heavy items that the French could supply in only limited quantities because of their higher transportation costs. Considering that the sales of

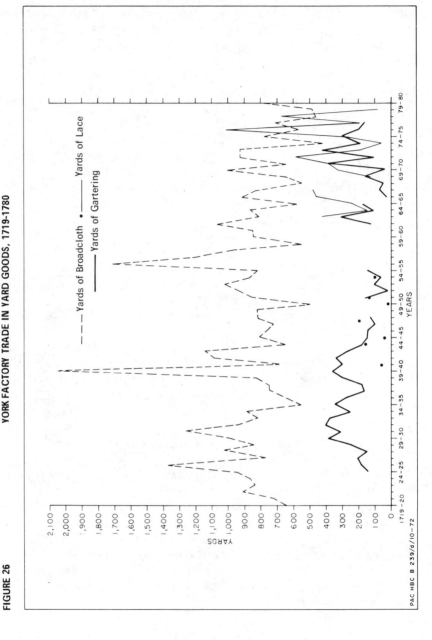

FIGURE 26

YORK FACTORY TRADE IN YARD GOODS, 1719-1780

PAC HBC B 239/d/10-72

FIGURE 27

YORK FACTORY TRADE IN HATCHETS AND KETTLES, 1719-1780

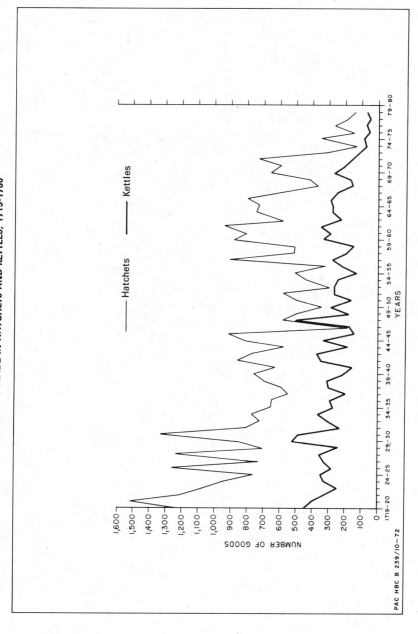

PAC HBC B 239/l0—72

FIGURE 28

YORK FACTORY TRADE IN KNIVES, ICE CHISELS AND FILES, 1719-1780

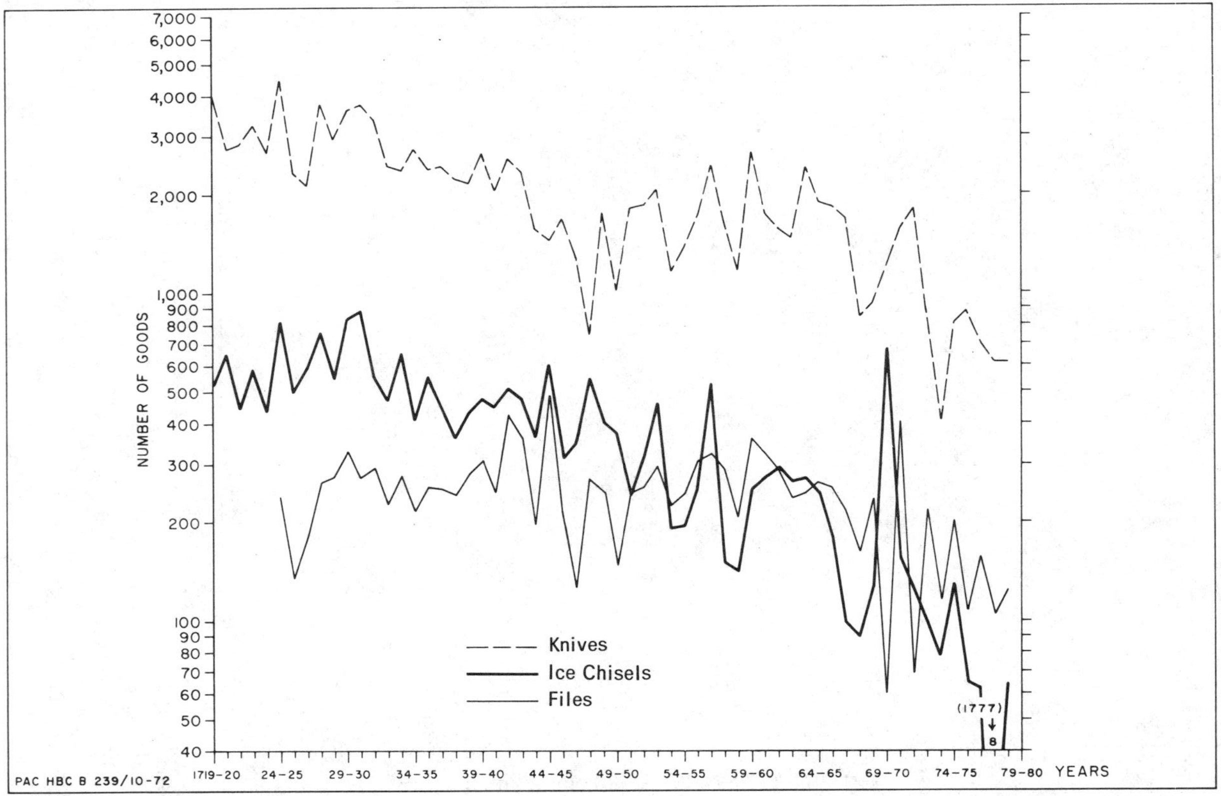

PAC HBC B 239/10-72

kettles at York Factory after 1774 amounted to roughly 30 per cent of those of the preceding years, it is apparent that the per-capita trade was fairly evenly distributed among the various bands which came to the post, even though kettles were reportedly more popular among woodland groups.

Regional variations in the consumption of luxury goods also show contrasting patterns. As illustrated by Figure 25, an average of 222 pounds of beads were bought by the Indians each year in the 1720s, compared to 107 in the 1750s, 109 in the 1760s, and 84 in late 1770s. The last two sets of figures indicate that perhaps over 75 per cent of the bead trade was going to bands living in the sections of the hinterland closest to the post. The sales of tobacco present quite a different picture from that of beads. Although exhibiting some wide fluctuations in volume, the tobacco trade remained relatively constant until 1774. The French had little impact on the English traffic in this commodity due to the fact that the Brazil tobacco of the Hudson's Bay Company was preferred to that of the French, and, since it was an item of low bulk and high value, Indian middlemen were taking it into the interior as will be discussed in greater detail below.

It is more difficult to discern spatial patterns in the consumption of rum and brandy. As Figure 29 demonstrates, there was an increase in the volumes exchanged from 1720 to 1753, when a peak was reached of 864 gallons. Thereafter, it remained relatively constant until a second peak was attained in 1771, when 761 gallons were bartered to the Indians. These peaks occur at times of maximum fur-trade rivalry, and, consequently, the graphs portray a picture which was the reverse of that of other goods. It is difficult therefore, to draw any conclusions regarding regional variations of traffic in this commodity. The data merely illustrate graphically a fact that is generally well known, namely that the consumption increased steadily through time and was especially high during periods of intense competition.

Summarizing the information gained from the York Factory account books, it would appear that the Cree living closest to the Bay, mostly the Home-Guard Indians, were buying large quantities of blankets, cloth, and beads. Inland groups, chiefly the Parkland Assiniboine and Western Cree were the principal consumers of tobacco. Other goods seem to have been more evenly distributed on a per-capita basis to the different tribes. However, since the Inland Indian tribes were far more numerous, 60 to 70 per cent of the total amounts of such items as kettles, knives, hatchets, and guns went to the interior regions. The total quantities that would have been involved during the period from 1720 to 1774 are listed in Table 2.

FIGURE 29

YORK FACTORY TRADE IN LUXURY GOODS, 1719-1780

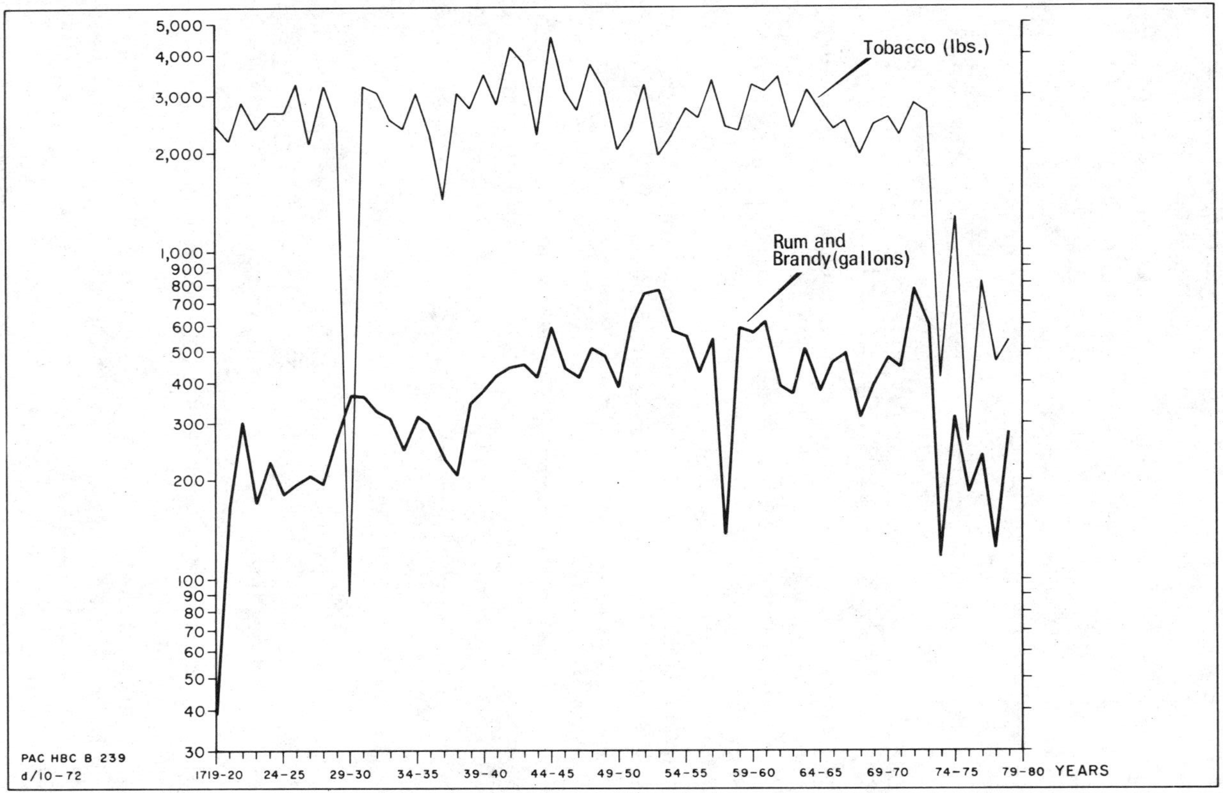

TABLE 2

Total quantities of goods traded at
York Factory 1720–74

Trade goods	Total traded*
Guns	9,927†
Powder	145,388 pounds
Kettles	14,780
Hatchets	39,365
Knives	110,624
Broadcloth	473,440 yards
Blankets	6,954
Beads	6,934 pounds
Tobacco	144,024 pounds
Rum and brandy	21,634 gallons

* SOURCE: York Factory Account Books, 1714–20,
  PAC HBC B 239/d/4-64
† Covers the period from 1714 to 1774

As has been pointed out, a large proportion of the trade goods which the
Assiniboine and Western Cree acquired were passed on to other groups
with whom the two tribes traded. Although the volume of this second-
hand trade is hard to ascertain, the journals of the few traders and
explorers who penetrated into western Canada provide us with some
clues. Also, their observations lend support to some of the inferences that
have been drawn from the above analysis of the York Factory account
books regarding regional trade patterns.

According to La Vérendrye, ammunition, tobacco, and metal goods
were the items most desired by the Assiniboine, Cree, and Ojibwa bands
living in southern Manitoba and the adjacent portions of Ontario. Typical
of his many comments on the subject were the following remarks which he
made in 1738 at Fort La Reine on the site of the present city of Portage la
Prairie. Describing the gifts he had given to a band of Assiniboine which
had assembled there, he said: 'I made them a present from you of powder,
ball, tobacco, axes, knives, chisels, awls, these all being things which they
value highly owing to their lack of everything.'[9] Four years later in 1742,
Arthur Dobbs also stressed the importance these items had for the Indians, saying that they would not have made the long trip to the Bay if they
did not need guns, powder and shot, hatchets, and other iron tools for
hunting as well as tobacco and brandy for luxury.[10]

These same commodities figured prominently in the Assiniboine trade with the Mandan. They bartered their used and deteriorated kettles, axes, knives, guns, and other trade goods for the corn they wanted, and for many other items which the Mandan manufactured or obtained through their trading contacts with other peoples to the southwest. The Mandan themselves had a considerable reputation for craft work in leather, beads, and feathers. Seemingly not having developed these crafts to the same degree of sophistication, the Assiniboine valued these products highly. In describing the Assiniboine intercourse with the Mandan in 1739, La Vérendrye wrote:

they had completed their purchases of all the things they were to buy, such as coloured buffalo robes, deer and buck skins carefully dressed and ornamented with fur and feathers, painted feathers and furs, worked garters, head-bands, girdles. Of all the tribes they [the Mandan] are the most skilful in dressing leather, and they work very delicately in hair and feathers; the Assiniboin cannot do work of the same kind. They are sharp traders, and clean the Assiniboin out of everything they have in the way of guns, powder, ball, kettles, axes, knives and awls.[11]

La Vérendrye's observation is significant in two important respects. In his accounting of the goods which the Assiniboine were obtaining from the Mandan, he does not mention horses even though he records that the Mandan were familiar with these animals and Indians to the southwest possessed them.[12] In light of the fact that he did not see any of them in Assiniboine territory of southern Manitoba, it is unlikely that any were being acquired by them through trade. Equally important, La Vérendrye's description lists only European trade goods among the wares that the Mandan took from the Assiniboine. This suggests the possibility that the Assiniboine did not carry on a regular trade with the Mandan in pre-European times. However, it is difficult to establish this with any degree of certainty because of the paucity of archaeological data. The excavations of the Stott mound and village site near Brandon, Manitoba, did yield a single item of European manufacture and a potsherd of Mandan origin. The presence of one European article has led archaeologists to conclude that it was a proto-historic Assiniboine site which was probably occupied at the time of initial European contact, since later habitation sites contain an abundance of trade goods such as beads and various metal objects.[13] Similarly, in the Missouri Valley of North Dakota, metal and glass objects appear in archaeological sites dating to ca. 1675 to 1700. This would have been soon after the establishment of the Hudson's Bay Company on the Bay in 1670, suggesting that regular contacts may have existed prior to that time.[14] Furthermore, Father Aulneau and La Vérendrye indicated that the tribe was making annual, perhaps even semi-annual, trips to the Mandan by the time of initial white penetration into southern Manitoba.[15]

Yet, even though these different lines of evidence do hint at the possibility of some antiquity for this trade, it seems likely that it was largely a historic phenomenon nonetheless. It is unclear just what the Assiniboine would have bartered to the Mandan before contacts with Europeans. In all probability, the Assiniboine developed their first extensive contact with the latter group between 1670 and 1720 when the Mandan sent trading parties down to the Bay. These expeditions would have had to pass through Assiniboine territory. They undoubtedly stopped and camped with the Assiniboine while en route, and this could account for the presence of a Mandan potsherd in the Stott archaeological site. Brandon lies along one of the major routeways between York Factory and the Missouri River, and it is more likely that the Mandan, rather than the Assiniboine, would have brought the pot in question to the site. The latter had their own pottery, Blackduck, and there is no evidence that they ever placed any value on Mandan ceramics. It was never mentioned as an item of trade between the two groups. Thus, the Mandan potsherd is probably the remains of a vessel which this Missouri tribe had used to carry food with them while travelling back and forth from the Bay. Similarly, the late seventeenth century trade goods found along the Missouri River were in all likelihood transported there by the Mandan themselves, and not the Assiniboine, as is commonly supposed.[16]

Farther to the west and to the northwest, the interior trade was quite different as Henday's observations of 1754–5 indicate. He had been sent inland from York Factory for the purpose of bolstering the trading position of the Hudson's Bay Company, and he therefore took detailed notes on the nature and organization of the interchange of goods between tribal groups. The influence which the French had on this traffic was noted as well. Furthermore, his notes provide us with a particularly good picture of the winter activities of the Parkland Indian middlemen at mid-century and show the degree of economic specialization which had taken place by then. While in eastern Alberta in the general vicinity of the Red Deer River during the month of December, he reportedly tried to persuade his companions to trap deer and wolves, but had little success.

Their presence in Blackfoot territory and their trading relations with that tribe were cited as the reasons. The former rendered it unsafe to trap, and the latter made it unnecessary. In Henday's words:

I asked the Natives why they did not Hap [trap] Wolves; they made the Answer that the Archithinue Natives would kill them if they trapped in their country: I then asked them when and where they were to get the Wolves, etc., to carry down in the Spring. They made no answer; but laughed one to another ...
Wolves are numerous. An Indian told me that my tentmates were angry with me last night for speaking so much concerning Happing & advised me to say no more about it, for they would get more Wolves, Beaver etc. from the Archithinue Natives in the spring, than they can carry.[17]

In spite of the Indians' advice, Henday persisted in his attempts to induce his men to trap. However, as he admitted, it served no purpose, and they passed the remainder of the winter in a rather leisurely fashion subsisting largely on bison.

Late in March, Henday's band headed to a river, probably a branch of the Red Deer River, and began building their canoes. The latter were launched on 28 April and on 12 May his fleet of canoes met the Blackfoot, as his Indian informant had told him would be the case. During the next nine days, his band, and a group of Assiniboine who had joined them, traded with over 277 tents of Blackfoot. After several other similar en-counters with the latter tribe, Henday remarked: 'We are above 60 Canoes and there are scarce a Gun, Kettle, Hatchet or Knife amongst us, having traded them with the Archithinue Natives.'[18] As middlemen in the fur trade, the Parkland Assiniboine and Cree were thus able to spend the winter in comparative ease subsisting on bison.[19] In the spring they discarded their used trade goods through barter with the Blackfoot for furs. Like the traffic between the Assiniboine and the Mandan, metal goods of European manufacture were the chief items the Plains groups demanded.[20] However, in contrast to the above trade, traditional hand-craft items such as ropes, feathers, and beaded belts were not bartered in any significant quantities. Instead, the acquisition of furs was the prime goal of the Assiniboine and Western Cree in the Saskatchewan region. Some horses were taken in trade also.

Once Henday's party had received all of the furs their canoes could carry, they continued their trip down the Saskatchewan River, passing the two French posts which were then in operation. At the first post, Fort à la Corne, located just below the Forks, Henday had the great displeasure of seeing the French obtain all of the 'prime winter furs' in exchange for ten gallons of 'watered brandy.' When the brigade reached Fort Paskoyac (The Pas) the operation was repeated, leaving Henday with only the bulky low value furs. At that point he remarked that if the French had had Brazil tobacco, they would have been able to engross all of the trade.[21] The importance of luxury goods in the Saskatchewan trade is thereby underscored. The French used alcohol liberally to relieve the Indian of his most valuable furs, while the English used the Brazil tobacco to lure them down to the Bay.

At Fort Paskoyac, a reshuffling of cargoes had apparently become common after 1740. For example, while Henday was at the post, he said that several of the Assiniboine who had been travelling with him distributed the heavy furs which the French had refused among the Cree canoes and 'gave them directions what to trade for.'[22] Many Cree families did likewise, according to Andrew Graham.[23] Therefore, not only were large numbers of Cree and some of the Assiniboine acting as middlemen in the sense that they obtained their furs by bartering away used European goods, but following the French intrusion they also were operating as representatives for their relatives and allies who did not choose to make the long voyage down to the Bay. It was undoubtedly trade of this sort that helps to account for the continued high consumption levels at York Factory of certain commodities like tobacco even though many of the Western Cree and Assiniboine had ceased to go beyond the French posts situated in the interior. Henday's observations also give us a good indication of the nature of the effects of French competition on the Hudson Bay trade. The French were skimming off the higher quality furs. In return, they were bartering low-bulk, high-value trade goods to the Indians. Because of the extended nature of their lines of communication and their more limited cargo capacities the French could not bring in sufficient quantities of kettles, arms, ammunition, and other heavy or bulky items to satisfy the Indian's demands.

The pattern of trade which thus emerged after the 1730s and persisted until the late 1750s was one that saw the Assiniboine and Cree trading with both the French and the English, taking a somewhat different array of goods from each, and likewise bartering different kinds of fur to the two groups in return.

NOTES

1 York Factory Account Books, 1689–1782, PAC HBC B 239/d/1–72

2 York Factory Journals, 1716, PAC HBC B 239/a/2, p. 22

3 According to John Fullartine who was stationed at Fort Albany in 1703 the Indians 'teased' him for not having any short guns. Davies, *Letters from Hudson Bay, 1703–40*, 9

4 Isham's Observations, PAC HBC E 2/1, p. 55

5 Burpee, 'Journal of Anthony Hendry,' 333

6 York Factory Account Books, 1690 to 1780, PAC HBC B 239/d/2–72

7 For a more thorough description of the ways in which blankets and cloth were used see, Williams *Graham's Observations* 145–50. Local materials still figured prominently in their clothing and there is little evidence to suggest that their traditional styles of dress had changed to any great degree as of that date.

8 Ice chisels were an important item for fur hunting. Indians used them to break open beaver lodges during the winter. Hatchets were used for the same purpose.

9 Burpee, *Journals and Letters of La Vérendrye*, 305. He made similar observations regarding the Cree on pp. 146–8 and the Monsoni on p. 136. Even though he states that these Indians valued ammunition and he gave them some as presents, Figure 22 shows that the French had little impact on the powder trade. They appear to have had a greater influence on the sales of flint and shot.

10 *An Account of the Countries Adjoining to Hudson's Bay*, 39. Dobbs probably overstated his case regarding their degree of dependence on Europeans since his purpose was to support his claim that the Hudson's Bay Company was overcharging the Indians. Also, Dobbs never travelled inland and therefore would not have been familiar with the ways in which these articles were being used by the Indians.

11 Burpee, *Journals and Letters of La Vérendrye*, 332

12 Ibid., 336–7. The Mandan did not possess any horses.

13 For a complete discussion of the artefact inventory of the site, see MacNeish, 'The Stott Mound and Village Near Brandon, Manitoba,' 31–41

14 Donald J. Lehmer, personal communication, 15 May 1969

15 Thwaites, *Jesuit Relations*, 68: 291–3, and Burpee, *Journals and Letters of La Vérendrye*, 253–4

16 La Vérendrye, for example, never mentioned that the ceramic wares of the Mandan were among the items the Assiniboine esteemed. Presumably, if the Assiniboine had taken any in trade La Vérendrye would have mentioned it in his list of goods. Ibid., 332

17 Burpee, 'Journal of Anthony Hendry,' 344

18 Ibid., 351

19 Henday also observed that they killed few moose even though the animal was relatively plentiful. The reason cited was that buffalo was the chief winter food.

20 When speaking of the Saskatchewan Cree, Andrew Graham said: 'having plenty of food they have no ambition or desire of obtaining more than is sufficient for the simplicity of their way of life, Tobacco, ammunition, fire-arms, knives, and hatchets, are the principal useful articles, consequently anything more than is necessary would be superfluous and burthensome.' Williams, *Graham's Observations*, 193. Clearly cloth, blankets and other similar items were of secondary importance to the parkland Indians.

21 Burpee, 'Journal of Anthony Hendry,' 353

22 Ibid., 353

23 Williams, *Graham's Observations*, 193

5
Migrations, epidemics, and population changes, 1763–1821

During the tumultuous period between 1763 and 1821, population movement continued unabated, but the principal direction of the Assiniboine and Cree migrations changed markedly. Until nearly the close of the eighteenth century, the main course of movement of the Assiniboine had been to the northwest. Thereafter, they began to drift increasingly to the south. In the 1790s Alexander Mackenzie reported that the most western Assiniboine bands were found in the area of Fort George on the North Saskatchewan River. Some occupied the woodlands to the north of the river, but most lived in the grasslands to the south. Even though they had penetrated this far to the northwest, Mackenzie added that the bulk of the tribe was still centred in the Assiniboine River valley.[1] In 1794, Duncan M'Gillivray of the Northwest Company, who was stationed at Fort George, made more detailed notes on the distribution of the western groups of Assiniboine and identified three separate bands: the Canoe Assiniboine of the lower Qu'Appelle, the Grand River Assiniboine of the South Saskatchewan (who frequented South Branch House), and the Strong Wood Assiniboine of Battle River. No references were made to tribal groups living in the Assiniboine River valley.[2]

Alexander Henry the Younger, provided abundant information about the Assiniboine River valley district as well as those areas covered in the above accounts. Writing in 1808 he recognized ten separate bands of Assiniboine which were distributed as follows (see Figure 30): 200 tents of the Little Girl Assiniboine living along the Souris River in the Moose Hills and at Tête à La Biche; 200 lodges of the Paddling and Foot Assiniboine

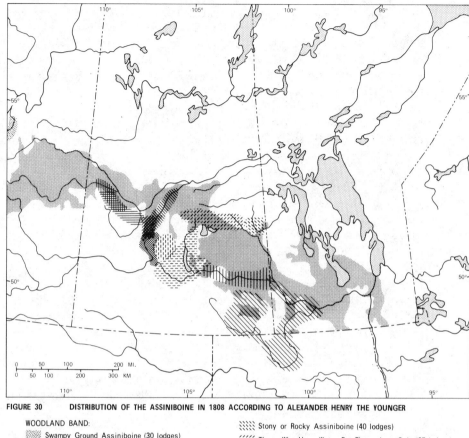

FIGURE 30   DISTRIBUTION OF THE ASSINIBOINE IN 1808 ACCORDING TO ALEXANDER HENRY THE YOUNGER

WOODLAND BAND:

:::: Swampy Ground Assiniboine (30 lodges)

PARKLAND-GRASSLAND BANDS:
(These are primarily winter locations.)

\\\ Little Girl Assiniboine (200 lodges)

|||||| Paddling & Foot Assiniboine (200 lodges)

:::: Canoe Assiniboine (160 lodges)

::::: Red River Assiniboine (24 lodges)

▓▓ Rabbit Assiniboine (30 lodges)

::::: Stony or Rocky Assiniboine (40 lodges)

:::: Those Who Have Water For Themselves Only (35 lodges)

/// Eagle Hill Assiniboine (38 lodges)

\\\ Saskatchewan Assiniboine (50 lodges)

≡ Foot Assiniboine (33 lodges)

|||||| Strong Wood Assiniboine (40 lodges)

▓▓ PARKLAND BELT

Source: E. Coues, "New Light", Vol.2, pp.522-523

of the Qu'Appelle valley and southward; 160 lodges of the Canoe and Paddling Assiniboine, situated to the west of the preceding groups; 24 lodges of Red River Assiniboine located farther to the west near the Canoe band; 30 lodges of the Rabbit Assiniboine found to the west of the

Red River band; 40 lodges of Stone or Rocky Assiniboine residing near the Skunk Wood Hills and Montagne de Foudre (Thunder Hill); 35 lodges of Those Who Have Water for Themselves Only, also living in the Skunk Hills; 38 lodges of Eagle Hills Assiniboine dwelling between the Bear Hills and the south branch of the Saskatchewan; 50 lodges of Saskatchewan Assiniboine who camped between the south branch and the Eagle Hills; and 33 lodges of Foot Assiniboine who roamed between Eagle Hills and Lac Diable.[3] This account shows that the tribe was centred in the area between the Souris and Qu'Appelle valleys. Nearly two-thirds of the Assiniboine population was found in this region, while the remaining one-third was scattered to the west and northwest, primarily between the South Saskatchewan and Battle rivers.

The Hudson's Bay Company district reports that were filed toward the close of the period indicate that the Assiniboine had abandoned the Red River valley as well as all of the territory north of the Assiniboine River and east of the Manitoba escarpment.[4] Furthermore, the Fort Pelly (Swan River) and Carlton House District reports state that the tribe did not frequent the forested portions of these departments either. The latter account, which covers the north and south branches of the Saskatchewan River, mentioned that 300 lodges of Assiniboine were found in the grassland portions of the district.[5] Most of the remaining groups were still to be found in the Qu'Appelle and Souris valleys. In 1815, Peter Fidler estimated that the Assiniboine living along the Assiniboine River downstream from Carlton House totalled 300 lodges.[6] This figure undoubtedly includes those bands living in the above two valleys, and therefore suggests that roughly equal numbers of the tribe were found in the two districts.

The 1819 report for the Brandon District, which included the Souris and lower Qu'Appelle valleys, does not give a detailed accounting of the locations of the various bands, but it does provide a sketchy picture of the population distribution. Two-thirds of the Assiniboine were found in the Qu'Appelle and Beaver River areas; one-sixth lived along the upper Assiniboine River near Fort Hibernia; and one-sixth made their camps in the lands near Brandon House.[7] The report for 1822 is far more explicit and identifies the different tribal bands. According to John McDonald who filed the account there were six different bands (see Figure 31): the Walking Stones, having 80 lodges and ranging between Brandon House and the Missouri River; the Young Girl's tribe of 140 lodges, living between Brandon House and the lakes of the Qu'Appelle River; the Assapascan, consisting of 40 lodges and centred around the lakes of the

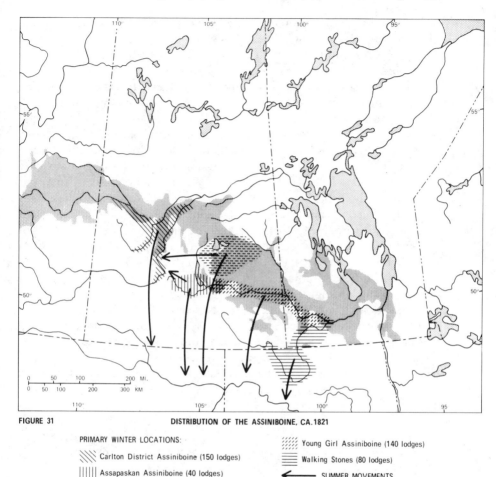

FIGURE 31   DISTRIBUTION OF THE ASSINIBOINE, CA. 1821

PRIMARY WINTER LOCATIONS:

⧵⧵⧵ Carlton District Assiniboine (150 lodges)

||||| Assapaskan Assiniboine (40 lodges)

Les Gens de Bras Fond Assiniboine (60 loges)
& Lonely Dog's Band (50 lodges)

Young Girl Assiniboine (140 lodges)

Walking Stones (80 lodges)

SUMMER MOVEMENTS

PARKLAND BELT

Source: Brandon House District Report, 1822, PAC HBC B 22/e/2, and Carlton House District Report, 1815, PAC HBC B 27/e/1.

Qu'Appelle; Les Gens de Bras Fond, comprising 60 lodges and roaming between the latter lakes and those of the upper Assiniboine River; and finally, Lonely Dog's Band of 50 lodges, who ranged over the grasslands between the South Saskatchewan River and the headwaters of the Red River.[8] Comparing the patterns portrayed by these reports to that of Alexander Henry the Younger for 1808, it becomes apparent that the distribution of the Assiniboine had changed very little during the thirteen-year period ending in 1821, and over half of the tribe's population continued to be centred in the Souris–Qu'Appelle valley region. The remainder were found in the territory between the South Saskatchewan River and the lower Battle river.

In addition to the groups listed above, a smaller number of Assiniboine lived in the woodlands to the north of the North Saskatchewan River outside of the principal territory of their relatives. According to the Edmonton District Report of 1823–4, thirty tents of Assiniboine, Cree, and Métis lived in the forests near Edmonton House. Farther to the northwest, a band of Strong Wood Assiniboine numbering some sixty tents were said to be located in the vicinity of the McLeod River, an upper tributary of the Athabaska River.[9] These two groups appear to have been the last of the once-more-numerous Woodland Assiniboine, or Northern Sinepoetts as they were formerly known. Presumably the ancestors of these two bands had been in the vanguard of the westward-moving Woodland Assiniboine in the early eighteenth century.

As with the Assiniboine, the Cree expansion to the northwest began ebbing in the late eighteenth century and had nearly ceased by 1784. In that year smallpox struck the tribe, three years before it hit their northern enemies the Chipewyans, and the reduction of their numbers which resulted seriously weakened them as a military power. Consequently, they began to withdraw from the Chipewyan lands they had taken earlier, and territories which the Cree held in the late seventies, such as those around Portage la Loche and Ile à la Crosse, were back under the control of Chipewyan groups by 1790.[10] With this retraction of the northern limits of their territory, the Cree turned southward and began pushing more vigorously into the grasslands and parklands located to the south of the North Saskatchewan River. In 1793 an important battle was fought with the Gros Ventre near South Branch House in which the Cree exterminated a band of the former tribe which numbered sixteen lodges. According to Duncan M'Gillivray the two tribes had held each other in mutual fear until that time and their skirmishes produced few deaths on either side. However, after the above massacre M'Gillivray claimed that the Gross Ventre dreaded the Cree and apparently began withdrawing from the upper Qu'Appelle and lower South Saskatchewan valleys, opening these areas to Cree and Assiniboine settlement.[11]

A comparison of the tribal distribution as portrayed by Alexander Mackenzie for 1790 with those of later years highlights the magnitude of change that was brought about by this reorientation of the principal direction of Cree expansion. Mackenzie wrote that the western territory of the Cree could be delimited by a line running from:

the middle part of the River Winipic, following that water through the Lake Winipic, to the discharge of the Saskatchiwine into it; from thence it accompanies the latter to Fort George, when the line, striking by the head of the Beaver River to the Elk River, runs along its banks to its discharge in the Lake of the Hills; from which it may be carried back East, to the Ile à La Crosse, and so on to Churchill by the Missinipi [Churchill River] ... Some of them, indeed, have penetrated farther West and South to the Red River, to the South of Lake Winipic and the South branch of the Saskatchiwine.[12]

The bands which Mackenzie said lived beyond these boundaries became known as the Plains Cree, but it is clear from his commentary that they were few in 1790 and lived close to the forests (Figure 32).

More detailed descriptions of the locations of the Plains Cree were provided by Alexander Henry the Younger and Daniel Harmon in the early nineteenth century. According to Henry they were found only infrequently on the Red River in the first decade of the century, in contrast to the situation of the 1730s. Rather, they lived to the west along the Assiniboine River in the vicinity of Portage la Prairie and beyond.[13] From another quarter, the upper Assiniboine valley region, Harmon said that they were present at Fort Alexandria, Duck Mountain, Montagne à la Bosse, the Fishing Lakes, and Fort Qu'Appelle during the years from 1800 to 1808.[14]

At the close of the period, the Hudson's Bay Company district reports show that rapid population dislocations were taking place in Manitoba and northern Ontario. For example, the Cree had abandoned all the territory between Lake of the Woods and Lake Winnipeg, as well as most of the interlake region of Manitoba. In the latter country only one small tribal band remained. This band reportedly traded at Halket's House, a minor post which was situated on the narrows of Lake Manitoba.[15] To the northwest, the report for the Swan River region indicates that the Cree had largely deserted the forested sections of the district. Apparently they had moved to the grassland margins of the department where they lived in company with the Assiniboine (Figure 33).[16]

In 1815, 100 lodges of Cree were found in the Carlton District west of Swan River, and, as in the Swan River area, most of the Cree were said to be living in the grasslands.[17] To the southeast, John McDonald listed three separate Cree bands in his report for the Brandon territory in 1822. The largest numbered 75 lodges and hunted in the Beaver, Touchwood, Strongwood, and Nut hills. They traded at Fort Alexandria. Next in size with 40 lodges was the band which traded at Brandon House. The smallest of the three groups lived in the area of Beaver Creek on the lower

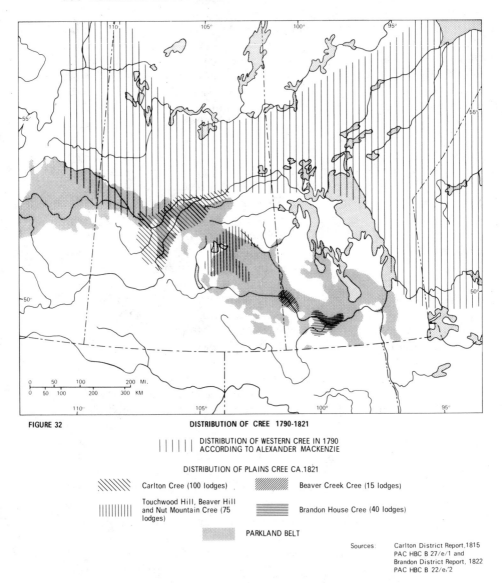

FIGURE 32

DISTRIBUTION OF CREE 1790-1821

| | | | | | DISTRIBUTION OF WESTERN CREE IN 1790
ACCORDING TO ALEXANDER MACKENZIE

DISTRIBUTION OF PLAINS CREE CA.1821

Carlton Cree (100 lodges)

Beaver Creek Cree (15 lodges)

Touchwood Hill, Beaver Hill
and Nut Mountain Cree (75
lodges)

Brandon House Cree (40 lodges)

PARKLAND BELT

Sources: Carlton District Report,1815
PAC HBC B 27/e/1 and
Brandon District Report, 1822
PAC HBC B 22/e/2

Qu'Appelle River and consisted of only 15 lodges. From these last two
district reports it is clear therefore that the Plains Cree were concentrated
in roughly the same areas as the Assiniboine but were fewer, totalling only
about 230 lodges. Also, their distribution within these territories differed

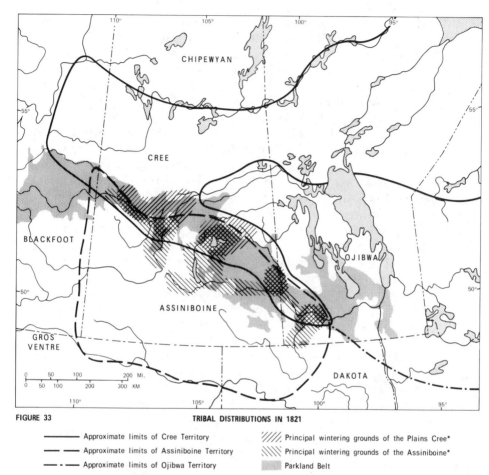

FIGURE 33   TRIBAL DISTRIBUTIONS IN 1821

———————— Approximate limits of Cree Territory   ⁄⁄⁄⁄ Principal wintering grounds of the Plains Cree*

— — — Approximate limits of Assiniboine Territory   ⟍⟍⟍ Principal wintering grounds of the Assiniboine*

— · — Approximate limits of Ojibwa Territory   ▓▓ Parkland Belt

*Brandon District Report 1822-23, PAC HBC B 27/e/2 and Carlton District Report 1815, PAC HBC B 22/e/1.

from that of the Assiniboine in that the bulk of the Plains Cree were found
to the north and northwest of the Qu'Appelle River. In this region nearly
175 of the 230 lodges were located.

As the Cree withdrew from the southeastern and south-central portions of Manitoba, the Ojibwa rapidly replaced them. To illustrate, in
1776 Alexander Henry the Elder, outlined the tribe's territory on a map
which he compiled for western Canada. According to his map, the tribal
territory of the Ojibwa extended southward from the canoe route running between Lake of the Woods and Lake Superior (Figure 34). How-

ever, by the early 1820s they had become the principal inhabitants of the
Fort Alexander Department, the Manitoba interlake area, the Dauphin
District, and the forested part of the Swan River territory (Figure 33).[18]
The Cumberland Department appears to have marked the northwestern
limits of their expansion by about 1820. They were present there as early
as 1792, but the district report for 1815 stated that half of the 110 Indian
families who traded at Cumberland House were newcomers from York
Factory, the North River (Nelson River), and the 'Rat' country north of
Cumberland Lake.[19] Considering the directions from which these immigrants were arriving, it is certain that they were chiefly Cree, many probably being Swampy Cree, if they did in fact come from York Factory as the
report claims. In this manner the Ojibwa movement into these lands was
counterbalanced by a southward drift of Cree.

The movements of Cree and Ojibwa were stimulated by a number of
pressures that were being exerted upon the two groups. The most frequently cited reason for the migrations is the decline of the fur and game
resources of the forested area.[20] As the subsequent discussion will show,
this was indeed a serious problem in the interior by the turn of the
century; yet, as an explanation of the migrations it is insufficient. In
particular, it does not make it clear why the Ojibwa were leaving lands
where the fur-animal populations had been depleted, but were settling in
areas which the Cree had abandoned for similar reasons. This apparent
anomaly can perhaps be resolved by considering the economic orientations of the two tribes in the light of the changing nature of the fur trade.

As noted earlier, many of the Western Cree bands had operated as
middlemen in the fur trade prior to 1763 and were accustomed to acquiring most of their pelts through barter with other tribes. When the
Montreal traders and the Hudson's Bay Company men moved into the
interior beginning in 1763, these Indian middlemen were bypassed as the
Europeans established direct contact with the trapping bands. To obtain
the European goods which they had become dependent upon, the Cree
were forced to take their own furs, or they had to find another commodity
which could be exchanged at the posts. Because of their long specialization as intermediaries in the fur trade, many of the Cree were not particularly skilful as trappers, and in fact had developed a disdain for this
activity.[21] Not surprisingly, therefore, when the growing size of the fur-
trade network generated a large demand for provisions, many of the
bands which formerly had exploited the bison resource of the parklands
only on a seasonal basis moved into the latter region where they could
serve as provisioners for the trading companies.[22]

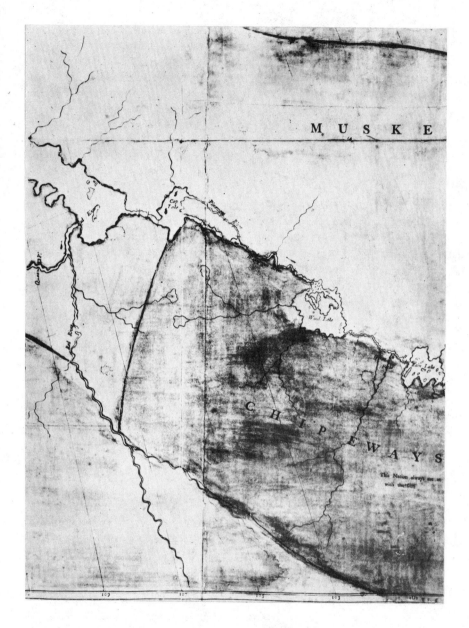

FIGURE 34   A section from Alexander Henry the Elder's map, 'The North West Parts of America' 1775 (copy in Public Archives of Canada)

The Ojibwa, on the other hand, were more proficient fur hunters, and the trading companies, especially the Northwest Company, actively encouraged them to move into Cree territory. Many Ojibwa did so, and with their more intensive trapping they were apparently able to secure furs in hunting grounds which the Cree had reported to be exhausted.[23] This combination of circumstances possibly explains not only why the Ojibwa bands moved from one impoverished department to another, which was presumably equally depleted, but it also could account for the peaceful nature of these incursions. With their different economic orientations, the two groups would not have come into serious conflict.[24]

In summarizing the population relocations which had taken place between 1763 and 1821, one of the more striking changes was the nearly complete abandonment of the Red River valley, the lower Assiniboine River, and the Manitoba interlake regions by the Assiniboine and Western Cree (Figure 33). As they withdrew, the Ojibwa moved in behind them. The Ojibwa also moved into the Swan River and Cumberland districts and penetrated as far up the Assiniboine River as its confluence with the Souris River. To the west and the southwest, the Assiniboine and Cree held most of the parkland and grassland regions of the present province of Saskatchewan. In the territories beyond, the Slaves held the lands to the west of a line running from the Battle River to the Red Deer River, and the Blood Indians held the country lying westward of a line drawn from the Red Deer River to the Bad River. The Gros Ventre had retreated southwesterly and were found to the south and west of the Bad River (Figure 33).[25] Along the southern frontier of the Assiniboine–Cree–Ojibwa territory, warfare with the Dakota Sioux continued unabated. Frequent hostilities were also reported between the Assiniboine and their old trading partners the Mandan, as well as with the Blackfoot groups to the southwest and west. Part of the reason for the increased conflict in the latter quarters was that the changing nature of the fur trade had undermined the economic basis for the cooperation between these groups which had evolved during the early eighteenth century. The inland penetration of the Europeans meant that the Assiniboine and Plains Cree were no longer able to operate as middlemen, but rather were forced to compete with other plains groups to obtain the same commodities for trade at the parkland posts.

Although post journals and travelers' accounts contain detailed information regarding tribal locations and movements, unfortunately data concerning population numbers and their changes over time are much more scanty and less precise. The earliest population estimate for the

Assiniboine was made by Alexander Henry the Elder in 1776 on the basis of information which he had gathered on his travels in western Canada. According to Henry, the Plains Assiniboine numbered roughly 300 lodges.[26] That would indicate that they would have had a total population of between 2400 and 3000, since eight to ten persons lived in each tent. Shortly after Henry made his estimate, smallpox swept throughout the west and greatly reduced their numbers as well as those of neighbouring tribes. Concerning the outbreak of this epidemic David Thompson wrote:

From the best information this disease was caught by the Chipaways (the Forest Indians) [Ojibwa] and Sieux (of the Plains) [the Dakota Sioux] about the same time, in the year 1780 ...
From the Chipaways it extended over all the Indians of the forest to it's northward extremity, and by the Sieux over the Indians of the Plains and crossed the Rocky Mountains.[27]

The Cumberland and Hudson House Journals of 1780–2 corroborate Thompson's observation and provide some additional information concerning the pattern of diffusion of the disease. Smallpox appears to have spread most rapidly in the grassland area, as might be expected considering the greater mobility of these tribes by that date. Having been first picked up by the Sioux, it was transmitted by them to the trading villages along the upper Missouri River. From these centres it quickly diffused in all directions. In the Canadian prairies, it was first reported in South Saskatchewan River area near the Red Deer River in the month of October. By November it extended to the forks of the Saskatchewan. Having reached the latter area it continued spreading to the north and east (Figure 35). In December it broke out in the Cumberland Lake region and by the end of January it erupted in The Pas area of Manitoba. Thus, it reached the Woodland Indians of North-central Manitoba from the west rather than the southeast even though it was sweeping through the Ojibwa territory along the Rainy and Winnipeg rivers at the same time (Figure 35).

Lacking any immunity to this European disease, the Indians suffered terrible losses. These losses were further increased by the Indians' reactions to smallpox after they contracted it. Once a victim came down with the disease, he and his companions generally considered his fate to be sealed and he was abandoned. Regarding these attitudes and practices, William Walker reported in 1781:

they are frightened of going nigh one to another as soon as they take bad, So the one half for want of indulgencies is starved before they can gather Strength to help themselves, They think when they are once taken bad they need not look for any recovery. So the person that's bad turns [so] feeble that he cannot walk, they leave them behind when they're pitching away, and so the poor Soul perishes.[28]

This fatalistic outlook and the associated practice of abandoning the afflicted rather than giving them aid diminished their chances of recovery due to the resulting problem of undernourishment. Furthermore, when the Indians were running high fevers, they sought relief by throwing themselves in lakes and rivers. This was said to have had a disastrous effect. It was this combination of factors that made the epidemic so devastating to the Indians and Thompson claimed that their populations were reduced by one-half to three-fifths.[29]

In the case of the Assiniboine the toll appears to have been much less, judging from Alexander Mackenzie's estimate for 1789 which listed 200 lodges.[30] Using the same ratio of people per lodge of earlier years it would imply that their numbers had been reduced by about one-third to between 1600 and 2000. However, their losses may actually have been greater since it is unclear how the epidemic affected the sizes and structures of families during the period of adjustment which followed. Presumably, if women and children were most affected, as was usually the case in European populations, then family sizes may have declined temporarily. This would have lowered the number of persons living in each tent. Yet, contrary to the European experience, David Thompson wrote that among the Indians: 'More Men died in proportion then Women and Children, for unable to bear the heat of the fever they rushed into the Rivers and Lakes to Cool themselves, and the greater part thus perished.'[31] Considering that the Assiniboine were heavily dependent upon hunting activities to provide the largest part of their diet, the remaining women and children may have been forced through economic necessity to move in with the surviving males. In this case, the lodge ratios may have remained nearly constant.

Regardless of the magnitude of the loss which the tribe suffered from smallpox, its population rebounded rapidly nonetheless. A comparison of the approximations of the two Henry's for 1776 and 1809 reveals that the Assiniboine roughly quadrupled their numbers in the thirty-three-year period in spite of the epidemic.[32]

Having recovered from this earlier disaster, the tribe experienced another setback in 1819 when a dual epidemic of measles and whooping

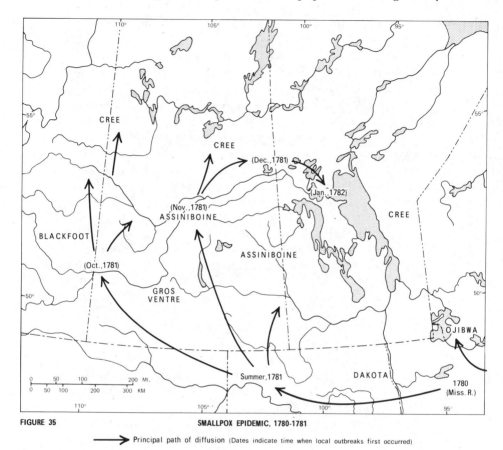

FIGURE 35   SMALLPOX EPIDEMIC, 1780-1781

————▶ Principal path of diffusion (Dates indicate time when local outbreaks first occurred)

cough swept throughout the Western Interior affecting Plains and Woodland Indians alike. According to the Edmonton District Report of
1819–20 these diseases broke out in the early winter. Regarding their
effects, the report went on to say:

scarcely had those unfortunate creatures proceded one days march from the Forts
when they were attacked with the Measeles which disease proved fatal to great
numbers of them ... This dreadful disease (for so it was at that season of the Year)
[parenthesis his] as well as the hooping Cough prevailed during the greater part of
the Winter among all the different tribes of Indians who trade with us at this
District and proved equally fatal to all.[33]

The size of the losses which the Assiniboine suffered can be determined more precisely in this instance. In 1809 Alexander Henry the Younger estimated that there were 460 lodges of Assiniboine in the Brandon District (Figure 36).[34] Six years later in 1815 Peter Fidler stated that an average of eleven Indians lived in each lodge.[35] These two sources therefore suggest that the pre-epidemic population of the Brandon Assiniboine amounted to approximately 5000 people. In 1822–3, John McDonald wrote that there were only seven people in each tent, but he reckoned that there were still 450 lodges. This set of figures gives a population of 3150 or nearly 40 per cent less than the pre-epidemic population. However, in all probability the loss was even greater. McDonald does not indicate how he arrived at his estimate of 450 lodges, which seems a bit high judging from the values for the Carlton District. A tally of McDonald's approximations of the populations of the various Brandon Assiniboine bands yields a total of only 370 lodges.[36] Using this number as the basis for projecting the total population, it would appear that the tribe numbered roughly 2600. If the later figure is the correct one, which seems likely, then the Assiniboine living in the Brandon region had lost almost half of their population. The losses in the Carlton District were only slightly less severe. For instance, the Carlton District report of 1815 listed a total of 300 lodges for the tribe.[37] Using the ratio of eleven persons per lodge, the Assiniboine would have numbered nearly 3300. Seven years later, the 1822 report for the department tallied only 200 lodges, or one-third fewer than in 1815.[38] If the post-epidemic figure of seven per lodge of the Brandon area is assumed to be applicable to the Carlton District, then the Carlton Assiniboine population would have been about 1400 in 1822 – approximately 42 per cent less than the pre-epidemic figures. The magnitude of the loss would therefore have been somewhat less than that of the Brandon District. Regarding the differential impact of the measles epidemic on various segments of the population, the data from the Carlton and Brandon districts suggest that the adult-male losses were again heavy. According to the Carlton report of 1822 there were still four men per lodge.[39] Since there were 100 fewer lodges, the male population would have declined by at least 400. With district losses amounting to roughly 900 persons, that would have meant that male deaths accounted for about 44 per cent of the total. In the Brandon District, the number of men per lodge dropped to two, giving a male population of 740 as compared to 1840 in 1815.[40] Thus, of the 2400 who died in 1819 in the Brandon area, 1100, or roughly 42 per cent, were males. Unfortunately, there is not sufficient data to permit estimations of

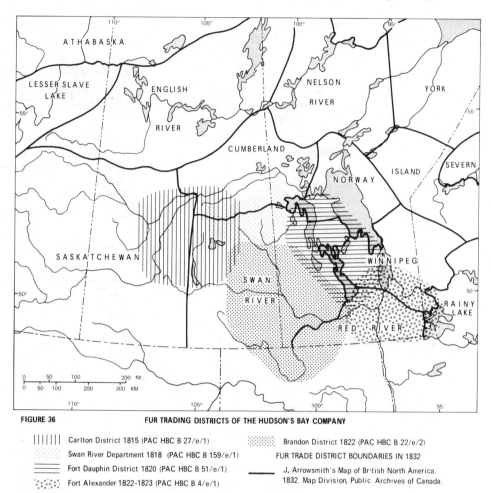

FIGURE 36   FUR TRADING DISTRICTS OF THE HUDSON'S BAY COMPANY

||||||| Carlton District 1815 (PAC HBC B 27/e/1)

Swan River Department 1818 (PAC HBC B 159/e/1)

≡≡≡ Fort Dauphin District 1820 (PAC HBC B 51/e/1)

Fort Alexander 1822-1823 (PAC HBC B 4/e/1)

Brandon District 1822 (PAC HBC B 22/e/2)

FUR TRADE DISTRICT BOUNDARIES IN 1832

J. Arrowsmith's Map of British North America,
1832. Map Division, Public Archives of Canada.

the relative losses of women, children, or older people as a portion of the total.

Unlike the Assiniboine, the Western Cree were scattered over a larger territory and generally lived in smaller groups; therefore, it is more difficult to determine their numbers. Further aggravating this problem is the fact that many of the earlier observers do not indicate which groups they included in their estimates. Some totals are comprised of the combined figures for the grassland and woodland bands, whereas others are based solely on approximations for those inhabiting the parklands and grasslands. In 1863, Dr F. Hayden estimated that there were 800 lodges of Cree living in the territories west of Lake Winnipeg in 1776.[41] When these numbers are viewed in relation to the later calculations which were made by Alexander Mackenzie, Alexander Henry the Younger, and the Hudson's Bay Company traders, it becomes apparent that Hayden's totals are much too high even allowing for the subsequent reductions of the group's population as a consequence of the smallpox outbreak of the 1780s. For instance, in 1789 Mackenzie listed only 110 tents for the Plains Cree and 200 for the Strongwood bands.[42] In 1809 Henry the Younger gave a figure of 300 tents, a value close to that of Mackenzie's. However, Henry said that his approximation excluded the Cree living north of the Beaver River in western Saskatchewan and eastern Alberta, and consequently his tally included only parkland and grassland bands.[43] It is thus difficult to draw any firm conclusions regarding the growth rate of the Western Cree during these early years. At best, these estimates tentatively suggest that their population remained fairly constant. This is somewhat surprising, considering that the Assiniboine were rapidly increasing in numbers at the same time.

Examinations of the Carlton District report of 1815 and the Brandon report of 1822 show that 100 Cree lodges were found in the former area and 130 in the latter region. Since the men who wrote these accounts indicate that the Plains Cree were quite similar in most respects to their Assiniboine neighbours, it is assumed that roughly the same tent ratios can be used to arrive at a measure of their population size. Accordingly, the Plains Cree would have numbered between 2000 and 2700 prior to the measles epidemic of 1819 and about 1600 shortly thereafter if we assume that they suffered from the disease to the same extent as the Assiniboine did.[44]

The population data for the western bands of Ojibwa is very limited. The best source of information on this group are district reports of the Hudson's Bay Company, and most of the enumerations are for the years 1819–22. According to the company's records, 136 Ojibwa were living in the Fort Alexander District in 1822 and 572 in the Dauphin District in 1820.[45] Elsewhere, only crude approximations are available. According to William Brown there were 100 Ojibwa males in the Manitoba Lake District in 1819, which would indicate that the total population was two-and-one-half to five-and-one-half times that number, or from 250 to 550 men, women, and children.[46] Only ten lodges of Ojibwa were said to be in the Brandon District in 1822 and none were reported in the Carlton District as of 1815.[47] In the latter year there were fewer than fifty-five families attached to the Cumberland District.[48] On the basis of this evidence it would appear that the population of the Ojibwa in Manitoba and Saskatchewan at the close of the period totalled probably no more than 1400.[49]

The demographic picture for the region between 1763 and 1821, therefore, suggests that the population of the Assiniboine grew rapidly even though the tribe suffered two serious setbacks in the epidemic years of 1781 and 1819. In the case of the Parkland-Grassland Cree a far more sluggish growth rate is indicated, especially for the period from the 1780s to 1810. If Mackenzie's and the younger Henry's figures are correct, there was in fact no significant growth during these years. The situation in the years prior to 1781 is uncertain as Hayden's estimate for 1776 is far too high. Considering that the Cree bands probably suffered losses from smallpox of the same magnitude as those of the Assiniboine, it can be assumed that the post-epidemic population was about two-thirds to one-half of what it had been. Taking Mackenzie's 1789 figure of 310 lodges and projecting backwards, it would appear likely that their numbers stood closer to between 460 lodges to 620 lodges or a population of from 2200 to 6800 in the 1770s, rather than the 880 lodges and some 7600 to 8800 people suggested by Dr Hayden. Comparing this total with that of 1822, it appears that the Cree population of the parkland-grassland region never reached its pre-1780 size. With respect to the Ojibwa, it is not possible to establish a growth curve due to the lack of early data and to the fact that they were recent immigrants to the region.

The sharply different population-growth rates of the Assiniboine and Western Cree are puzzling considering that the two groups were living in roughly similar environmental settings and were often in close contact with each other. It is unlikely that the differences were simply the result of observational errors since the estimates for the two groups come from the same sources. Furthermore, there is no evidence to suggest that the Cree suffered more heavily than did the Assiniboine from the various epidemics. It may be that the general mortality rates of the Cree were higher than those of the Assiniboine because of somewhat lower standards of living. David Thompson did point out in his journal that the Cree populations increased very slowly over time.[50] An analysis of Peter Fidler's population data for the Red River area in 1815 also suggests such a possibility (Figure 37). As the population pyramids indicate, the Cree had the lowest percentage of their population in the lower and upper age categories, 33 and 7 per cent respectively, while the Assiniboine had 46

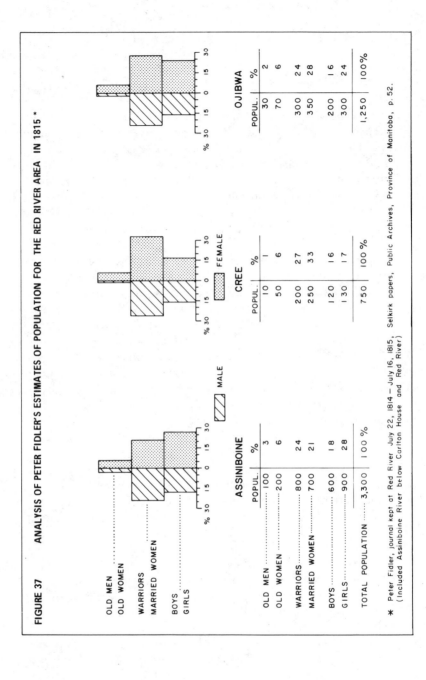

FIGURE 37   ANALYSIS OF PETER FIDLER'S ESTIMATES OF POPULATION FOR THE RED RIVER AREA IN 1815 *

ASSINIBOINE

	POPUL.	%
OLD MEN	100	3
OLD WOMEN	200	6
WARRIORS	800	24
MARRIED WOMEN	700	21
BOYS	600	18
GIRLS	900	28
TOTAL POPULATION	3,300	100 %

CREE

	POPUL.	%
OLD MEN	10	1
OLD WOMEN	50	6
WARRIORS	200	27
MARRIED WOMEN	250	33
BOYS	120	16
GIRLS	130	17
	750	100 %

OJIBWA

	POPUL.	%
OLD MEN	30	2
OLD WOMEN	70	6
WARRIORS	300	24
MARRIED WOMEN	350	28
BOYS	200	16
GIRLS	300	24
	1,250	100 %

MALE   FEMALE

* Peter Fidler, journal kept at Red River July 22, 1814 – July 16, 1815, Selkirk papers, Public Archives, Province of Manitoba, p. 52.
(Included Assinboine River below Carlton House and Red River)

and 9 respectively, and the Ojibwa 40 and 8 per cent. It may well be that the Assiniboine, who were the most fully acculturated to the grasslands, and the Ojibwa, who engaged in some agriculture and had access to wild rice, had more abundant and reliable food supplies.[51] These two groups therefore would have been able to support larger numbers of people in the so-called 'nonproductive' age groups. With a very high percentage of its total population in the lower age category, the natural growth potential of the Assiniboine would have been the greatest of the three tribes. As will be demonstrated subsequently, the Assiniboine did continue to increase rapidly in numbers without any appreciable emmigration for outside areas up to 1838.

NOTES

1 *Voyages From Montreal*, lxx
2 Morton, *The Journal of Duncan M'Gillivray*, 34–5
3 Coues, *New Light on the Early History of the Greater Northwest*, 2:522–3
4 Cumberland House District Report, 1815, PAC HBC B 49/e/1, p. 4; Manitoba Lake–Big Point District Report, 1818–19, PAC HBC B 122/e/1, p. 7; and Fort Dauphin District Report, 1820, PAC HBC B 51/e/1, p. 15
5 Fort Pelly District Report, 1818–19, PAC HBC B 159/e/1, pp. 5–6; and Carlton House District Report, PAC HBC B 27/e/1, p. 2
6 'Journal Kept at Red River,' Selkirk Papers, 69: 52. The Carlton House in this instance was a post which the Hudson's Bay Company had built on the upper headwaters of the Assiniboine River in 1790. It was sometimes referred to as Fort Assiniboine. Voorhis, *Canadian Historic Forts and Trading Posts*, 44
7 Brandon House District Report, 1819, PAC HBC B 22/e/1, p. 11
8 Brandon House District Report, 1822, PAC HBC B 22/e/2, pp. 3–4
9 Edmonton District Report, 1823–4, PAC HBC B 60/e/6, p. 3. In the report for the previous year a lower set of figures were given. The parkland Assiniboine, Cree, and Métis near the post were said to number twenty tents and the Strong Wood Assiniboine forty tents. The reasons for the upwards revisions were not given, but presumably they were based on more detailed information. Edmonton District Report, 1822–3, PAC HBC B 60/e/5, p. 4
10 For a more thorough discussion of Indian migrations in this quarter see, Hlady, 'Indian Migrations in Manitoba and the West,' 28–9, 40–2
11 Morton, *Journal of Duncan M'Gillivray*, 62–3
12 *Voyages From Montreal*, xcii
13 Coues, *New Light on the Early History of the Greater Northwest*, 1:46
14 Hlady, 'Indian Migrations in Manitoba and the West,' 31

15 Manitoba Lake–Big Point Report, 1818–19, PAC HBC B 122/e/1, p. 7; and Fort Alexander District Report, 1822–3, PAC HBC B 4/e/1, p. 3

16 Fort Pelly District Report, 1818–19, PAC HBC B 159/e/1, pp. 5–6

17 Carlton District Report, 1815, PAC HBC B 27/e/1, p. 2

18 Manitoba Lake–Big Point Report, 1818–19, PAC HBC B 122/e/1, p. 7; Fort Alexander District Report, 1822–3, PAC HBC B 4/e/1, p. 3; and Fort Dauphin District Report, 1820, PAC HBC B 51/e/1, p. 7

19 Cumberland House District Report, 1815, PAC HBC B 49/e/1, p. 4; and Cumberland House Post Journals, 1792, PAC HBC B 49/a/23, p. 27

20 Cited, for example, in the Brandon District Report for 1822–3 and the Lac la Pluie Report of the same year. PAC HBC B 22/e/2, p. 3 and PAC HBC B 105/e/2, p. 1, respectively

21 In particular, they frequently complained that it was difficult work to break open frozen beaver lodges in the winter.

22 The changing nature of the fur trade and the Indian responses to it will be discussed in greater detail subsequently.

23 For example, the Fort Pelly (Swan River) District Report for 1818–19 stated that the Ojibwa living there were not indigenous to the region, but rather had been brought there by the North West Company. PAC HBC B 159/e/1, pp. 5–6

24 Alternative hypotheses could be suggested. There may have been a short time lag between the abandonment of a region by one group and its reoccupation by another. If this period were only of three or four years duration it would have been sufficiently long for the fur-animal populations to have made a substantial recovery. On the other hand, perhaps population densities in the territories held by the Ojibwa were less than they had been during the period of Cree occupance. Ojibwa pressures on resources therefore would have been less intensive.

25 Edmonton District Report, 1815, PAC HBC B 60/e/1, p. 4

26 Wissler, 'Population Changes among the Northern Plains Indians,' 7. The problem with Henry's estimate, as well as those of many other observers is that he did not travel through much of the tribe's homelands. Henry probably underestimated the population of the Assiniboine since he said that they had several villages each of which had from 100 to 200 lodges: *Travels and Adventures*, 303.

27 Glover, *David Thompson's Narrative*, 236

28 Rich, *Cumberland and Hudson House Journals, 1779–82*, 265

29 Glover, *Thompson's Narrative*, 236

30 *Voyage from Montreal*, p. lxx. Unlike Alexander Henry the Elder, Mackenzie recognized two divisions of Assiniboine, a Plains group numbering 120 lodges and a woodland group totalling 70 lodges in the Saskatchewan area. However,

like Henry, he too probably underestimated their numbers since his figures do not appear to have included the Assiniboine living in southeastern Saskatchewan. In effect, his estimates probably covered the same groups as Henry's.

31 Glover, *Thompson's Narrative*, 236
32 Coues, *New Light on the Early History of the Greater Northwest*, 2:522–3. Henry the Younger's tally listed 847 lodges.
33 PAC HBC B 60/e/3, p. 6
34 Coues, *New Light on the Early History of the Greater Northwest*, 2:522–3
35 'Journal Kept at Red River,' 52
36 Brandon District Report, 1822–23, PAC HBC B 22/e/2, p. 3
37 Carlton District Report, 1815, PAC HBC B 27/e/1, p. 2
38 Edmonton District Report, 1822–23, PAC HBC B 60/e/5, p. 4. The Carlton figures were included in the Edmonton Report since Carlton House had been attached to the Edmonton District.
39 Ibid., 4
40 Brandon District Report, 1822–23, PAC HBC B 22/e/2, p. 3
41 'Contributions to the Ethnology and Philiology of the Indian Tribes of the Upper Missouri Valley,' 236. According to J.C. Ewers, Hayden's account is believed to have been copied from the missing portions of E. Denig's account. E. Denig, *Five Indian Tribes of the Upper Missouri*, xxv-xxxvii and 109
42 Wissler, 'Population Changes among the Northern Plains Indians,' 9
43 Coues, *New Light on the Early History of the Greater Northwest*, 2:516
44 These values were obtained by using Wissler's pre-epidemic tent ratio of from eight to eleven and the post-epidemic figure of seven. Furthermore, the lodge count for the Carlton District for 1822 was estimated at eighty-eight (that is, decreasing it by 12 per cent to allow for the effects of the epidemic) and the Brandon Department figure for 1815 was set at 145 (that is, the 1822 tally was increased by 12 per cent). The resulting totals were then rounded off to the nearest hundred.
45 Fort Alexander District Report, 1822–3, PAC HBC B 4/e/1, p. 3, and Fort Dauphin District Report, 1820–1, PAC HBC B 51/e/1, p. 15. These counts are probably fairly accurate since the Ojibwa had close ties to the posts and credit records were kept for the various families.
46 Manitoba Lake-Big Point District Report, 1818–19, PAC HBC B 122/e/1, p. 7. The ratio used in this instance was based upon data contained in the Dauphin District Report for 1820–1, the Fort Alexander Report for 1822–3, and the Lac la Pluie Report for 1829–30. The latter district had the highest ratio and that of Fort Alexander the lowest.
47 Brandon District Report, 1822, PAC HBC B 22/e/2, p. 4, and Carlton District Report, 1815, PAC HBC B 27/e/1, p. 2

48 Cumberland District Report, 1815, PAC HBC B 49/e/1, p. 4
49 This figure was obtained by averaging the high and low estimates and rounding off the result to the nearest one-hundred.
50 Glover, *Thompson's Narrative*, 92
51 It might be suggested that different social practices were responsible, yet,
historical accounts indicate that the marriage practices of the three goups were
quite similar. All three groups practised some polygamy; conversely, infan-
ticide was rare except in instances were twins were born. Henry, *Travels and
Adventures*, 305–9, and Williams, *Graham's Observations*, 176–8. Also, Henry
pointed out that all three groups took male and female slaves. However, he
added that the Assiniboine treated the latter most cruelly and rarely married or
incorporated them into their society. Therefore, the latter tribe would not
have acquired a larger number of potential mothers through raiding activities.
Henry, *Travels and Adventures*, 312–13

6

The destruction of
fur and game animals

During the fifty-eight-year period between the Treaty of Paris in 1763 and the merger of the Hudson's Bay and North West companies in 1821 trading rivalries reached their peak in the Western Interior of Canada. This intensive competition favoured a ruthless exploitation of the region's fur and game animals, and by the end of the period many sections of central and southern Manitoba and Saskatchewan had been nearly depleted of these resources. Although the population levels of the various species fluctuated locally under natural conditions, thereby potentially skewing the picture of the general situation of the country which individual post records present, the annual district reports filed by the various traders and those of George Simpson do provide us with a reasonably accurate notion of the degree to which the resource base had been eroded by the 1820s (see Figure 36 for district boundaries).[1]

In the forested area of the southeast, the Lac La Pluie Report for 1822–3 indicated that beaver had long been exhausted and that most of the pelts taken consisted of less valuable furs, chiefly marten and muskrat.[2] Similar conditions existed to the north and west. In 1820, Peter Fidler, who was in charge of the Fort Dauphin District which stretched from the west shores of Lake Winnipeg to the Shell River, claimed that beaver were very scarce, as were marten even though the latter had been numerous as late as 1817. The decline of marten was well illustrated by the District's fur returns which show that in 1817, 2196 marten were traded, but thereafter the number dropped rapidly, totalling only 1430 in 1819, 513 in 1820, and a mere 366 in 1821, or one-seventh of the 1817 total. With the exception of lynx, all other furs showed similar decreases during these years.[3] In the Cumberland Lake region to the north the effects of over-hunting had apparently been felt at an even earlier date. In 1795, the Cumberland House Journals indicated that the lands around the post had been trapped out for a number of years. A report for 1815 shows that the situation had not improved and beaver were still scarce. Only muskrat were relatively plentiful but they too were over-hunted as Indian families moved into the district from exhausted territories to the east and, especially, the north. In 1819, for example, 37,007 muskrat skins were taken in trade.[4] Prime furs had also been depeleted in the forested Ile à la Crosse and Lesser Slave Lake districts to the northwest of Cumberland Lake.[5]

Like the woodland region, the parkland belt was initially well endowed with fur-bearing animals. The river valleys and larger 'islands' of woods provided habitats where beaver, muskrat, marten, and fisher thrived. However, since their habitats were concentrated in a few areas, these animals were quickly discovered and destroyed, and by the 1820s they had been largely exterminated from the middle and upper portions of the Assiniboine River valley. As a consequence, Govenor George Simpson of the Hudson's Bay Company decided that it would be wise to close a number of posts and rearrange district boundaries in order to reduce the expenses which the company was incurring. In his 1824 report to the company in London he justified his actions writing:

The Upper Red River District is nearly exhausted in Fur bearing Animals, and the Posts cannot be kept under a very heavy expense in Clerks men and Goods ... it produces nothing but Provisions Leather Robes and Hides of which we can obtain from other quarters a larger quantity than required ... it therefore appeared highly expedient to abandone this superfluous and costly department entirely. The neighbouring Department, that of Swan River, comprises three Posts ... but the Returns of this District have decreased so much of late years as to render the Trade thereof very unprofitable ... [therefore] my attention was directed to the reduction of this Department likewise.[6]

Furs were equally scarce in the country lying adjacent to the Saskatchewan River between the forks and Edmonton House. The Carlton District Report of 1815 recorded that, 'This part of the country is nearly exhausted in Beaver, but abounds in Wolves and Foxes, particularly when the Buffalo are Plenty.'[7] However, the latter skins were of relatively low value. In the wooded country to the northward traders began to suggest that beaver trapping be suspended to give the animal a chance to recover.[8]

Although intensive hunting pressures were largely responsible for draining the country of its furs, other factors played a contributing role. The historical record shows that natural disasters, primarily disease, fires, and droughts, often took heavy tolls. The effect that diseases could have on the fur resources of a territory was amply illustrated by John Tanner's observations made near the present city of Pembina, North Dakota, in the early nineteenth century. When describing one of his trapping operations he said:

I knew of more than twenty gangs of beaver in the country around my camp, and I now went and began to break up the lodges, but I was much surprised to find nearly all of them empty. At last I found that some kind of distemper was prevailing among these animals which destroyed them in vast numbers. I found them dead and dying in the water, on the ice, and on the land. Sometimes I found one that, having cut a tree half down, had died at its roots; sometimes one who had drawn a stick of timber halfway to its lodge was lying dead by his burthen. Many of them which I opened, were red and bloody about the heart. Those that lived in large rivers and running water suffered less. Almost all of those that lived in the ponds and stagnant water died. Since that year the beaver have never been so plentiful in the country of the Red River and Hudson's Bay, as they used formerly to be.[9]

Tanner's story is corroborated by the report that Peter Fidler filed for the Dauphin District nearly twenty years later in 1820. When discussing the resource conditions of the district he wrote:

Beaver formerly a well known Animal is now very scarce – formerly more Packs of Beaver skins at 90 lb. weight was taken out of this District than are now got [in] single Skins – about 19 years some disorder occasioned by the Change of the Air or Some other unknown cause suddenly reduced them to the very few that is now to be found. This was the Case South of the Athapescow [Athabasca] all along the Coast of Hudson's Bay as far West as the Eastern borders of the Rocky – This unknown cause extended at the same time in the same direction to near Moose Factory, there and to the Northward of the Settlement the Disorder seems not to have extended its fatal affects.[10]

Thus, in the case of beaver, it may have been the combination of a particularly fatal epidemic at the beginning of the nineteenth century and the continued intensive trapping of the animal which led to its near extermination in many districts of the west.

David Thompson suggests the possibility that perhaps smallpox may have been transmitted to certain animal species. Regarding the effects of the epidemic of 1781 on wildlife he wrote:

All the Wolves and Dogs that fed on the bodies of those [Indians] that died of the Small Pox lost their hair especially on the sides and belly ... the Dogs were mostly killed ...
I have already mentioned that before the dreadful disease appeared among the Indians they were numerous, and the Bison, Moose, Red, and other Deer more so in proportion and Provisions of Meat ... in abundance ... it was noticed by the Traders and Natives, that at the death of the latter ... the numerous herds of Bison and Deer also disappeared both in the Woods and in the Plains, and the Indians about Cumberland House declared the Same of the Moose and the Swans, Geese, and Ducks.[11]

This observation is difficult to interpret. The scavaging dogs and wolves may very well have contracted a disease by preying upon the decomposing bodies of the Indians. However, it is doubtful that they became infected with smallpox. If it were some other disease presumably it could have spread to other animals as Thompson suggests. In any case, it seems unlikely that it would have spread to waterfowl. It is distinctly possible that the reported decline in the numbers of all species was in a large part related to the decline of Indian populations. The traders depended upon the Indians to supply them with most of their provisions, but following the epidemic the Indians were unable to do so. In addition, the Indians who survived were understandably demoralized by the epidemic. Hence, their perceptions of their surroundings may well have been somewhat distorted for a brief period after 1781. Indeed, Thompson indicates that this was the case. In this way, the combination of disillusionment and short provision supplies at the posts may have given the impression that smallpox had also taken its toll among animal populations.

Periodic droughts wrought devastation in a variety of ways. Forest fires often burned over extensive tracts of territories at these times. For instance, the Lac la Pluie Report for 1825–6 claimed that fires were extensive in the district in 1804–5 burning throughout the autumn until heavy snows extinguished them. These fires were said to have killed large numbers of beaver. Furthermore, the report went on to say that such fires had been common in the region at the beginning of the century, suggesting that perhaps there had been a series of dry years.[12]

Besides the increased incidence of fires, prolonged dry periods caused water levels to fall and, as noted earlier, animals such as the muskrat were adversely affected by these changes. These cyclic variations became increasingly critical to the Indians and traders of Manitoba and Saskatchewan in the early nineteenth century since nearly all other fur-bearing animals had been wiped out. Thus, by the 1820s, the trapping economies of the Indians in southern Manitoba and eastern Saskatchewan were heavily dependent upon their muskrat returns placing them in a difficult position. This problem was perhaps most acute in the Cumberland District and led Governor Simpson to report in 1825:

The Trade of this Department is very precarious depending almost entirely on the state of the Water[,] Muskrat being the only Fur it provides in any quantity. When the Waters are low this Animal entirely disappears but with the return of high Water it Multiplies with incredible rapidity; the Indians of Cumberland are therefore at times the most Wealthy and independent in the Country and at others the most Wretched.[13]

Similar conditions existed in the Swan River, Red River, and Winnipeg districts. Thus, by the 1820s the combination of intensive trapping and natural calamities had largely destroyed the fur resource base of the parklands and bordering forests of the Western Interior of Canada. In these areas the fur trade became highly dependent upon the single and very unreliable resource – muskrat.

In the forested territory adjacent to the parklands big-game populations were also dwindling in the face of relentless hunting pressures. By the late eighteenth century the moose and woodland caribou of the region to the east of Lake Manitoba and the Red River valley had been seriously reduced in numbers. Alexander Mackenzie remarked that game in the Rainy Lake–Lake of the Woods area had become so scarce that the few natives who remained there were forced to rely upon fish and wild rice. He added that this situation differed from that which had existed at the time of French control, but that conditions in the region were improving and the game was recovering.[14]

Mackenzie seems to have been somewhat optimistic in his predictions that the numbers of game were increasing. The Lac la Pluie reports of the Hudson's Bay Company in the 1820s clearly indicate that this was not the case, and a serious shortage of moose and deer was still plaguing the district. According to the report for 1825–6:

Moose Deer [Moose] formerly were numerous in the Department at present however they are only to be Met with towards the Plains. In the spring of 1824 the

Indians killed a great number, but this year the same Indians in the same places are almost starving to death – however I have heard of a couple of Families who have lived all winter on Moose meat. Formerly the Rein Deer was also very numerous, and more to the northward, than to the southward of the boundary line [United States boundary]; which I believe is still the case, but deplorably scarce on both sides. Roe and Roe Buck or Chevuille [red deer] is sometimes to be Met with towards the Plains.[15]

Three years earlier a report for the same district claimed that big game was so scarce that the Indians lacked sufficient skins to make their clothes and moccasins.[16] The situation was equally desparate in the neighbouring Winnipeg District. In 1824, Govenor Simpson wrote of this district: 'the country is so much exhausted that I can see no prospect of future amendment and think it is not unlikely that in the course of a few years the Indians will remove to other parts in order to avoid starvation as there are no large Animals to be found and the fisheries not to be depended on.'[17] Similar circumstances prevailed in the forested portions of the interlake region of Manitoba. The North West Company maintained a post on the western shores of Lake Winnipeg in 1804–5, and Alexander Henry the Younger stated that the men stationed there suffered from serious food shortages. He attributed these shortages to a lack of large game animals in the lands near the Fort and added that the Indians refused to come there for those reasons.[18]

Game conditions in the lands adjacent to Saskatchewan were apparently much more favourable. The Cumberland District Report for 1815 declared that the country around the post abounded in moose and reindeer and that these two animals constituted the principal part of the diet of natives.[19] In the Ile à La Crosse area these two animals were still abundant as of 1822–3 while some bison were found in the southern margins of the area as well.[20] Peter Fidler's reports for the Fort Dauphin District in 1820 and 1821 indicated that moose were still abundant near the Manitoba escarpment while some 'jumping deer' (pronghorned antelope) and red deer were found along the southern fringes of the Department. Of these two animals Fidler said, 'these are the only meat animals we have in this district that keeps constantly in it of large size.'[21] No mention was made of bison, although they were undoubtedly found in the parkland limits of the area along with the antelope and red deer which he mentioned. Clearly moose was the chief game animal and was still present in adequate numbers.[22]

Within the parkland belt, the reports of the Brandon, Swan River, and

Carlton districts (Figure 36) make it evident that bison were still present in large numbers, and that they comprised the major portion of the diet of both the Indians and the fur traders living there. Moose and red deer were important secondary food sources which were used whenever the bison herds were not found locally. The numbers of these two animals which were present varied considerably from department to department. In 1822 John McDonald reported that neither animal was abundant in the Brandon territory. He cited the lack of any dense woods as the reason for the scarcity of moose.[23] The Swan River District included both forest and parkland environments and moose and red deer were more plentiful there. Moose were especially numerous along the Red Deer River. The bison population, on the other hand, was rather limited.[24] Farther west in the Carlton region red deer and moose were both sufficiently abundant to provide adequate stocks of food when bison were absent for short periods. The same was true around Edmonton House.[25]

As of 1821, therefore, the fur resources of the forests and adjacent parklands had been nearly depleted of high-quality furs. A similar situation existed with respect to game animals in the eastern forest districts, while elsewhere game supplies were still adequate.

NOTES

1 Simpson's reports were synthesized from the various district reports which were sent to him on a yearly basis. His accounts therefore provide a good overview of changing resource conditions.

2 PAC HBC B 105/e/2, p. 1

3 Fort Dauphin District Report, 1820–1, PAC HBC B 51/e/2, p. 7

4 Cumberland House Journals, 1815, PAC HBC B 49/a/26, p. 33, and Cumberland District Report, 1815, PAC HBC B 49/e/1, p. 4

5 Ile à la Crosse District Report, 1822, PAC HBC B 89/e/1, pp. 1 and 2, and Lesser Slave Lake District Report, 1822, PAC HBC B 115/e/4, p. 3. It should be pointed out, however, that the Lesser Slave Lake Report for 1822–3 stated that in that year the fur returns equalled those of nine years previous and the chief trader there expressed the opinion that the commonly held view that declining fur returns were a consequence of the exhaustion of fur resources was not entirely correct. He felt that the period of intensive competition had made the Indians less diligent.

6 Report to Governor and Committee in London, 5 June 1824, PAC HBC D 4/87, p. 11

7 PAC HBC B 27/e/1, p. 1

8 Ile à la Crosse District Report, 1822, PAC HBC 89/e/1, p. 2

9 Tanner, *Captivity and Adventures*, 88–89

10 Fort Dauphin District Report, 1820, PAC HBC B 51/e/1, pp. 5–6

11 Glover, *Thompson's Narrative*, 237

12 Lac la Pluie District Report, 1825, PAC HBC B 105/e/6, p. 3

13 Report to the Governor and Committee in London, 1 September 1825, PAC HBC D 4/88, p. 81

14 *Voyages From Montreal*, lvii–lxii

15 PAC HBC B 105/e/6, p. 2

16 Lac la Pluie District Report, 1822, PAC HBC B 105/e/2, p. 1

17 Report to the Governor and Committee in London, 10 August 1824, PAC HBC D 4/87, p. 48

18 Coues, *New Light on the Early History of the Greater Northwest*, 1:451–2

19 PAC HBC B 49/e/1, p. 2

20 Ile à la Crosse District Report, 1822, PAC HBC B 89/e/1, p. 1

21 Fort Dauphin District Report, 1820, PAC HBC B 51/e/1, p. 5. Significantly, he said in his account for 1821 that moose had been scarce in the preceeding four years due to drought conditions which had diminished the grasses in the area. However, in 1821, rains were frequent and the grasses recovered as did the moose population.

22 However, the population of this animal was variable depending upon grazing conditions. As noted above, moose was plentiful during wet years and often scarce during dry conditions.

23 Brandon District Report, 1822, PAC HBC B 22/e/2, p. 2

24 Red Deer River Post Journal, 1812–13, PAC HBC B 176/a/1, p. 2, and Fort Pelly District Report, 1828, PAC HBC B 159/e/3, p. 2. The latter report indicated that the Fort Pelly men had to subsist largely on moose and red deer.

25 Edmonton House District Report, 1815, PAC HBC B 60/e/1, p. 2

7

New economic opportunities

Between 1763 and 1821 the character of the Northwest fur trade changed substantially, and these changes strongly inflenced the evolving tribal economies of the Indians of western Canada. Although the Seven Years' War was concluded with the Treaty of Paris in 1763, the trading posts which had been abandoned by the French in Manitoba and Saskatchewan were not reoccupied by the British traders until later in the decade. This delay was partly related to the Hudson's Bay Company's continuing policy of relying on Indian middlemen to bring furs down to the Bay. In addition, the attempts of the Montreal-based merchants to take over the old trading network of the French failed initially. Pontiac's rebellion blocked inland expansion until after 1764, and when the canoes were finally dispatched from the St Lawrence River in 1765 they were plundered on the Rainy River by a band of Ojibwa who were said to be destitute of European goods.[1] The Indians had been without these commodities since the late 1750s when the French began to withdraw from the region.

After 1765 the tempo of expansion quickened, and as early as 1767 the Montreal pedlars had reached as far up the Saskatchewan River as Finlay's House (Figure 38). Furthermore, they had opened three trading houses in the Red River–Assiniboine River region. In 1768 the trade regulations that had been imposed by the proclamation of 7 October 1763 requiring all traders to obtain licences and restricting trade to designated posts were rescinded, opening the Northwest to all traders.[2] Intensive competition for the Indians' furs resulted immediately, and in the following year the Hudson's Bay Company men complained that the interior had been so flooded with their rivals that the commerce of the posts on the Bay was being seriously undermined.[3] In response to this increased pressure the company directors in London relented in their opposition to suggestions that inland posts be constructed, and in 1774 the Hudson's Bay Company built its first post on the Saskatchewan River at Pine Island in Cumberland Lake. The company's opponents reacted to this new challenge quickly and surrounded the post, cutting off its hinterland. Also, they formed various alliances, such as that of J. McGill, B. Frobisher, and M. Blondeau of 1775. These alliances were continually being formed and dissolved, but they ultimately led to the establishment of the first North West Company in 1779 and its successors, the North West companies of 1780–2, 1783–7, 1787–1804, and 1804–21, as well as the short-lived XY Company of 1798–1804. These competitors of the Hudson's Bay Company collectively are usually referred to as the Nor'Westers.

These various organizations allowed the Nor'Westers to pool their resources, thereby enabling them to establish a supply system which could support the further territorial expansion of their operations. Expansion was necessary if they were to bypass the Assiniboine and Cree middlemen tied into the Hudson's Bay Company trading network. Reflecting this increased capability Peter Pond was able to outfit himself at Cumberland Lake in 1778 and penetrate into the Mackenzie River basin of what was to become the Athabasca District, the richest fur district in the western part of the continent. With the expansion of the fur trade into the Athabasca, the whole ecological situation of the trade changed from that of the pre-1763 period, and the resources of the forests alone could no longer support it. Instead, to maintain the increasing number of posts and the lengthening lines of communications, the Hudson's Bay and North West companies found it necessary to establish food supply networks which drew heavily upon the bison of the parklands and grasslands.

The Hudson's Bay Company came to a quick realization of this fact as a result of its experiences at Cumberland Lake in the 1770s. After four years of continuing hardship there, Matthew Cocking concluded that the local resources could sustain no more than twelve men.[4] Since the supplies were barely able to meet the requirements of the trading post, it was clear that little surplus would be available to feed the canoemen travelling between them. Indeed, it was the lack of such a supply which prevented the Hudson's Bay Company from exploiting to the fullest extent its locational advantage vis-à-vis the North West Company in the early years of the Athabascan trade. David Thompson pointed this out in 1796 after having surveyed the inland route from the Bay to Lake Athabasca via the Nelson–Burntwood–Churchill River route. By keeping careful observa-

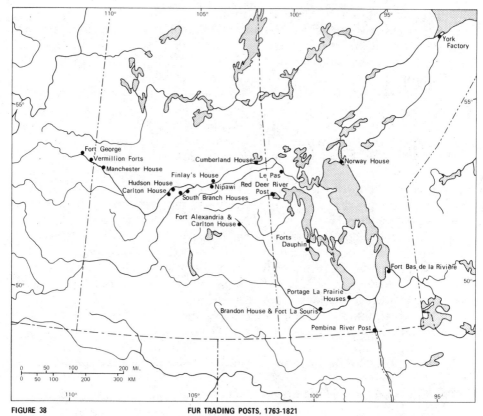

FIGURE 38   **FUR TRADING POSTS, 1763-1821**

Sources: A. S. Morton, "A HISTORY OF THE CANADIAN WEST TO 1870-71" and E. Voorhis, "HISTORIC FORTS AND TRADING POSTS"

tions of distances as he travelled, he concluded that the route was considerably shorter than the one that bent southward to Cumberland Lake.
Although it was a difficult and dangerous traverse, he felt it would be
useable if adequate provisions could be assured. Lacking these, the
sparseness of the Indian population and meagre resources of the area
rendered it useless.[5]

To deal with these logistical problems the company established its first
post in the parkland area in 1779 – Hudson House on the North Saskatchewan River (Figure 38). Once this new resource area was tapped it
grew rapidly in importance, and the company's men became increasingly
skilful in their attempts to deal with the environment of the boreal forest.
This was illustrated by the developments at Cumberland House. As time
passed the post's chief function changed, and rather than serve as a fur

trading centre it became primarily a provision depot. To function in this new capacity it was necessary to exploit the local environment more intensively and more widely. The food-gathering activities were carried on as far away as Beaver Lake, which was located roughly fifty miles to the north. This lake yielded over 3000 pounds of fish each year; yet, Cumberland House continued to depend on the parklands for a major portion of its food supplies. For example, in the winter of 1819–20 the Franklin polar expedition visited the post. While there, one of the members of the expedition, Dr Richardson, made some notes on the daily diet of his party and that of the traders. He said that besides the large quantities of fish which were consumed 'The rest of our winter's provisions consisted of geese, salted in the autumn, and of dried meats and pemmican, obtained from the provision posts on the Plains of the Saskatchawan[sic]. A good many potatoes are also raised at this post, and a small supply of tea and sugar is brought from the depôt at York Factory.'[6]

In short, at the close of the period the prairies continued to supply a large percentage of the provisions in stock at the post even though the food resources of the area were being exploited far more effectively, and agriculture had been introduced on a limited scale.

In addition to Cumberland House, the Hudson's Bay Company also maintained a supply base at Norway House situated on the north end of Lake Winnipeg (Figure 38). This post was built in 1801, and by 1820 it was being used as the chief provisioning station for the Athabasca brigades. Furs were brought from the latter region to Norway House where they were exchanged for European goods, which were shipped inland from York Factory. To feed these brigades, foodstuffs were sent from the upper Saskatchewan River and from southern Manitoba – mostly from the Assiniboine River Valley by 1820. In 1812 the Selkirk colony was established on the Red River and it supplied the Hudson's Bay Company with some agricultural produce. However, before 1821 these supplies were insignificant when compared to the quantities of dried buffalo meat, grease, and pemmican which were consumed.[7]

The North West Company likewise maintained a post at Cumberland Lake. In describing its function in 1808, Alexander Henry the Younger said: 'this post is kept by us less for the purpose of trade than for the convenience of a dépôt to supply our northern brigades. In the spring we bring down [from the upper] Saskatchewan to this place from 300 to 500 bags of pemmican, and upwards of 200 kegs of grease.'[8]

In addition to the Cumberland Lake post the company men maintained two other provision stations in the interior, one at Bas de la Rivière and the other at Rainy Lake (Figure 39). The former was supplied by the

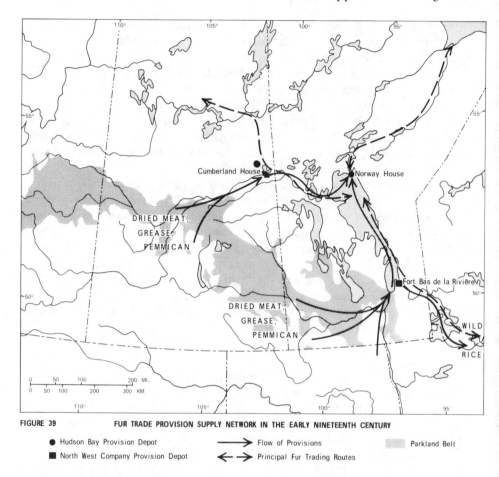

FIGURE 39   FUR TRADE PROVISION SUPPLY NETWORK IN THE EARLY NINETEENTH CENTURY

● Hudson Bay Provision Depot   ⟶ Flow of Provisions   Parkland Belt
■ North West Company Provision Depot   ⟵ ⟶ Principal Fur Trading Routes

Red, Assiniboine, and Qu'Appelle river areas. The latter establishment played a role similar to that of Norway House of the Hudson's Bay Company in that it was the terminal point for the North West Company's Athabasca brigades. Like the post at the mouth of the Winnipeg River, it too received pemmican and grease from the prairies of southern Manitoba and Saskatchewan. This source was augmented considerably by large quantities of wild rice and some corn obtained locally.[9] Although it is not possible to determine the exact size of the provision requirement that the fur trade generated, a rough approximation of this demand can be made by examining the records of the two largest companies. Regarding the consumption of food at the posts in the parklands Peter Fidler indicated in his 1819 report for the Brandon District: 'The allowance of fresh meat for one man exclusive of Bone is 5 lb., a woman half that, for every child 1 to 1 1/2 lbs. per day of any provisions 2 lb., 1 and 3/4 respectively the same allowance for any other kind of provision. Fish 7 1/2 lb. per day per man but in general they have more when they can be got.'[10]

Meat was thus the staple and fish a supplementary food which was eaten whenever it was available. With these ample allowances, the quantities of food which were necessary to sustain even small posts were sizable. For instance, Alexander Henry the Younger of the North West Company indicated that the forty-one people stationed at his trading house on the Pembina River used the supplies listed in Table 3 during the winter of 1807–8.[11] From these figures it can be seen that at this one post, which was not an especially large one, over 63,000 pounds of bison meat was used. Recalling that the intensive rivalry between the various companies led to a proliferation of posts in the years before 1821, these totals take on added significance. For instance, in 1795 there were twenty-one trading houses in operation on the Assiniboine River alone and if it is assumed that their rates of consumption averaged only one-half that of Henry's post, this region alone would have produced a demand on the order of at least 1,323,000 pounds.[12] If the sex ratios of the kills were similar to that tallied by Henry, it would have taken the meat of over 3082 bison to satisfy this requirement.[13]

As noted earlier, besides the people attached to the posts, the voyageurs manning the canoe brigades had to be provided for. Being engaged in physically demanding work, these men were hearty eaters, having a food intake which averaged eight pounds of fresh meat, or a pound to a pound-and-a-half of pemmican a day.[14] As the volume of canoe traffic steadily increased, the quantities of meat and fat which were required to feed these canoemen rose accordingly. By the first decade of the nineteenth century the North West Company was purchasing an average of 140 ninety-pound bags each year in the Red River Department and 300 to 500 bags from the Saskatchewan District. This yielded an annual total average of nearly 48,600 pounds. Besides pemmican, 1.2 tons of grease was also being supplied each year by the Red River Department and 18,000 pounds by the Saskatchewan District.[15] As Table 4 shows, the size of this company's provision requirement was still growing in 1813; the Red River Region was expected to furnish 395 bags of pemmican and the Saskatchewan territory 250.5 for a total of 644 bags, or roughly 9000 more pounds than in the earlier years of the preceding decade. In short, during the period from 1763 to 1821, declining fur

TABLE 3
Food consumption at Pembina River, winter of 1807–8 (for forty-one people)

Numbers	Weight	Season taken
112 cows	45,000	1 September – 1 February
35 bulls	18,000	
3 red deer	905	Autumn
5 large black bears	460	Winter
4 beavers		
3 swans		
1 white crane		
12 outards		
36 ducks		
1150 fish of different kinds		15 November – 1 April with nets under the ice
775 sturgeon	50–150 each	
grease	410	20 April – 20 May
bear meat	140	
325 bushels of potatoes and assorted vegetables		

resources and the efforts to bypass Indian middlemen as well as increasing levels of competition between rival trading groups led to a rapid spatial expansion of the fur trade in western Canada. This expansion created great logistical problems for the fur companies who had to maintain transportation routes that continued to grow in length. To cope with these difficulties, trading houses were established in the parklands to draw upon the bison resource. At strategic transportation points supply depots were constructed to receive and store the pemmican, dried meat, and grease coming from the posts (Figure 39). The stock of food which accumulated in these depots was used to provision the canoe brigades which were engaged in the transportation of furs and trade goods. In this manner a new economic link was welded between the parkland-grassland region and the forest country.

Of significance to the Assiniboine and Western Cree, the increasing size of the provision requirement of the fur trade offered them new economic opportunities when their traditional role as middlemen in the fur trade was being undermined by the flood of pedlars into western Canada. The Assiniboine were the first to respond to the changing conditions, and the historical records suggest that they shifted the primary focus of their trading activities from the exchange of furs to the bartering of dried meat and grease in a relatively short period of time. To illustrate,

TABLE 4
North West Company provision requirements for 1813*

Department	Number of canoes	Bags per canoe	Total of 90-lb. pemmican bags supplied	
Cumberland House				
Athabasca	28	2.5	70	} outbound
English River	11	2.5	28†	
Athabasca	22	3	66	} inbound
English River	10	3	30	
Fort des Prairies	12	2	24	
Athabasca River	5	3	15	
Misc. Requirements			15	
Total	88		248	
Red River				
Athabasca	28	2	56	
English River	11	3.5	39†	
Lake Winnipeg	3	3.5	11†	
Fort des Prairies	14	3.5	49	outbound
Athabasca River	5	3.5	18†	
Rainy River			10	
Red River	6	3.5	21	
Athabasca	21	3	63	
Athabasca River	4	3	12	
English River	12	3	36	
Red River	6	3	18	inbound
Fort Dauphin	5	3	15	
Lake Winnipeg	4	3	12	
Fort des Prairies	12	3	36	
Total	131		395	
Total requirements	*219*		*644*	*(58,095 lbs.)*

* Wallace, *Documents Relating to the North West Company*, 277–9
† Total rounded upwards

as late as the 1760s and 1770s, the journal accounts of the Hudson's Bay Company indicate that the tribe was an important source of furs, and the European traders valued their contacts with them. In 1768, Andrew Graham, who was stationed at York Factory, claimed that the Assiniboine were rich in furs, and that their beaver pelts were among the best that the company acquired in trade. He went on to say that it was unfortunate the company was unable to induce a larger number of the tribe to make the trip down to the Bay.[16] The economic orientation of the tribe changed quickly thereafter, however, as they began to appreciate more fully the important role which they could play in the fur trade as provisioners. This new awareness was first evident in the fall of 1780 when the Assiniboine living in a territory around Hudson House on the North Saskatchewan River burnt the prairies adjacent to the post. Robert Longmoor wrote of their reasons: 'their design is that they may get a great deal for provisions as very few is hunting of furs.'[17] By burning the prairies in the autumn, the Indians did not give the grass a chance to recover before winter and local pasturage was therefore poor until the next spring. Thus, not only were they quick to perceive the new opportunity, the Indians also realized that the provision requirements of the companies made the Europeans vulnerable, and they began to exploit the vulnerability to their own ends.

Although as late as 1790 Edward Umfreville wrote that the Assiniboine were notable fur trappers, it is clear that trapping activities were becoming of secondary importance to most of the tribal bands, with the exception of those living in the forest to the north of the North Saskatchewan River.[18] For instance, when comparing the Assiniboine to the Cree and Objibwa, Alexander Mackenzie reported:

They are not beaver hunters ... They confine themselves to hunting the buffalo and trapping wolves, which cover the country. What they do not want of the former for raiment and food, they sometimes make into pemmican, or pounded meat, while they melt the fat, and prepare the skins in their hair for winter. The wolves they never eat, but produce a tallow from their fat, and prepare their skins; all of which they bring to exchange ... The Algonquins [Ojibwa] and the Knistineaux [Cree], on the contrary, attend fur-hunting.[19]

John MacDonnell, a North West Company trader, who was stationed by the Qu'Appelle River from 1793 to 1795, made similar comments about the Assiniboine. In 1797 he wrote his observations on the Qu'Appelle region and said that the men of the latter tribe were 'the worst hunters of any Indians in the North-West who have traders amongst them. Their whole hunt consists of wolves, foxes, kitts, and buffalo robes; for beavers, otters and other good furs they seldom take any.'[20]

As the demand for foodstuffs continued to grow and with it the significance of the Assiniboine and Plains Cree as suppliers, these tribes, especially the former, became increasingly troublesome, and they frequently exerted their economic power either to obtain more favourable rates of exchange for themselves, or to prevent their enemies from trading at the various parkland posts.[21] In the Saskatchewan River valley the traders lived in constant fear of threatened food boycotts, and, therefore, they frequently had to yield to Indian demands. For example, the journals of the second of the Franklin Polar Expeditions, that of 1819–23, indicated that at Carlton House 'Through fear of having their provisions and supplies entirely cutoff, the traders are often obliged to overlook the grossest offenses, even murder.'[22]

As was the case initially, fire was the chief weapon which the tribes used to apply economic pressure. Numerous references showed that it became a common practice for the Indians to burn the prairies around the post in the late autumn to prevent the bison from approaching them during the winter season. Unfortunately for the local Indians, they, too, frequently suffered as a result. The Hudson House journal for the winter of 1780–1 shows that many Indians arrived starving, being unable to obtain any bison since the Assiniboine had burnt the surrounding prairies.[23]

In this way, after 1763 the fur trade offered the Indians of the southern regions of Manitoba and Saskatchewan a new means by which they could obtain the European goods which they had come to rely upon. This new opportunity appeared at a critical moment in the economic history of these groups. The fur resources of the adjacent forests were giving out and the English traders were bypassing the Cree and the Assiniboine middlemen. These groups were therefore forced to obtain other commodities which could be bartered at the posts. Since they were initially encouraged to bring in dried meat and pemmican with their furs, the former produce constituted an increasing percentage of the total trade of these tribes. In this manner the fur trade favoured an increased exploitation of the grassland-parkland environment by many groups living in south-central Manitoba and Saskatchewan. Those Indians who remained in the forest on the other hand, centred their activities on trapping fur animals during the winter and fishing in the summer. A few of them also served as hunters at the various posts, or provided a number of other services for the fur companies such as the manufacturing of canoes. The latter activity became increasingly important as the fur companies took over the carrying trade. Several of the Indian bands living in the Rainy Lake–Lake of the Woods region were said to have developed a preference for making canoes as opposed to trapping furs. They built traditional Indian canoes as well as the larger canôt du nord developed by the North West Company. However, the forest-oriented activities could support relatively few Indians.

NOTES

1 Many of the bands living along the canoe route between Lake Winnipeg and Lake Superior were apparently unable to satisfy their demands for goods through trade with the Hudson's Bay Company and Indian middlemen. Their situation was thus desperate by 1765. For a more detailed discussion of these early attempts to expand the Montreal based fur trade see Morton, *Manitoba*, 36–40 and Rich, *The Fur Trade*, 130–45.

2 These restrictions were part of the 'Imperial Plan of 1763' and required that the fur traders have licenses, and that the trade be officially conducted only at designated posts. However, these provisions were never effectively enforced. Rich, *The Fur Trade*, 133

3 Judging from the data plotted in Figure 19 it would appear that the company's employees may have exaggerated the effectiveness of this competition somewhat. At York Factory the value of furs and goods did not drop sharply before 1774. The value of the overplus did show a marked decline, however, and this no doubt was a reflection of the improved bargaining position of the Indians.

4 Rich, *Cumberland and Hudson House Journals, 1779–82*, 1:112

5 Rich, *The Fur Trade*, 183

6 John Franklin, *Narrative of a Journey to the Shores of the Polar Sea*, 84–5

7 During its first decade of existence the colony suffered severe setbacks as a consequence of both the climate and hostility of the North West Company.

8 Coues, *New Light on the Early History of the Greater Northwest*, 2:475

9 As early as 1775 Alexander Henry the Elder recognized the importance of wild rice to the prosecution of the northwest fur trade. He bought over 100 bushels of the grain in that year and said that he could not have completed his voyage to Beaver Lake without it. Henry, *Travels and Adventures in Canada*, 242

10 Brandon District Report, 1819, PAC HBC B 22/e/1, p. 4

11 Coues, *New Light on the Early History of the greater Northwest*, 1:444. Most of the fish were given to the Indians.

12 Rich, *The Fur Trade*, 188

13 It is probable that they would have been the same since the meat of the female was preferred. Thus, it has been assumed cows would have comprised 71 per cent of the kill.

14 Merriman, 'The Bison and the Fur Trade,' 7

15 Ibid., 7

16 Williams, *Graham's Observations*, 194. Graham indicated that only about forty canoes of Assiniboine came to York Factory each year. Since he said that canoes averaged three persons each, roughly 120 Assiniboine men were involved. Considering that Alexander Henry the Elder's 1776 estimate for the tribe suggested they had a total of about 600 adult men, it would appear that at least 20 per cent of the tribe had trading contacts with the Hudson's Bay Company. This figure can probably be taken as a minimal approximation because the furs of any one canoe customarily belonged to several families.

17 Rich, *Cumberland and Hudson House Journals*, 2:166

18 *The Present State of Hudson's Bay*, (1954), 101–2

19 *Voyages From Montreal*, lxiv

20 Masson, *Les Bourgeois de la Campagnie du Nord-Ouest*, 1:28

21 By the time of the merger of the Hudson's Bay and North West companies in 1821, many of the Cree had followed the early lead of the Assiniboine and had begun focusing most of their activities on the hunting of bison to satisfy their own food requirements and to obtain a surplus for trade. Thus, the Carlton District Report for 1815 and the Brandon Report for 1822 indicated that in those areas the Plains Cree were similar to the Assiniboine in most respects. PAC HBC B 27/e/1 p. 2, and B 22/e/2 pp. 3–4, respectively.

22 It was reported that the Assiniboine threatened to cut off supplies going to Forts Augustus and Edmonton to prevent their enemies from obtaining ammunition. Franklin, *Narrative of a Journey*, 106–7.

23 Rich, *Cumberland and Hudson House Journals*, 2:175

8

Economic dependency and the fur trade: contrasting trends

In spite of the rapidly rising levels of competition between the Hudson's Bay Company and its rivals during the period from 1763 to 1821, most of the trading conventions which had been worked out between Europeans and Indians in earlier years remained intact. Yet, in the context of sharp economic rivalries, old, established trading customs served additional functions and, therefore, had different implications for culture change among the Indians. Furthermore, the relative importance of the various modes of exchange shifted over time.

As had been customary in the late seventeenth and eighteenth centuries, gift-giving continued to be an important ceremony which was conducted prior to trade. Although these exchanges had initially served largely to reaffirm friendship between the participating parties, under intensively competitive conditions, European traders dispensed gifts for the added purposes of enhancing the status of band leaders in the eyes of their Indian followers and to reward them for their efforts on behalf of their respective fur companies. Traditionally, the authority of band leaders was limited. A chief's ability to hold the allegiance of a group of Indians depended largely upon his success as a hunter and warrior. The virtues of kindness and generosity were also important.[1] In an effort to simplify their relations with the various Indian bands, the fur companies preferred to deal with the same leader year after year whenever possible. The increased use of credit over time also made it desirable to stabilize chieftanships. In their attempts to assure themselves of a portion of the returns of future Indian hunts, the various European trading groups gave the Indians sizeable advances of goods, particularly in the autumn and to a lesser extent in the spring, hoping that they would be able to collect these debts the following season. Debt collection was not always successful, but prior to 1763 the Hudson's Bay Company was apparently able to keep the amounts which the Indians owed down to a manageable size by using what amounted to a variable line of credit. Humphrey Martin provides us with some insights into the ways in which the system worked. In 1762, Martin turned over control of York Factory to Ferdinand Jacobs and left him a detailed set of instructions which outlined the procedures he was to follow in dealing with the Indians. He informed Jacobs that 'good' Indians were to be given credit in order to encourage them to return in subsequent years. However, Jacobs was told not to expect that these Indians would always clear their debts the following year. Regarding those who failed to do so, Martin wrote: 'the next year we trust them tho not so much as before which enables them to pay all they owe.'[2]

Under monopolistic conditions or situations of limited competition as was characterized by the French-English rivalries before 1763, the system of credit appears to have worked reasonably well, and credit abuses were kept down to an acceptable level. However, with the proliferation of inland posts which took place after 1763, the credit system became unmanageable. Indians often took their debts at one post in the autumn and traded their furs in the spring at another establishment usually belonging to a rival company. They were thereby able to obtain a double return on their hunts. It was partly in an effort to reduce these abuses that the fur companies attempted to win the loyalties of the band leaders, and at the same time increase the authority of these leaders in the eyes of the Indians. Presumably, if successful, these chiefs could then have been prevailed upon to bring their respective bands to particular posts on a regular basis, thereby making debt collection feasible.

Martin's instructions to Jacobs detailed the ways in which the Hudson's Bay Company traders were using gifts to further their aims of increasing the authority and status of band leaders prior to the invasion of the Western Interior by the Nor'Westers. They also illustrate the manner in which these leaders were rewarded for their efforts on behalf of the company. In outlining the procedures Jacobs was to follow in carrying out trade ceremonies, Martin wrote:

As soon as a gang of Indians come to the Fort, if near ones We take their goods in directly, if not we lett them put their goods in their tents which we commonly lend them[.] The Leader, or Leaders are taken into the Chiefs State room, if far away Indians they have a Coat, Waistcoat and Breeches, Shirt, Hatt, Sash, often Hankerchiefs, Stockings and Garters given them, they are commonly Kist by tne Chief [Factor] then he gives them Brandy, Tobacco, pipes, prunes, and bisket, the next Morning if the Chief or Leader is sober not only he but his whole gang are admitted into the Governor's State room to Smoak ... After they have traded all their goods Except a few, the Leader is admitted into the Govenor's Cabbin where he receives his present which is more or less According to the number of Canues he has brought, after him the Indian Doctors Are admitted when they get Medicines for part of which they pay, and part is given them.[3]

As this set of instructions indicates, the band leaders, particularly those coming from more distant areas, were accorded preferential treatment, receiving gifts at the beginning and conclusion of trading transactions. The suit of clothing which was given to them before trade began was called the 'Captain's Outfit,' and as this term suggests it served to make the trading captains stand out from the rest of the Indians. Andrew Graham provides us with a more detailed description of this outfit. He indicated that it consisted of:

A coarse cloth coat, either red or blue, lined with baize with regimental cuffs and collar. The waistcoat and breeches are of baize: the suit is ornamented with broad and narrow orris lace of different colours; a white or checked shirt; a pair of yarn stockings tied below the knee with worsted garters; a pair of English shoes. The hat is laced and ornamented with feathers of different colours. A worsted sash tied around the crown, an end hanging out on each side down to the shoulders. A silk handkerchief is tucked by a corner into a loops behind; with these decorations it is put on the captain's head and completes his dress. The lieutenant is also presented with an inferior suit.[4]

It is clear from Graham's description that these suits were patterned after European military uniforms. Furthermore, the difference in status between the band leaders and their more important followers was recognized and emphasized by the kinds of outfits which were given away. In subsequent years, the North West Company also followed this practice, but added a flag as another symbol of headship.

Once the Indians had accepted these European symbols of political authority and allegiance, the trading companies attempted to use the symbols to manipulate the Indians. For example, if a band failed to obtain a sufficient quantity of furs or provisions to pay off its debts, the band leader was denied these symbols of office.[5] On the other hand, as Martin's instructions indicate, if they were successful in persuading their followers to trap and bring their furs to the appropriate company posts, the band leaders received their uniforms as well as an additional present at the conclusion of trade the amount of which was proportional to the number of Indians they had brought with them.

Although the trading companies made considerable attempts to enhance the political authority of band leaders in such ways, they were largely unsuccessful because the efforts of one company were usually undermined by those of rival groups. For example, at York Factory prior to 1763 Humphrey Martin indicates that lavish gifts were given to only fifteen Indian captains. These leaders customarily brought down thirty or more canoes along with them to trade each year. In addition, Martin stated that there were many lesser Captains who led parties of from five to thirty canoes. They were accorded less generous receptions.[6]

After 1763, as the competition between the Hudson's Bay and North West companies intensified, this situtation changed. The multiplication of inland posts meant that the large trading parties of as many as one hundred canoes became a thing of the past. Smaller groups of thirty canoes (approximately seventy-five men or less) assumed greater importance. Therefore, the companies found it necessary to bestow sizable gifts upon the leaders of fairly small bands. Furthermore, as the North West and Hudson's Bay companies attempted to win the loyalty of these bands and exert their respective influences upon them, they often selected Indians to serve as spokesmen on their behalf. Consequently, many bands had two or more trading chiefs each of whom pledged loyalty to a different company. Under these circumstances the number of Indians who were treated as chiefs and were entitled to receive presents increased substantially. Even at relatively small posts, the number of captains who were being outfitted exceeded the number similarly treated at York Factory in earlier years. For instance, in 1795, Duncan M'Gillivray was stationed at the North West Company post of Fort George located on the North Saskatchewan River. On 24 April he reported:

we were interrupted by the arrival of a large band of Indians consisting of Circees, Crees, Piegans and Blood Indians ... Mr. Shaw made them a present of 3 kegs of Rum, separated in proportion to the number of men in each band, with which they were well satisfied. After they had indulged themselves with a few drams they began to make their presents according to custom, and before midnight we had clothed 22 Chiefs, a greater number than was clothed before in one day at any settlement in the North West.[7]

As the number of Indian leaders entitled to obtain gifts increased, the values of their gratuities rose also. This was largely a consequence of the fact that one of the traditional virtues of an Indian leader was generosity, and chiefs found it necessary to demonstrate this virtue by making more substantial presents to their follows than did their rivals. The companies, therefore, had to make an attempt to back their band leaders with more lavish support than their competitors did. Duncan M'Gillivray again provides us with a good illustration of this practice. After concluding his trade with the Sarsi, Piegan, Cree, and Blood Indians who had visited Fort George on 24 April 1795, he wrote:

All the above mentioned Indians departed apparently well satisfied with their reception. The *English Indians* on the contrary complained bitterly of their treatment and threatened to return no more to that House [Buckingham House]. Our neighbours [Hudson's Bay Company] are scarce of Goods this Spring, a circumstance which they have hitherto carefully concealed from the natives, but the demands made upon them at this time are so great that they could not supply them or satisfy the Indians in the usual manner. To increase this dissatisfaction and to make the contrast more glaring, we have been rather more lavish than usual.[8]

Even though such actions often did have the desired result on a short-term basis, their final effect was only to set off a further upward spiral in the cost of carrying on trade as competing companies attempted to match or exceed these bids for the Indian trade. Among the Indians it appears to have had the affect of making wealth a prerequisite of chieftainship.[9] Ultimately, these various efforts to stabilize and enhance the authority of Indian chiefs failed. Rather, they had the effect of increasing factionalism and tensions within bands, creating a more unstable political and social climate.

Of significance to the process of material culture change, the increased importance of gift-giving and the extensive use of credit as an allurement to trade without an adequate system of collection meant that between 1763 and 1821 there was a continual decline of relative cost of goods to Indians. Furthermore, the proliferation of inland posts had the effect of making these commodities geographically more accessible throughout the Western Interior.

However, although increasingly intensive company competition was making it easier for the Indians to obtain trade goods, their demand for utilitarian and ornamental items did not rise at the same rate as prices fell. In fact, as subsequent discussions will demonstrate, it actually declined in some quarters. In effect, the consumer demand of the Indians continued to be inelastic on a short-term basis and this had serious repercussions in the new setting in which the fur trade was conducted after 1763. Most important, it favoured a rapid increase in the consumption of alcohol and tobacco. These two commodities figured prominently in gift-giving ceremonies and, therefore, as gift exchanges played a more critical role in the fur trade, greater quantities were given away. For example, by the late-eighteenth century it became commonplace for band leaders to dispatch a few of their men to the trading houses a few days in advance of their arrival in order to pick up tobacco. After obtaining it, these men would return to the band and the group would begin celebrating and smoking before they reached the posts. By the beginning of the nineteenth century, many of the traders adopted the practice of sending their own men out to greet Indian trade parties as soon as they learned they were in the vicinity in the hopes of luring them to their posts. This was necessary because in many localities, such as the area near Brandon, Manitoba, several trading establishments were close together, often within view of each other. Thus, a trader had to dispense gifts to Indians before they arrived at his post in the hope that he could persuade the Indians not to stop at the neighbouring houses. In fact in some districts, such as Cumberland Lake, the North West Company began sending their men to the Indians' hunting camps making it unnecessary for the Indians to visit the posts.

The tendency toward greater per-capita consumption of alcohol and tobacco by Indians, which this lavish gift-giving encouraged, was reinforced by the addictive nature of these two commodities. Moreover, because the Indians could satisfy their needs for other trade goods with less effort due to the falling prices demanded for them, they spent much more of the free time which they gained at the local trading posts drinking and smoking and leading what the traders termed the 'indolent life.' In this way competitive conditions further strengthened the tendency toward greater addiction.

As a result of this combination of circumstances, the possession of adequate stocks of alcohol and tobacco became prerequisites for the successful conduct of the fur trade. As early as the 1770s, access to cheap supplies of these commodities had become a paramount concern of the traders. For instance, in 1775 Samuel Hearne, who was stationed at the Hudson's Bay Company post of Cumberland House, was plagued by shortages of alcohol which were hampering his trading activities. This problem led him to complain:

for want of a greater assortment of goods and Brandy in Proportion it is Noways in the power of those inland to ingroce the trade. For tho we undersell the Canadians [Montreal pedlars] by far in some articles while our goods last, yet when Brandy is out, the Indian's leave off Trading, a strong proof of which I had last Spring before I had embark'd for York Fort, for notwithstanding there ware plenty of amanition and some other useful articals left, the Indians would not trade their Furs because I had no brandy.[10]

Although Hearne thus indicates that alcohol had assumed a central role in the trade, it is also clear from his remarks that brandy or rum alone was not sufficient to bring the Indians to trade even though the exaggerated claims of some traders might suggest this was the case. Rather, the key to success was to have a large quantity of this commodity and an equally sizeable stock of good quality trade goods. That the quality of trade goods was equally important to the Indians in spite of their growing addiction to rum and brandy was made clear by the comments of James Bird who managed the Hudson's Bay Company post of Carlton House (Saskatchewan River) in 1796–7. Bird was fearful that the better quality ʳᵒᵒds that his North West Company rivals were beginning to bring in would deprive him of the portion of the trade which he had managed to hold until that time in spite of the fact that the Nor'Westers dispensed brandy more liberally than he did. Thus, on 20 November 1796 he wrote:

I have only traded about 300 MB ... but poor prospects of getting anything considerable this season, owing to the scarcity of Beaver ... [and] also to the late improvements the Canadian Traders have made in the quality of their goods; a few years since many Indians who from the large quantities of Spiritous Liquors given to them or were induced to go to the Canadian Houses, the superiority of our Cloth, Guns etc. tempted [them] to trade those articles with us, but they now find themselves as well satisfied by the Canadians.[11]

Besides having access to plentiful supplies of alcohol and good quality utilitarian items in proportion, it was also necessary to have a considerable stock of tobacco on hand. As discussed previously, as early as the 1750s the superior Brazil tobacco of the Hudson's Bay Company was a key item which kept the inland Indians coming down to the Bay. Each year 2000 to 3000 pounds of this commodity were bartered at York Factory and these groups took between 1600 to 2400 pounds of the total.[12] It is difficult to determine how far into the interior this tobacco was being carried, but as of the middle of the eighteenth century apparently very little of it had reached the Blackfoot even though the latter tribe had close trading contacts with the Assiniboine and Western Cree. This was suggested by a rather amusing remark which Henday made while visiting the tribe in 1755. Regarding the subject of tobacco he quipped, 'They think nothing of my tobacco; & I set as little value on theirs; which is dryed Horse-dung.'[13]

Besides Brazil tobacco, the Hudson's Bay Company also bartered English roll and Virginia leaf, but neither of these types were ever of major importance: in 1770 2765.5 pounds of Brazil tobacco were traded in at York Factory compared to only 211 pounds of English roll and 49 pounds of Virginia leaf.[14] These proportions were typical of most years. The Brazil tobacco was usually twisted into a long rope which was then rolled into a ball. The Indians were given their allotments of it in lengths, a foot or two at a time. As in the case of alcohol, these lengths were generally given away 'free' to encourage the tribes to trade their furs. A shortness of supply or a poor quality of stock at the post was a serious problem and could cause the trader to lose a large proportion of his normal business.[15]

Although alcohol and tobacco were central to the trade in all areas, the relative importance of these commodities to other goods that the Indians were acquiring varied regionally. These differences were largely a consequence of spatial variations in the levels of fur-company competition, disparate lines of cultural development among the Indians, and changes in local resource conditions.

The uneven intensities of European trade rivalries meant that in some quarters the Indians had to pay relatively more for trade goods than they did in other areas. For instance, the Hudson's Bay Company did not move into the Red, Assiniboine, and Qu'Appelle valleys in force until the 1790s, and, consequently, the Indians living in these territories secured most of their trade goods from the North West Company or from Indian middlemen. Since the latter company was burdened by heavy transportation costs because it had to ship its goods overland from Montreal, it was therefore obliged to charge the Indians more for them than the Hudson's Bay Company did (see Table 5). Alternatively, this merchandise could be obtained from Cree and Assiniboine middlemen, but at an even greater expense. For instance, in 1769 William Tomison reported that the Cree were selling good guns to the Assiniboine for a price of thirty-six MBS, when the Nor'Westers were charging twenty and the Hudson's Bay Company only ten. Even 'half-wore' guns were being exchanged at a rate of twenty-five to thirty beaver.[16]

TABLE 5
A comparison of the Hudson's Bay and North West companies' standards of trade

| Trade goods | Value in beaver | |
	Hudson's Bay Co., 1760–1*	North West Co., Fort des Prairies, 1776–7†
guns (all sizes)	14	20
blankets	7	10 (stroud)
		8 (white)
axes	1	3
gun powder	1 per lb.	1 per pint
shot	1 per 4 lbs.	1 per 10 balls

* York Factory Account Books, B 239/d/50, pp. 23–6
† Henry, *Travels and Adventures*, 303–4

In addition to these higher prices many items were either not available or were present in only limited quantities in those areas where the North West Company and Indian Middlemen were the chief suppliers. Heavy bulky goods were especially scarce in these districts since they were costly to transport over long distances. For instance, kettles were highly prized by the Assiniboine, but many of the groups living in the parklands of central Saskatchewan apparently had few of them as late as the 1770s in spite of over one hundred years of direct or indirect trade with the Hudson's Bay Company. This fact was brought to light by Alexander Henry the Elder's experiences during his visit to the parklands in 1776. He described his first meal in an Assiniboine encampment: 'Our supper was made of the tongues of wild ox, or buffalo, boiled in my kettle, which was the only one in the camp.'[17] Later, as the band prepared to leave for Fort des Prairies he added: 'we collected our baggage, which however, was but small; consisting in a buffalo robe for each person, an axe and a kettle. The last was reluctantly parted with by our friends, who had none left to supply its place.'[18]

The initial inland penetration of the Hudson's Bay Company does not appear to have alleviated this shortage to any significant extent. At the outset the company lacked the needed transportation capacity, and therefore could not fully exploit its advantage of location vis-à-vis the Montreal pedlars. As a result, it sent relatively few kettles to the Saskatchwan area in the 1770s.[19] It was in these ways that regional variations in the vigour of fur-trade competition influenced the lines of material culture change by determining the quantities, types, and prices of European goods which were available to the Indians. These discrepancies were especially important before 1800. After that date, economic rivalries appeared to have been intensive in all quarters.

The different environment and economic orientations of the tribes strongly influenced their preferences for certain types of goods. As was the case before 1763, there were significant differences in this respect between the forest and parkland-grassland groups. Furthermore, there were a number of forces in operation that tended to accentuate these dissimilarities through time. Alexander Henry the Elder was one of the first travelers to comment on these various trading habits in the years after 1763. After visiting Fort des Prairies in 1776 he claimed that the principal profits of the post were derived from the sales of knives, beads, flints, steels, awls, and other 'small articles,' while, as was general practice, rum and tobacco were given away. Other items such as guns, blankets, axes, gun powder, and shot were exchanged, but presumably in much smaller quantities. A short while later Henry compared this trade, especially that portion which was accounted for by the Assiniboine, with that of other tribes living to the northeast. He wrote: 'It is not in this manner that the Northern Indians [Chipewyans and Woodland Cree] dispose of the harvest of the chase. With them, the principal purchases are of necessaries; but the Osinipoilles are less dependent on our merchandise. The wild ox alone supplies them with everything which they are accustomed to want.'[20]

Writing three years later Philip Turnor of the Hudson's Bay Company made some similar observations, but he was more explicit in the ways the forest trade differed from that of the parklands. In this instance Turnor was contrasting the barter of goods at Gloucester House, a small outpost of Fort Albany located in the boreal forest, and Cumberland House, which at that time conducted the bulk of the company's trade with the parkland and grassland Indians living to the west of the Manitoba escarpment. Concerning the trade of these two posts he wrote:

The trade of this place [Gloucester House] and Cumberland House differ very much, at Cumberland House Brandy is the chief trade all Powder Shot, Tobacco, Knives, Flints, Steels, Paint and small articles are given and at this place the chief trade is in Cloth, Blankets, Powder, Shot, Guns and Ironwork and some Tobacco ... they will have a good drink before they trade ... when they get sober they trade Cloth, Blankets, Powder, Shot, etc., which they can not do without having no Leather in their Country, on the contrary at Cumberland House cloth is almost a Luxury they having plenty of leather and can live without a Gun most of them being able to kill Buffalo with Bow and Arrows.[21]

The continued expansion of the fur trade tended to favour these disparate lines of development. For example, as many of the parkland groups of Assiniboine and Cree directed their attention more and more to the hunting of bison to help satisfy the growing provision requirements of the Hudson's Bay and North West companies, they became less dependent on the trapping and trading of furs to obtain the European goods they had come to rely upon. In this manner they were able to complete the transition from woodland- to grassland-oriented economies. One of the results of these transformations was that, over time, many tribal bands became less reliant on Europeans for many of the necessities of life. The bison increasingly satisfied these requirements. Furthermore, with the declining emphasis placed on the trapping of furs, items such as hatchets, ice chisels, and traps were of lesser importance.

The position of the groups that remained in the bordering forest contrasted sharply with that of the parkland tribes. For these bands, Woodland Assiniboine, Cree, and Ojibwa, participation in the fur trade led to a growing dependence on the trading companies. Whereas the problem of overhunting had been largely confined to the lands around the Bay in the pre-1763 period, by the early nineteenth century it had become widespread in the lands lying around the eastern and northeastern margins of the parkland area. In the Lac la Pluie District to the east of the Red River valley large game animals had been reduced in numbers to the point that the Indians were facing difficulties in finding enough materials to make their clothing. For instance, according to the 1825–6 report for that department: 'In other parts of the Country where large Animals are Numerous, an Indian may cloath himself with leather: but here it is impossible, he can have no other recourse whatever but to our goods. Nay, we are obliged to bring in drest leather & parchement to supply him with the means of making his shoes & snowshoes.'[22]

Under these deteriorating conditions, the Woodland Indians came to rely increasingly on their trapping operations in spite of the fact that the fur resource base was declining too. Moreover, to carry on these activities successfully they had to turn to the traders for their ice chisels, axes, traps, and other equipment. In brief, the tribal bands living in the forested tracks of land required a greater variety of metal goods, consumed more ammunition, and placed a higher value on cloth and blankets than did the Indian groups living in the parklands and grasslands. But in addition, like the latter groups, they also had become addicted to alcohol and tobacco.

These regional differences perhaps can be best illustrated by examining the account books of three Hudson's Bay Company posts, those of Brandon, Carlton, and Cumberland houses for the period between 1810 and 1814.[23] By that time Cumberland House had ceased to handle the trade of the Parkland Indians, and thus the patterns of exchange which it exhibited typified those of the forest posts. On the other hand, Carlton and Brandon houses were located in the parkland area and a considerable portion of their trade was carried on with the Assiniboine and Plains Cree. The data from these posts has been summarized in Table 6. Quite striking is the fact that over 26 per cent of the value of the Indian expenditures at Cumberland House were accounted for by cloth sales, while at Brandon and Carlton houses the figures were only 13 and 10 per cent respectively. Expressed in crude per-capita figures, the variance was even greater. Thus, during the four-year period, each of the families of the Cumberland district would have bought a total of about 15$^{1}/_{5}$ yards as opposed to only 2$^{7}/_{10}$ yards in the Brandon district and a mere 4/5 of a yard in the Carlton territory.[24] Similarly, the blanket trade was of relatively greater importance in the Cumberland area. This was especially true of the per-capita consumption. In the parkland areas the total volume of trade amounted to less than one blanket per family whereas at Cumberland House it would have equalled more than two.

The traffic in metal goods also appears to have been greater in the latter district, judging from the ratios between the quantities sold and the number of families in each area. Likewise, the rate at which ammunition was being bartered in the Cumberland District suggests that the Indians in that department were expending it six to twelve times more rapidly than were the Indians living in the parklands. Only in the case of tobacco did the consumption levels of the latter Indians exceed those of the forest bands. Indeed, this commodity alone accounts for over a quarter of the value of all of the goods which the Hudson's Bay Company was trading at its parkland posts. On the other hand, in the Cumberland Department it was worth less than 10 per cent of the total.

Granting that the contrasting buying habits of the Woodland and Parkland-Grassland Indians can be readily documented, variations of these habits among the latter Indians who occupied southern Manitoba and Saskatchewan are more difficult to determine. In part this difficulty results from the conflicting observations left by the fur traders. For instance, in 1793–4 Donald McKay claimed that ammunition, cutlery, and cloth were 'Useless' at Brandon House, and that the only thing which was necessary to the conduct of the trade there was a good supply of rum.[25] George Sutherland, who was stationed on Shell River near the northern margins of this district in the following year, largely concurred with McKay's observations, but he added that powder, beads, and knives were important as well.[26]

TABLE 6

Goods traded at Brandon, Carlton, and Cumberland houses, 1810–11 to 1813–14*

	Awls			Beads			Blankets			Brandy		
	No.	Value†	% of Total‡	Lbs.	Value	%of Total	No.	Value	% of total	Gals.	Value	% of total
Brandon House												
1810–11	200	ND**	–	61³/₄	ND	–	230	ND	–	791	ND	–
1811–12	48	0/2/0	–	15¹/₂	2/14/3	–	45	46/12/1	10.8	50	16/5/0	3.9
1812–13	132	2/8/7	–	40	8/0/0	–	282	11/16/5¹/₂	3.1	243	79/19/9	7.8
1813–14	109	2/5/5	–	24³/₄	5/6/1	–	63	77/10/9	4.8	22	7/4/10	4.3
Average % of total			–			–			6.2			4.0
Total quantity per family††	.82			.24			.6			1.9		

* PAC HBC B/27/d/1–4, B 22/d/1–4, and B 49/d/1–4
† Values in journals were expressed in British sterling
‡ Percentage of the total value of all goods traded which includes unlisted items
** ND = no data available
†† For the four-year period
‡‡ Includes rum for 1813–14

TABLE 6 (continued)
Goods traded at Brandon, Carlton, and Cumberland houses 1810–11 to 1813–14*

	Awls			Beads			Blankets			Brandy		
	No.	Value	% of total	Lbs.	Value	% of total	No.	Value	% of total	Gals.	Value	% of total
Carlton House												
1810–11	90	0/3/9	<5.5	6¾	ND	–	16	14/4/11	4.3	71¼	57/0/0	16.5
1811–12	78	0/3/3	<.5	16¾	2/18/7½	.8	13	8/13/6	2.6	81¾	53/2/9	15.4
1812–13	100	0/4/2	<.5	27	5/5/0	1.3	5½	3/2/11½	.8	19	6/5/1	1.6
1813–14	none	–	–	21	5/1/6	1.5	7½	8/11/4½	2.7	ND	–	
Average % of total			–			–			2.5			13.2‡‡
Total quantity per family††	.67			.17			.4			.42		
Cumberland House												
1810–11	96	2/4/0	–	7	1/4/6	–	39	54/5/4	8.7	271	108/8/0	17.0
1811–12	89	0/3/8½	–	10¼	1/15/10½	–	40	26/19/9	3.6	242¼	72/17/7½	9.8
1812–13	128	2/6/4	–	9½	1/17/0	–	85½	87/7/5	9.0	144⅛	47/8/8	4.0
1813–14	148	3/1/8	–	13	2/12/0	–	109	113/0/10	9.2	none	–	–
Average % of total			–			–			7.6			6.9
Total quantity per family††	4.2			.35			2.5			6.0		

TABLE 6 (*continued*)
Goods traded at Brandon, Carlton, and Cumberland houses, 1810–11 to 1813–14*

	Cloth			Duffel			Guns			Hatchets		
	Yds.	Value	% of total	Yds.	Value	% of total	No.	Value	% of total	No.	Value	% of total
Brandon House												
1810–11	745	ND	–	124	ND	–	39	ND	–	71	ND	–
1811–12	128¹/₄	68/1/5	16.4	38	13/6/0	3.4	5	14/10/0	3.3	46	10/20/8	2.6
1812–13	219¹/₂	59/8/3¹/₂	7.5	34¹/₄	ND	–	21	60/12/9	7.6	60	14/17/6	1.9
1813–14	194³/₄	260/9/4	16.2	111⁷/₈	ND	–	34	86/5/6	5.9	96	24/2/9	1.5
Average % of total			13.4						5.6			2.0
Total quantity per family††	2.7			–			.17			.46		
Carlton House												
1810–11	85	51/0/9	14.8	ND	–	–	12	34/16/0	9.8	39	9/5/6	2.6
1811–12	76³/₄	40/8/10	11.6	ND	–	–	8	24/4/0	6.9	67	14/15/11	4.3
1812–13	62⁷/₈	31/16/2¹/₄	8.7	ND	–	–	12	34/13/0	9.3	43	9/2/3	2.4
1813–14	105¹/₂	48/15/4	14.9	ND	–	–	1	2/17/9	.9	27	5/18/7	1.8
Average % of total			9.9						6.7			2.7
Total quantity per family††	.82			–			.08			.44		
Cumberland House												
1810–11	232¹/₂	149/12/8	24.1	ND	–	–	14	40/12/0	6.4	59	12/6/8	1.9
1811–12	423	203/1/7¹/₂	27.0	ND	–	–	21	60/18/0	8.1	67	16/3/5	2.1
1812–13	474¹/₄	238/19/4	25.0	ND	–	–	23	66/10/3	7.0	72	17/5/1	1.7
1813–i4	544	326/5/4	31.0	ND	–	–	31	78/13/3	6.4	100	22/10/8	1.8
Average % of total			26.7						6.9			1.8
Total quantity per family††	15.2			–			.80			2.7		

TABLE 6 (continued)
Goods traded at Brandon, Carlton, and Cumberland houses, 1810–11 to 1813–14*

	Ice Chisels			Kettles			Knives			Powder		
	No.	Value	% of total	Lbs.	Value	% of total	No.	Value	% of total	Lbs.	Value	% of total
Brandon House												
1810–11	5	ND	–	12	ND	–	1071	ND	–	565	ND	–
1811–12	ND	–	–	23½	6/0/0	1.4	224	5/8/4	1.2	363	54/10/6	9.4
1812–13	27	4/14/6	–	128	45/13/9	5.8	430	19/15/5	.7	497	74/11/0	8.0
1813–14	25	4/7/6	–	129	46/0/0	2.8	1008	22/17/1	1.4	854½	128/2/9	10.0
Average % of total			–			3.3			1.1			11.1
Total quantity per family††	.1			.5			4.6			3.9		
Carlton House												
1810–11	18	2/17/0	–	27	7/6/4	2.3	160	3/4/10	.86	153½	23/0/6	6.6
1811–12	ND	–	–	ND	–	–	272	5/3/8	1.4	181	27/3/0	7.8
1812–13	19	3/6/6	.82	ND	–	–	183	8/11/10	2.4	250	37/10/0	10.1
1813–14	15	2/12/6	.62	ND	–	–	352	7/16/5¾	2.4	160	24/0/0	7.4
Average % of total			–			–			1.7			8.0
Total quantity per family††	.01			–			2.4			1.9		
Cumberland House												
1810–11	28	4/8/8	–	33¾	8/14/4½	1.2	ND	–	–	472	70/16/0	11.3
1811–12	44	7/14/0	–	102	26/7/0	3.5	266	6/5/2	.8	532	79/17/6	10.8
1812–13	30	5/5/0	–	97	34/11/1½	3.5	345	10/15/9	1.0	758	113/14/0	11.7
1813–14	62	10/17/0	3.0	134¼	44/1/8	3.6	396	10/1/7	.8	854½	128/3/6	10.5
Average % of total			–			2.9			.6			11.1
Total quantity per family††	1.5			3.3			9.1			23.7		

TABLE 6 (continued)
Goods traded at Brandon, Carlton, and Cumberland houses, 1810–11 to 1813–14*

	Rum			Shot			Tobacco		
	Gals.	Value	% of total	Lbs.	Value	% of total	Lbs.	Value	% of total
Brandon House									
1810–11	26	ND	–	778	ND	–	867	ND	–
1811–12	138½	52/10/3	12.8	678	16/33/6½	4.1	1410	71/15/0	17.4
1812–13	170	62/6/8	7.8	ND	23/4/9	2.9	1004¾	209/18/4	26.7
1813–14	685⅞	253/0/0	15.8	ND	35/0/0	2.1	1707	426/16/3	26.6
Average % of total			12.0			3.0			23.5
Total quantity per family††	1.7			–			8.4		
Carlton House									
1810–11	ND	–	–	270	7/15/9	2.6	445	111/5/0	32.0
1811–12	ND	–	–	238	6/1/1¼	1.7	559	97/16/6	28.0
1812–13	ND	–	–	ND	9/6/6¼	2.4	500	91/15/2	25.2
1813–14	182⅛	66/15/7	20.8	ND	11/0/3½	3.4	373	93/5/0	28.8
Average % of total			–			2.5			28.2
Total quantity per family††	.5			–			4.6		
Cumberland House									
1810–11	3¼	1/19/0	.16	532	20/0/2	3.2	314¼	78/12/6	12.0
1811–12	122½	48/8/11	6.2	892	22/7/0	2.9	406½	71/2/9	9.5
1812–13	241	88/9/2	9.0	ND	27/10/9	2.8	379¼	69/10/7	7.1
1813–14	510⅛	189/0/4½	15.6	ND	41/8/1	3.3	472¼	118/1/3	9.7
Average % of total			7.7			3.0			9.5
Total quantity per family††	7.9			–			1.4		

In the other parkland departments lying to the northwest of Brandon House, cloth seems to have been of much greater consequence, and after tobacco, rum, and brandy it was one of the commodities which was in the greatest demand. Reflecting this fact, the shortage of yard goods, especially in conjunction with the low stock of liquor, was a cause for considerable concern at South Branch House in 1790–1. Expressing his uneasiness about this state of affairs, William Walker who was in charge of the post wrote: 'Indians coming in dayly but I do not get any Trade from them for want of Liquor and Cloth which is the Two Chiefest Articles belonging to us.'[27]

The journals of other posts located along the North and South Saskatchewan rivers show that the same stress was placed on the importance of maintaining an adequate inventory of cloth in the trading houses.[28] In addition, because of its significance to the successful conduct of the fur trade, the different companies kept a close eye on the quality of their opposition's supplies.[29]

After cloth and blankets, hatchets and ice chisels were among the most sought after articles in the upper Saskatchewan River area. As with cloth, shortages of these goods plagued the Hudson's Bay Company posts in that country in the 1790s. The heavy demand there for these items often meant that the supply requirements of these parkland posts conflicted with those of the woodland trading establishments farther to the east. To illustrate, even though Cumberland House often functioned as a distributing centre for the York Factory network of posts on the Saskatchewan River, it frequently was unable to satisfy their requests for merchandise. When James Bird wrote to Peter Fidler at Cumberland House in 1797 asking him to send up a supply of ice chisels, hatchets, and files, Fidler replied saying that he could not spare them. He informed Bird that the Indians in his department depended on him for those articles, and if he failed to provide them they simply would go elsewhere.[30]

Thus, the journal records of the Hudson's Bay Company suggest that the barter of European goods at the posts on the Saskatchewan was somewhat different from that of the Brandon Department in the late eighteenth century. The patterns of exchange in the former area showed more similarities to those of woodland districts than did those in the latter territory. This difference can perhaps be explained by the fact that many of the Cree bands living in the Saskatchewan River valley were recent immigrants from the forest and therefore retained many of the characteristics of their older way of life. In contrast, in the Brandon Department the Assiniboine were the most numerous, and they were much more accustomed to the parkland and grassland environment.

Somewhat puzzling is the fact that a re-examination of Table 4 summarizing the trade data for Carlton and Brandon houses between 1810 and 1814 suggests a pattern of trade for the parklands which is quite different from that outlined above. The only similarity between the two periods seems to have been in the liquor traffic, with the volume of consumption continuing to be greater in the Brandon District. In contrast to the earlier situation, cloth and blankets were of slightly greater consequence in the latter department than they were in the Carlton area. This development is difficult to explain. It may partly reflect the fact that Cree and Ojibwa groups were moving into the northern and eastern portions of the Brandon territory – they would have purchased larger quantities of cloth than the Assiniboine. However, the latter tribe still comprised over three-quarters of the district's population. Furthermore, trade groups were continuing to move into the Carlton Department from the adjacent woodlands, and they too would have generated a considerable demand for clothing materials. With respect to the trade in metal goods it appeared that there were no longer any substantial differences between these two sections of the parklands. This change would reflect the declining importance of trapping in the parklands along the Saskatchewan River in central and western Saskatchewan.

In brief, with the exception of the consumption of alcohol, there do not appear to have been any notable dissimilarities in the barter of European goods in the southeastern and northwestern parklands of Canada by the beginning of the second decade of the nineteenth century. It is uncertain whether the discrepancy between this pattern and that indicated for the 1790s reflects any real changes, or merely throws doubt on the reliability of earlier observers. Traders tended to overstate the role which certain commodities played in the trade whenever they ran short of them. In addition, because of the disruptive effect which the heavy traffic of liquor was having on tribal populations, this subject received a good deal of attention in the journals of the traders and travelers. As a consequence, the use of other items by the Indians probably was largely unnoticed, or certainly underplayed, thereby giving the impression that they were unimportant.

Surprisingly, the commentary dealing with the trading preferences of tribal groups, in this case the Assiniboine, Cree, and Ojibwa, is more consistent. In almost all instances the former tribe was said to be the least dependent upon the trading houses. They came to the latter establishments primarily to obtain rum, brandy, tobacco, knives, ammunition (largely used for warfare), and trinkets.[31] The trading habits of the Cree and Ojibwa were much more varied. The Plains Cree were similar in most respects to the Assiniboine with the exception that they made greater use of firearms.[32] Other Cree groups living in closer proximity to the parkland-forest boundary were economically more closely linked to the trading posts, as were the Ojibwa. For example, when discussing the economic position of Cree and Ojibwa bands living near Bird Mountain, Saskatchewan, in 1801 Daniel Harmon wrote:

The Indians in this quarter have been so long accustomed to use European goods, that it would be with difficulty that they could now obtain a livelihood without them. Especially do they need fire arms, with which to kill their game, and axes, kettles, knives, etc. They have almost lost the use of bows and arrows; and they would find it nearly impossible to cut their wood with impliments made of stone or bone.[33]

Not all of the borderland Cree groups were as dependent as the band described above was, and, in general, they usually differed sharply in this respect from their Ojibwa neighbours. Thus, when Peter Fidler filed his report on the Dauphin District in 1820 he stated that the Ojibwa in the area traded largely for cloth, blankets, guns, kettles, and Capots, whereas the Cree took mostly rum. Besides these items he indicated that all of the Indians were given 'gratis' ammunition and tobacco. For every ten animals they killed, regardless of the size, they received a quart of 'high wines' plus some gifts for their wives such as beads, knives, awls, fire steels, and gartering.[34] Other accounts highlight the same contrasts between these two tribal populations. These dissimilarities were undoubtedly largely a function of the varying lengths of time they had resided in the parklands and the different roles which they played in the fur trade.

Besides the traffic with Europeans, inter-tribal trade continued to exert a strong influence on the direction of the material culture change among the Indian populations, particularly in the parkland-grassland region. It was through this medium that the Indians of Manitoba and Saskatchewan acquired horses. The historical record indicates that the Plains Assiniboine, Cree, and Ojibwa obtained them from two different sources. In the west, bands of Assiniboine and Plains Cree living in the central and western portions of Saskatchewan got their horses from the Blackfoot and Gros Ventre, while further east the tribal groups living in southern Manitoba and the adjacent sections of Saskatchewan acquired these animals through their trade contacts with the Mandan villages on the Missouri River. The timing and relative rates of the diffusion into these two portions of the parklands appear to have differed considerably.

The horse reached the western parklands sometime between the close of the seventeenth century and the middle of the eighteenth century. When Henry Kelsey visited the parklands of central Saskatchewan in 1690 and 1691, he did not record the presence of horses among any of the tribes which he visited, but when Anthony Henday undertook his expedition to the eastern Alberta region in 1754–5, he encountered the animal as far east as Buffer Lake, Saskatchewan.[35] Judging from his subsequent commentary it was among the Gros Ventre and Blackfoot living beyond this lake to the west that he found horses, yet he did not meet any Assiniboine bands using horses until he reached the area of Sounding Creek, Alberta, at a longitude of about 110 to 111 degrees west. The band he met there was a small one, having only seven lodges, and he bought his first horse from them. Other Mountain Assiniboine groups were seen in the same vicinity, but most of them were traveling with Archithinue Indians.[36]

Significantly, while making his return trip to the Bay, he visited ten tents of Eagle Indians on the South Saskatchewan River approximately 122 canoe miles from Fort à la Corne. He wrote: 'They are a tribe of the Asinepoet Nation; and like them use the Horses for carrying the baggage and not to ride on.'[37] It is clear from Henday's remarks that the Assiniboine of west-central Saskatchewan had possessed horses for only a relatively short period, considering that they were still using them essentially as they had employed their dogs. Furthermore, since there were few reports of horses being seen east of the South Saskatchewan River, it would appear that this river marked the approximate limit of their distribution in the western parklands in the middle of the eighteenth century.

By the 1770s this situation changed substantially, and horses had become relatively plentiful in the parklands, as well as in the grasslands to the south. For instance, when William Pink traveled up the Saskatchewan River in 1766 he met a band of Indians near the site of the present city of Prince Albert, Saskatchewan:

This Day Came a large Bodey of Indians, consisting of Sixteen Tents and a Great Maney Horses and piched thare Tenting a little to the s e of me ... Those Indians that I am with call them Pw Sym a Wock But I find that they are the Same that we Call Syn Na poits that come Down to your Fortes ... they say the chief of thare bode is farther in Land to the So Wards than those are that come down to your Settlements [Bay-side posts] that we call Syn Na poits, So they say they never saw any English Settlement, Nor Cannot paddle in Canue.[38]

Pink's observation is of value not only in that it indicates that this particular Assiniboine band was well supplied with horses, but it is one of the first references to suggest that the acquisition of this animal was leading the Indians to discontinue using the canoe. Passing through roughly the same territory six years later, Mathew Cocking made many similar remarks. He too met Assiniboine bands which seemed to still use the canoe; however, he also made it clear that other groups of the tribe had completely given it up. While journeying up the North Saskatchewan River just below its confluence with Eagle Creek, a small southern tributary, Cocking mentioned that the hills nearby were frequented by Assiniboine bands every spring. He said that they came there to secure the 'birchrine' (birch bark) which they used to cover their canoes.[39]

In 1776, Alexander Henry the Elder, made his visit to the parklands lying to the south of the Saskatchewan River. His trip took him to the area around the present city of Humboldt, Saskatchewan, east of the territory traversed by Cocking. Of considerable importance, Henry observed several large horse herds grazing near Assiniboine villages. Furthermore, he added that the tribe was noted for the many horses it possessed.[40] Thus, by the late 1770s horses were relatively abundant in the parklands and grasslands of south central Saskatchewan.

Further eastward the horse apparently reached the parkland zone somewhat later, and after its initial introduction its use spread at a much slower rate. When La Vérendrye made his various excursions in the area of southern Manitoba and North Dakota in the 1730s he did not see any horses, but in 1739 when he went to the Mandan villages on the Missouri River he reported that the tribe had contact with mounted Indians who came from the south and west.[41] Therefore, horses had reached the Missouri valley by that time and the eastern Assiniboine were familiar with the animal.[42] Shortly thereafter, in 1742, Maurepas wrote to Beauharnois that La Vérendrye's son-in-law had taken two horses from the Missouri River to Fort La Reine on the Assiniboine River, and this may have been the first time horses had been brought into the southern Manitoba area.[43] When Joseph Smith and Joseph Waggoner made their three expeditions to southwestern Manitoba and the adjacent portions of Saskatchewan in the late 1750s and early 1760s, they did not record having seen any horses. In fact, they made only one specific reference to the animal. Toward the conclusion of their last trip, which was taken in 1763–4, they mentioned that while they were constructing their canoes an Indian arrived who had lost two women and two horses as a result of a clash which he had had with the 'Archecadrenes,' presumably Gros

Ventre.[44] Yet, even though they apparently did not see any horses during the course of their travels, Smith and Waggoner visited bands of Assiniboine who they said had forgotten how to use canoes.[45] As has been noted previously, other observers have generally attributed the declining use of the canoe to the acquisition of horses. It seems reasonable to assume therefore that these animals were present among the tribal groups living in the borderland areas of the present provinces of Manitoba and Saskatchewan by the 1760s, but they were probably few in number. In this important respect this section of the parkland differed from those lying farther to the west-northwest. It may be that the more severe winter temperatures characteristic of this region meant that it was more difficult to keep the animals, especially in the first years after a tribe had acquired them (Figure 40). Once they learned how to care for horses they could reduce these winter losses, but even by the last quarter of the eighteenth century most of the parkland Indians of Manitoba and Saskatchewan had not developed the skills required to care for the animals adequately. Likewise, many of the characteristic features of the plains Indian horse culture had not yet appeared. At the time Alexander Henry the Elder visited the Assiniboine in 1776, he noted that they did not use their horses in the winter season because of the harshness of the weather. However, he learned from an informant that they did not look after the animals in the winter season either. Henry said that the Indians told him:

it was their uniform custom to leave their horses in the beginning of winter, at the first wood where they were when the snow fell, at which the horses always remain through the season, and where their masters are sure to find them in the spring. The horses never go out of sight of the island assigned them, winter or summer, for fear of wanting its shelter in a storm.[46]

Such practices stand in marked contrast to those of other plains tribes like the Blackfoot who did look after their stock during the winter season. Indeed, the latter tribe frequently moved their herds short distances when local pastures were exhausted and often gave the animals supplemental feed, most commonly cotton wood bark, when it was needed.[47] The failure of the Assiniboine to take similar precautions must have caused the tribe to lose a significant portion of its animals every winter. Cocking hinted that this was the case in the parklands to the west of the South Saskatchewan River. When recording the death of an Indian man on 16 February 1773, he added that several horses had died from lack of food also. He said that his Indian companions informed him that this usually happened at that time of the year.[48]

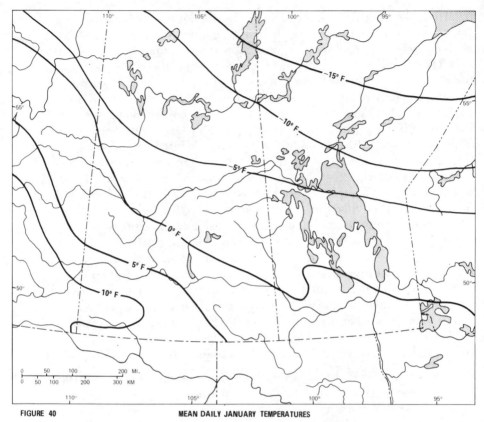

FIGURE 40   MEAN DAILY JANUARY TEMPERATURES

Source:

'' ATLAS OF CANADA''
Department of Mines· and Technical Surveys,
Geographical Branch, Ottawa, 1957

Judging from the paucity of references to Assiniboine horse stealing
as late as the 1770s and the fact that the tribe had not yet acquired the
reputation for being a notorious band of horse thieves for which it was
later noted, it appears that the 'horse raiding complex,' a dominant
feature of the equestrian plains cultures, had not developed fully in the
parklands to that time.

By the end of the century the above conditions had changed substantially in the Saskatchewan area and the 'horse culture' had matured
considerably. Thus, in 1790 Edward Umfreville wrote that the Cree spent
most of their time looking after their horses. Elaborating further he

said, 'Many of the men shew more affection for their horses than for their wives.'[49] By this time horse raiding had become a common practice, and John MacDonell, who was stationed on the Assiniboine River to the west of Brandon House in 1793, stated that it was an 'endless source of quarrel amongst the savages.'[50] However, he also mentioned that the Indians still left their horses to provide for themselves during the winter, indicating that the earlier habit of leaving their herds unattended after the first snowfall had not changed in spite of these other developments.[51] Considering that one of its chief functions was to enhance the status of warriors who gained prestige by their daring exploits, horse raiding was probably mostly a summer activity since it would have required little bravery to steal unattended animals in the winter. The seasonality of this activity meant that the trading posts had to maintain a constant vigil over their herds during the warmer months of the year. Reflecting the problem, Archibald McLeod, who was stationed at Fort Alexandria on the upper Assiniboine River in 1801, cautioned on 25 March: 'The time [end of March] approaches now that we must watch our horses as otherwise the Stone Indians will steal them in consequence of which I keep mine in the Fort day & night.'[52]

Although the horse was clearly well integrated into the economies of the parkland tribes by the turn of the century, the dog continued to be an important beast of burden. As an illustration, when Alexander Henry the Younger was stationed at Fort George on the north Saskatchewan in 1810, he had trading connections with the Gens du Pied Assiniboine band which included thirty-five men. Henry stated that this band was a notorious set of horse thieves but then added, 'I had the curiosity to count the Assiniboine dog travailles, and found no fewer than 230.'[53] That would have indicated a ratio of slightly over six dogs per man or thirteen per family since there was an average of two men per lodge. Using these animals the group would have been able to transport up to 2300 pounds of goods.[54] While the dog continued to be used by other plains tribes to the south and the southwest, it appears that the Assiniboine, Plains Cree, and Plains Ojibwa remained more dependent on them. This difference was largely related to the fact that these three tribes were 'horse poor.' This was especially true of those bands which lived in southern Manitoba. For instance, as late as 1800 horses were not common among Indians in the lower Assiniboine and Red river areas. In the latter year Alexander Henry the Younger bought two horses from a band of Cree camped near Portage la Prairie, and he took them to his Pembina River post located in the Red River Valley near the present international border (Figure 38).

Henry claimed that these were the first horses he had had on the Red River. In addition, he claimed that the Ojibwa living in the vicinity had none and used only canoes.[55] During the next fifteen years the situation changed very little, and horses were still relatively scarce in southern Manitoba in 1815 when Peter Fidler made his 'census' of the Assiniboine and Red River valleys. At that time he estimated that the Assiniboine had only 500 mounts. This figure would suggest that there were not enough horses for all of the warriors since there were about 800 men. Moreover, considering that there were 300 lodges, there would have been fewer than two horses per family. Surprisingly the ratios seemed to have been more favourable among the Cree, a tribe which was not noted for its herds of horses. Fidler said that they had about 200 animals, or nearly enough for each warrior to have one. Each family would have had an average of three mounts since he reckoned that the tribe had a total of approximately seventy-one lodges. He listed only 100 horses for the Ojibwa. This would give them only one per lodge, as there were 100 of the latter, and only one mount for every three warriors.[56] In brief, it is clear that there were few horses along the northeastern fringes of the grasslands. The reasons for the lower totals are not well understood, but are probably partly related to the harsher winter conditions there and to the fact that a portion of the population, the Ojibwa, were recent immigrants to the area. Therefore, they still retained many of their woodland cultural traits including the use of a canoe. Those groups who did acquire horses also adopted many of the features of the equestrian cultures which characterized most of the tribes bordering them to the south and to the west. Although the horse would have made it possible for the Indians to carry more European goods greater distances, and therefore presumably furthered the process of Europeanization of their cultures, there is little evidence that this occurred. This was a consequence of the fact that the increasing dependence which they placed on the bison resource reduced their demand for most European articles.

NOTES

1 David Rodnick, 'Political Structure among the Assiniboine Indians,' 412
2 York Factory Correspondence Books, 1762, PAC HBC B 239/b/23, pp. 14–15
3 Ibid.
4 Williams, *Graham's Observations*, 317
5 Morton, *The Journal of Duncan M'Gillivray*, 74
6 York Factory Correspondence Books, 1762, PAC HBC B 239/b/23, p. 15. This

treatment was not accorded to the leaders of 'near' Indians, for example the Homeguard Indians; when they arrived, trade began immediately without the elaborate preliminary exchange ceremonies.

7 Morton, *The Journal of Duncan M'Gillivray*, 74–5

8 Ibid., 75. Equally lavish gift-giving occurred at the neighbouring Hudson's Bay Company post of Buckingham House. For example, on 19 March William Tomison wrote: 'I was obliged to cloth eleven [Indians] to prevent them from going to the Canadian House [Fort George],' PAC HBC B 24/a/1, p. 24.

9 Rodnick, 'Political Structure among the Assiniboine Indians,' 412

10 Tyrrell, *The Journals of Samuel Hearne and Philip Turnor*, 188

11 Carlton House Post Journals, 1796–97, PAC HBC B 27/a/2, p. 11–12

12 York Factory Account Books, PAC HBC B 239/d/40–50

13 Burpee, 'Journal of a Journey Performed by Anthony Hendry,' 338–9

14 York Factory Account Books, 1770, PAC HBC B 239/d/61, pp. 26–58

15 For example, in 1787–8 South Branch House and Manchester House had insufficient supplies of tobacco and what they had was of poor quality. This difficulty was the subject of a considerable amount of correspondence. South Branch House Post Journal, 1787–8, PAC HBC B 205/a/2, p. 36

16 York Factory Journal, 1769, PAC HBC B 239/a/64, p. 13

17 *Travels and Adventures in Canada*, 281

18 Ibid., 314

19 For example, between 1774 and 1778 only seventy-two kettles were shipped to the Cumberland District, an amount which was roughly equal to the number traded in an average year at York Factory during the period before 1774. York Factory Account Books, PAC HBC B 239/d/64–68.

20 Henry, *Travels and Adventures in Canada*, 317

21 Tyrell, *The Journals of Samuel Hearne and Philip Turnor*, 274

22 Lac la Pluie District Report, 1825, PAC HBC B 105/e/6, p. 4

23 These years were selected because they are the only ones for which data is available for all three posts.

24 The family counts are based on the Brandon District Report of 1822 which listed 590 families, the Carlton Report of 1815 which gave a total of 400 families, and the Cumberland Report of 1815 which gave an estimate of 110 families. PAC HBC B 22/e/2, pp. 3–4; PAC HBC B 27/e/1, p. 2; and PAC HBC B 49/e/1, p. 4 respectively. This per-capita approximation probably reduces the difference somewhat since family sizes were smaller in the Cumberland area.

25 Brandon House Journal, 1793–4, PAC HBC B 22/a/1, p. 21

26 Ibid., 1794–5, PAC HBC B 22/a/2, p. 30

27 South Branch House Post Journal, 1790–1, PAC HBC B 205/a/5, p. 30. He claimed these shortages caused the company to lose most of the prime spring fur trade.

28 For example, shortages of cloth prompted comments at Buckingham House in
   1792–3 and again in 1796–7, at Carlton House in 1795–6, and at South Branch
   House in 1787–8. Buckingham House Journal, 1792–3 and 1796–7, PAC HBC B
   24/a/1, pp. 37–8 and 24/a/4, p. 16; Carlton House Post Journal, 1795–6 PAC HBC
   B 27/a/1, p. 23; and South Branch House Post Journal, PAC HBC B 205/a/2, p. 32.

29 For example, James Bird who was stationed at Carlton House in 1796–7 noted
   the improvement in the quality of the North West Company's cloth and was
   disturbed by this development. Carlton House Post Journal, 1796–7, PAC HBC B
   27/a/2, p. 11

30 Carlton House Post Journals, 1797–8, PAC HBC B 27/a/3, pp. 19–20

31 The Woodland Assiniboine would have been an exception in this respect. These
   Indians who lived to the north of the North Saskatchewan River in Alberta were
   more dependent on the trading companies. Franklin, *Narrative of a Journey to the
   Shores of the Polar Sea*, 105. Franklin points out that among the trinkets which the
   Plains Assiniboine prized, buttons were the most valued. They were worn as
   ornaments on clothing and in the hair.

32 Harmon, *Sixteen Years in Indian Country*, 41

33 Ibid., 64–5

34 Fort Dauphin District Report, 1820, PAC HBC B 51/e/1, p. 7

35 Doughty and Chester, *The Kelsey Papers*, pp. 1ff

36 Burpee, 'Journal of Anthony Hendry,' 329–35

37 Ibid., 351

38 York Factory Journal, PAC HBC B 239/a/56, p. 13

39 Burpee, 'An Adventurer From Hudson Bay,' 104

40 *Travels and Adventures in Canada*, 295

41 Burpee, *Journals and Letters of La Vérendrye*, 335–7

42 Actually they knew of the animal much earlier. In 1688 Jacques de Noyon met
   with some Assiniboine near Lake of the Woods. They told him about a people to
   the southwest who rode horses. These people were said to live in fortified
   villages. In all probability this was a second hand account of the Spanish.
   Ruggles, 'The Historical Geography and Cartography of the Canadian West,'
   300. This story was widespread and N. Jérémie heard a similar version of it from
   the Chipewyan during the French occupancy of York Factory, however, their
   account of the Spanish did not include reference to horses. Jérémie, 'Relation du
   Detroit et de le Baye de Hudson,' 5: 318

43 Burpee, *Journals and Letters of La Vérendrye*, 387–8

44 York Factory Journals, 1764, PAC HBC B 239/a/52, p. 18

45 York Factory Journals, 1757, PAC HBC B 239/a/45, p. 4

46 *Travels and Adventures in Canada*, 316

47 Ewers, 'The Horse in Blackfoot Indian Culture,' 40–3

48 Burpee, 'An Adventurer from Hudson Bay,' 114
49 *The Present State of Hudson's Bay*, 96–8
50 Gates, *Five Fur Traders, 113–14*
51 Ibid., 114
52 Ibid., 167
53 Coues, *New Light on the Early History of the Greater Northwest*, 2: 579
54 John MacDonell indicated that dogs were used in winter and summer and that each was able to haul from fifty to one-hundred pounds. Gates, *Five Fur Traders*, 114
55 Coues, *New Light on the Early History of the Greater Northwest*, 47
56 Journal Kept at Red River, Selkirk Papers, 69, nos. 18,430–18,536, p. 52

9
Land and life: a changing mosaic

Continuing Indian migrations, the modifications of the resource base, and the different responses of tribal groups to the changing nature of the fur trade had a varied impact on the seasonal movements and economic activities of the Assiniboine, Cree, and Ojibwa bands living in the forest-grassland borderlands of western Canada between 1763 and 1821. In the Saskatchewan and upper Assiniboine river areas, the earlier practice of exploiting woodland, grassland, and parkland resources on a seasonal basis persisted among a large proportion of the Indian population in spite of the economic changes under way.

As an example, journal accounts indicate that in the early nineteenth century, large-scale seasonal shifts of population were still occurring in the territory bordering the Saskatchewan River between Cumberland Lake and Lake Winnipeg, even though considerable numbers of Ojibwa and some Swampy Cree were moving into this country from the northeast and southeast. For instance, when Alexander Henry the Younger passed through this area in 1808 he stopped at Cedar Lake in the month of August to meet a band of 'Saulteurs' or Ojibwa who he claimed normally spent the summer at the lake. Presumably, they maintained a fishing camp there, although Henry did not actually state that this was the case. Regarding the winter activities of this group, he said that they usually moved to the Red Deer River department located to the west.[1] Several days later Henry reached Cumberland House as he continued his journey up the Saskatchewan River. Upon his arrival at this post he noted that there were several groups of Swampy Cree and Ojibwa camped nearby.

He learned that the latter bands wintered to the south in the vicinity of the Carrot River and the Pasquia Hills.[2]

Other observers recorded similar patterns of movement for the Swampy Cree. The journal of the Hudson's Bay Company's Red Deer River post for the year 1812–13 shows that the Cree who lived near Moose Lake, Manitoba, in the summer months abandoned the area in early winter to establish small camps in the Red Deer River District. The journalist indicated that these Cree usually arrived some time before the end of December and they remained for two to three months. Since they were usually starving when they arrived, the primary motive for these movements appears to have been the search for game. Also at that time, muskrat, the principal fur-bearing animal which they trapped, was still abundant in the Moose Lake area.[3]

Although there is no suggestion in any of the instances above that the migratory habits of these Swampy Cree and Ojibwa were taking them as far as the parkland zone, other sources provide evidence which shows that many of the Woodland Cree living to the south of the lower Saskatchewan River did make the trip. For example, sometime between 1801 and 1804 John Tanner and a small band of Ottawa Indians with whom he lived spent the winter in the Red Deer Country.[4] This group, which initially had eight male hunters, passed the autumn season trapping furs in the vicinity of the lower Red Deer River. Tanner reported that beaver were abundant there and his party killed a great number of them. In the early winter two more Indian hunters joined the group. Soon afterwards local game supplies were exhausted and they began suffering from a shortage of food. To cope with this increasingly difficult situation Tanner said:

We now determined to make a sunjegwun, and deposit such of our property as would impede us in a long journey, and go to the plains in pursuit of buffalo. We accordingly followed the path of the Crees, and overtook them in the Prairie ... It was about the middle of winter when we arrived among them ...
We stayed about one month in the Prairie, then returned to the lodge where we had left the old woman, thence to our trading-house on the Elk River [Red Deer River].[5]

Several important pieces of information are contained in this narrative. Tanner states that his band followed the paths of the Cree to the prairies thereby indicating that the Cree were in the habit of making such trips.[6] Furthermore, Tanner's group arrived in the Cree camp after it had been established and departed before it was broken up, making it clear that the Cree resided in the parklands for periods of over a month.

In comparing the seasonal migration patterns described in the above accounts it becomes apparent that population movements in the lower Saskatchewan River area were quite complex. The Swampy Cree and Ojibwa bands, who had summer fishing camps along the Saskatchewan River, moved out of the area in winter because of meagre game conditions and settled in the Carrot, Red Deer, and Swan River valleys where large moose populations were found.[7] Somewhat paradoxically, the Cree, who spent the summers in the latter areas, appear to have abandoned them in winter, claiming that there were limited game supplies, and travelled to parklands where they hunted bison. Since many of the Western Cree had acquired the habit of wintering in the parklands in the pre-1763 period when they served as middlemen in the trade between the Grassland-Parkland Indians and the Europeans, it may be that the winter bison hunt in this territory was a carry-over from the earlier period. With many Cree apparently taking part in these winter hunts, there was a considerable shift of population toward the parklands. It was this shift of population that enabled the Swampy Cree and Ojibwa to move into the area from the north and northeast during the winter months. Being fewer in number and hunting in smaller bands, they were able to obtain adequate supplies of food in an area where other groups may have had difficulty doing so.

Although older hunting and gathering habits persisted in the region and were being adopted by many of the newer immigrant tribal bands as Tanner's journal showed, the latter groups also introduced some new subsistence activities. One of these was sugar-making. Tanner, for instance, stated that after bartering his furs at the trading house on the Red Deer River, he travelled down the river a short distance to set up a sugar camp.[8] By 1812 these camps were numerous along this river. Most of them were located on points in the river where groves of Manitoba maple could be found. Generally, a grove was exploited by the same band every year and they had exclusive control over it.[9] The Cree do not appear to have become involved in this activity. Rather, most of the groves were held by the Ojibwa who, presumably, had known real sugar maples in Ontario.[10]

Westward up the Saskatchewan River valley in the vicinity of the middle and upper Carrot River an annual round of movement and economic activity quite similar to that of the Red Deer River district was common amongst local Indian groups at the close of the eighteenth century, judging from the information contained in the Fort Nipawi Post Journal for 1794–5. James Bird had been sent by the Hudson's Bay Company to man the post and he reached it in early October 1794. Upon his arrival, he learned that all of the local Indians had already come in with their autumn hunts and had left for their wintering grounds. The locations of the grounds were not given, but subsequent passages suggest that many of them were located towards the south. For example, most of the winter trade of the post consisted of provisions which were brought in by small groups of Indians. Until 6 December most of this produce consisted of moose and red deer meat; thereafter, bison meat became important. Furthermore, the Indian whom Bird hired to hunt for the post set up his camp in the parklands to the south.[11] The difficulties Bird had in getting meat from this camp to his post became the subject of several letters he sent to Mr Twatt at Cumberland House and to William Tomison at Buckingham House, and these letters throw some additional light on the factors which were favouring seasonal population movements in the district. According to Bird, the major problem he faced was the absence of horses and the lack of a sufficient number of dogs to haul large quantities of food long distances overland.[12] Lacking these, he faced the same problems as did the men at Cumberland House in obtaining adequate stocks of provisions during the winter, even though Fort Nipawi was located much closer to the parkland zone than was Cumberland House.[13] The local Indians experienced the same difficulty: they, too, had few dogs and no horses. Presumably, if the animals had been available tribal bands would have been able to trap furs all winter in the forest by making occasional hunting trips to the parklands, bringing back the meat they would have obtained.

Although Bird indicated that some 'Bungees' or Plains Ojibwa did remain in the country surrounding the post all winter, they seem to have been few in number. On 15 January 1795, he wrote that most of the Indians from his department, as well as those of the Red Deer River and Swan River territories, had gathered in the parklands where they were preparing to make war on the Gros Ventre. As part of this preparation, they were constructing a large bison pound in order to kill enough animals to provide food for their families while they were away.[14] Granting that this encampment was probably not a typical winter camp, since it was set up to make war, nonetheless, it does serve to demonstrate that the tribes of the areas involved were familiar with the construction of the buffalo pound and therefore had the means to kill large numbers of the animal. In addition, it shows that these groups turned to the parklands whenever the need arose to support large concentrations of population. Finally, this particular encampment was forming in the middle of the winter after the early winter fur hunt would have been completed, and at the time of the greatest food scarcity in the woodlands. Its formation was thus probably planned to coincide with the period when the woodland groups made their usual journeys out of the forests.

Unfortunately, the Nipawi journal does not cover the spring and summer seasons; consequently, information dealing with the population movements and economic activities during these seasons is lacking. However, since the local tribal bands were mostly Cree, fishing along the lakes and rivers was probably the dominant activity.

Further to the west, the conditions were quite different from those of the above-mentioned territories. In the North Saskatchewan River area, as well as along the lower South Saskatchewan River, the trading houses were located in the parkland belt. Partly for this reason horses were common among most of the Indians who had contacts with these establishments. Only the Woodland Assiniboine and Cree living to the north of the North Saskatchewan River were exceptions. Besides these contrasts, the Indian population of this country was more heterogeneous in terms of tribal composition than it was in the lands lying to the east. The Assiniboine and Cree were the most numerous, but bands of Gros Ventre and different groups from the Blackfoot confederacy also traded at the posts, especially those situated on the North Saskatchewan River upstream from its confluence with the Battle River.

The establishment of trading houses in the above districts beginning in the late 1770s exerted a considerable impact on the annual rounds of migration and economic activity which had developed among the local Indian populations. By eliminating the necessity of making long canoe voyages down to Hudson Bay or to the lower Saskatchewan River area, many of the Assiniboine and Cree were no longer required to maintain their links with the forest environment. Furthermore, the severing of these ties was encouraged by the growing demand for provisions. In response to these developments many bands of these two tribes abandoned the practice of making summer fishing camps. Instead, they moved into the grasslands.[15]

Their winter routine remained largely unchanged, however, and they continued to follow bison herds into the parkland zone in search of food and shelter. Thus, for example, Duncan M'Gillivray's 1794–5 journal for Fort George indicated that there were two groups of Assiniboine camped in the vicinity of the post during the months of December, January, and February: the Strong Wood and Grand River Assiniboine bands. Both of them had constructed buffalo pounds, with those of the Strong Wood being located on the lower Vermilion River.[16] M'Gillivray provided little information about the Cree locations with the exception that he said large numbers of the latter tribe were in the Beaver Hills during the winter where they had built their pounds.[17]

His other commentary makes it clear that in addition to the pounding of bison during the winter, many of the local bands still conducted two fur hunts, one in the late autumn and early winter, and the other in the late winter and early spring. In the trading year of 1794–5, M'Gillivray reported that the earlier of these two hunts was largely completed by 13 December, while the second was nearly finished by 30 April. The latter date was said to be unusually late because of the severity of the winter weather that year.[18] Not all of the Indians took part in these activities, however, as some groups appeared to have lost interest in trapping operations. As an illustration, M'Gillivray complained that the 'Grand Soteau's' band of Cree located in the Beaver Hills 'amused themselves driving Buffalo into a pound – a very unfavourable circumstance for our returns.'[19] Judging from the trading returns of the two groups camped closest to the Fort, the Grand River Assiniboine were the least inclined to trap furs.

Even though many of the Indians were loosening their ties to the adjacent woodlands, others continued to migrate back and forth between this area and the parkland zone with the changes of the seasons. These movements were recorded by Alexander Henry the Younger, who had a considerable amount of interchange with the Swampy Ground Assiniboine and Woodland Cree while he was stationed at Fort Vermilion in 1808–9. Both of these groups lived in the country north of the North Saskatchewan River. The notation below is typical of many of the remarks which he made about the migratory habits of the Woodland Cree families. On 20 January 1810, he wrote:

Missisticoine, a Cree, arrived with his family from the strong wood on his way to the Cree camps below. This is the first of my Crees who has come out of the woods this season; when once they take the route for the pounds below, we expect no more fur from them during the season, as they idle, playing and eating buffalo.[20]

Other families followed later with the last of them passing by Fort Vermilion on 30 March. However, this date was considered to be exceptionally late and it prompted Henry to remark, 'It is uncommon for a Cree family to stay so long alone in the strong woods.'[21]

Of considerable importance, Henry's journal shows that while the families were in the forest they lived as small isolated families, but once they settled in the parklands they gathered into large camps. Further-more, it is clear that these families maintained close contacts with the Parkland Cree bands since they travelled to buffalo pound encampments which were already established. At a later date similar movements and associations were recorded for the Cree of the Carlton District.[22] In fact, the only significant change that appears to have taken place is that some of the Woodland Cree were forced to abandon the forests earlier in the winter than they had previously because of the declining game resources of the forests. Thus, the Carlton District Report for 1826–7 indicated that these Indians were heading for the parklands in December, which was said to be sooner than normal.[23]

The persistence of the parkland-forest exploitation cycle among the Cree Indians in these departments was favoured by a number of factors. One of these was the continuation of the southward drift of the Cree which had begun in the late eighteenth century. As immigrant bands settled in the southern sections of the Boreal forest of central and Western Saskatchewan they followed the practices of other Cree groups, which they displaced, by tapping the game resources of the adjacent parklands. Indeed, as time passed it became increasingly necessary to hunt in the parklands because of the continuing depletion of the game-animal popu-lations in the woodlands. The fur traders also played a role in encourag-ing the Indians to exploit both the parklands and the grasslands since they repeatedly made attempts to persuade the Indians not to abandon their fur-trapping operations. In conjunction with this aim the traders tried to encourage them not to sever their links with the forest completely. As an example, in the autumn of 1808 Alexander Henry the Younger visited a small Cree camp on the North Saskatchewan River in the vicinity of the present city of North Battleford, Saskatchewan. When concluding his trade with them he reported: 'I remained with my guide to settle with the Indians and prevail on some of them to return above [north of the river], this fall, to make their hunt as usual in the strong wood Country.'[24] Considering that Henry made this remark in the middle of September, it is clear that this particular band was spending a major portion of its time in the parklands. Therefore, in this instance, Henry was attempting to slow an adaptive process which was already well advanced.

To the south of the Saskatchewan River, in the territory of the upper Assiniboine River (upstream from its confluence with the Qu'Appelle River), similar seasonal interactions of woodland-, parkland-, and grassland-oriented tribes occurred in the late eighteenth and early nineteenth centuries. Two Nor'Westers, Archibald McLeod and Daniel

Harmon, were in this district at the beginning of the last century and they made a number of valuable observations on this aspect of the economic geography of the area. The former trader was stationed at Fort Alexandria in 1800. This post had trading connections with the White Sand River, the Qu'Appelle Lakes, and the Porcupine, Nut, and Touchwood Hills (Figure 2). With the exclusion of the Nut and Porcupine Hills, all of these areas lay within the parkland zone. Significantly, McLeod's writings show that the Cree occupied all of these lands in the winter with the exception of the Qu'Appelle Lakes area, which was a winter camping ground of the Assiniboine, and the Porcupine Hills country which was a winter trapping area of the Ojibwa.

Regarding the Nut Hills territory, the one woodland section which was inhabited by the Cree during the winter, McLeod's journal shows that some of the bands of the latter Indians did not spend the entire winter season there, but rather passed a portion of it in the parklands hunting bison. He learned this from one of his men who had returned from those hills on 16 November 1800. McLeod said that this man informed him that three of the Cree with whom he traded were in the Nut Hills hunting beaver, but they intended to depart shortly for the Plains to hunt 'their Beloved Buffalo.'[25] Two years later, Daniel Harmon was stationed in the woodlands to the east of the Nut Hills near Bird Mountain (the present Thunder Hill, Saskatchewan) just to the north of the Swan River. He recorded similar movements, and suggested that they involved nearly all of the local population. For instance, on 8 February 1802, he wrote: 'All of the Indians of this place except my Hunters are gone to pass a couple of Months (as they are wont yearly to do) on their beloved food – Buffaloe Meat.'[26] In subsequent passages, Harmon indicated that the majority of these Indians returned to Bird Mountain by 20 March. After spending the next four weeks camped near his post, most of them departed on 22 April to make their spring fur hunts. Most of the latter were completed by 20 May, when Harmon concluded his trade with them and they left for the summer.[27]

The winter movements of the Assiniboine in this section of the parklands are somewhat uncertain. The Good Spirit Lake (formerly Devil's Lake) area of Saskatchewan was one of the locations which they frequented at that time of the year, and some of them may have camped as far north in Saskatchewan as Fishing Lake which lies to the east of the Quill Lakes.[28] Consequently, during the winter these Assiniboine would have been in contact with the Cree groups visited by McLeod and Harmon. In the spring and summer, when the Cree returned to the woodlands, the Assiniboine headed southward into the open grasslands reaching as far as the Missouri River.[29] In brief, the patterns of seasonal population migration in this territory were quite similar to those of the upper Saskatchwan River area.

By the early nineteenth century, the economic organization of southern Manitoba had changed considerably from that of earlier years and there is little evidence to suggest that any extensive seasonal movements of Indians back and forth across the forest-grassland boundary were still taking place on a regular basis. In the Brandon District the Assiniboine were the dominant group. They focused their economic activities on the hunting of bison and on the trapping of wolves and fox, and accordingly, they spent most of their time in the parklands and grasslands. Within this vast territory they generally wintered along the lower Souris, middle Assiniboine, and lower Qu'Appelle rivers. In these areas the rivers had cut deep trenches below the surrounding plains which provided shelter from the winter wind; furthermore, the trenches were heavily wooded. In addition to these retreats, the Assiniboine frequented the forested Moose Mountain and Turtle Mountain regions.[30] Having access to these environmental niches, it was not necessary to travel farther northward or eastward into the parkland belt in winter. Therefore, the distances they covered in their seasonal wanderings were probably less than those travelled by their predecessors who lived farther to the east in the early eighteenth century. Yet, the types of environment they exploited would have been very similar since the habitats of the above valleys and uplands closely resembled those of more eastern and northern territories, particularly in terms of the animal species which were present (Figure 41). During the summer months, they followed the practice of Assiniboine groups living in other districts to the northwest and moved into the open grasslands, usually travelling southward to the Missouri River.[31]

The Cree living in the Brandon District were few in number compared to the Assiniboine. Most of them pitched their winter camps in the vicinity of Brandon House. A few of them camped near the confluence of the Assiniboine and Qu'Appelle rivers. These groups were said to be similar in most respects to their Assiniboine neighbours, the only difference being that some of the Cree killed a few bears and trapped some fisher and fox during the winter in the lands to the north of the Assiniboine River. However, as the fur resources gave out, more of them were abandoning this custom and following the ways of the Assiniboine.[32] Besides the Cree there were a small number of Ojibwa in the department. They lived in the northern part of the district and appear to have roamed rather randomly over the country remaining mostly in the parklands.[33]

In the lower Assiniboine and adjacent Red River valleys the Ojibwa had become the dominant group by the early nineteenth century. In contrast with the practice of the earlier Cree and Assiniboine inhabitants of the territory, the Ojibwa did not exploit the woodlands and parklands on a seasonal basis. Rather, they lived in small bands and shifted their locations frequently in response to local game conditions. The movements of the small Ottawa band with whom John Tanner lived were fairly characteristic of most of the Indian groups living in southeastern Manitoba at the beginning of the last century. This band ranged rather widely over the latter territory wintering some years along the lower Red River and other years along the Assiniboine River. Occasionally they camped in the southern Riding Mountain area. Because his band's primary winter activity was directed toward the trapping of furs, as was also the case with most of the Ojibwa groups, movements were strongly influenced by local fur resource conditions.

Since the Ojibwa continued to rely mostly on their trapping operations to obtain furs which could be bartered at the trading houses for the European goods they desired, they retained many of the features of their woodland culture. For example, they had a very flexible social organization well suited to an economy that focused heavily on the exploitation of the forest resources. The social units were small, centring around the nuclear family, small winter band, and the larger spring hunting band. The most important unit was the winter hunting band consisting of a few families that were often related. Its primary purpose was an economic one, with the families usually rallying behind the leadership of a successful hunter. In the spring several of these bands often joined together to produce a larger unit, having from two to seven hunters. This unit served primarily to make a final intensive sweep through an area to obtain enough furs to allow them to outfit themselves for the long, dormant summer season when they had nothing to trade with Europeans.[34] These spring bands operated for very short periods, usually not more than three or four weeks during the period between the break-up of the ice in the rivers and the time when they transported their furs to the trading posts. In the summer these bands were absorbed into the larger lakeside fishing villages.[35] Such a social system helped the Ojibwa cope with the harsh environment of the forests during the winter without having to have recourse to the bison herds of the parklands.

Other factors were influential also. Judging from the Fort Alexander, Brandon, and Fort Dauphin District reports of 1822–3, the Indian population of the southern sections and boreal forest in Manitoba may have been much smaller than it had been in the previous period. For example,

FIGURE 41

VEGETATION CROSSECTIONS

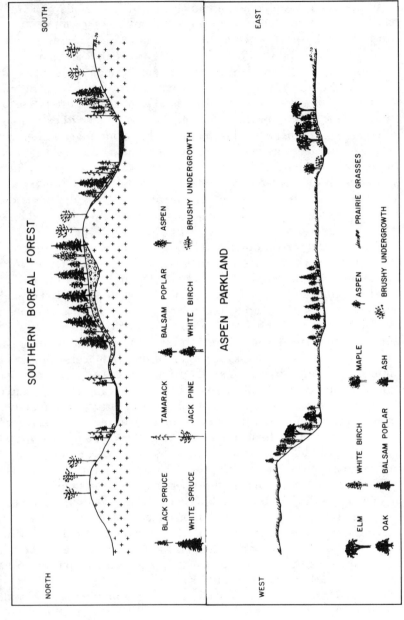

SOUTHERN BOREAL FOREST

BLACK SPRUCE	TAMARACK	BALSAM POPLAR	ASPEN
WHITE SPRUCE	JACK PINE	WHITE BIRCH	BRUSHY UNDERGROWTH

ASPEN PARKLAND

ELM	WHITE BIRCH	MAPLE	ASPEN	PRAIRIE GRASSES
OAK	BALSAM POPLAR	ASH	BRUSHY UNDERGROWTH

NORTH

SOUTH

WEST

EAST

the total Ojibwa population in these three departments at that time amounted to fewer than 800 persons.[36] In contrast, it should be recalled that many of the winter villages of the parkland Assiniboine in earlier years often had over a hundred lodges and 700 to 1200 inhabitants.[37]

Besides the lower population densities, the game-resource conditions in southern Manitoba in the early nineteenth century were apparently quite different from those of the parklands to the northwest, and these differences probably played a role in bringing about the earlier breakdown of the forest-parkland oriented economies in this area. For instance, the number of bison in the lower Assiniboine valley was apparently never as great as it was in the borderlands farther to the west, and, furthermore, this resource was in decline there by the second decade of the nineteenth century. As early as 1820 the bison herds no longer reached the forks of the Red River in significant numbers. Hence, the Indians in the Red River country would not have had an adequate subsistence base to support large winter villages as the Assiniboine formerly did in the early eighteenth century.[38] Toward the south in the upper Red River area (beyond the forks) the situation was quite different. This territory was a buffer zone between the Dakota Sioux and the Ojibwa and their allies until the early nineteenth century when the Ojibwa began settling there. Since the valley had been a no-man's-land prior to that time, it had served largely as a game refuge. As a consequence, fur and game animals were plentiful in the valley in the early nineteenth century. In this respect the area differed sharply from the wooded lands to the north and west where more stable political conditions allowed groups to exploit local environments intensively, thereby reducing subsistence resources below the levels which were required to sustain even small groups during the winter season.[39] It was these more favourable conditions which drew the Ojibwa to the southern Manitoba area.[40] Finally, many of the Ojibwa who moved into the area practiced some horticulture on a part-time basis to supplement the food they obtained by hunting and fishing. Although their horticultural activities do not appear to have been as important as the latter pursuits, nonetheless they could have played a role in obviating the necessity for some groups to move about on a seasonal basis, since agricultural produce, mostly corn, could be stored for use in winter when other foods were in short supply.[41]

In brief, the ecological orientations of Indian groups living in southern Manitoba were changing rapidly by the 1820s. The older practice of hunting in the woodlands and parklands on a seasonal basis was not followed to any great extent by the Ojibwa who had replaced the Cree as the chief inhabitants of the region. The early contraction of the bison range in this territory, the plentiful supply of other game in the upper Red River valley, as well as the practice of part-time farming by some bands, were all partly responsible for this development. In addition, the economic orientation of the Ojibwa and their social organization were influential. Finally, the population density of southern Manitoba appears to have been much lower than it had been in earlier years. This change was undoubtedly a factor. The lower density was brought about by migration, warfare, and disease. The combined effects of these population controls may have reduced the numbers of Indian inhabitants to a level which was approaching equilibrium with local resource conditions.

Farther to the northwest, the situation was different. The overlap of forest-parkland and parkland-grassland Indian economic systems continued. The perpetuation of these two systems in the latter territories was favoured by the progressive diminution of game in the forests and the continued presence in the parklands of large numbers of bison on a seasonal basis. Also, the Indian population pressure on the resources of the southern margins of the forests in Saskatchewan and eastern Alberta was being maintained by a steady southward drift of Cree. Finally, the fur traders encouraged the Indians to continue to hunt in the woodlands for at least a part of the year to obtain furs.

1 Coues, *New Light on the Early History of the Greater Northwest*, 2:466
2 Ibid., 477
3 Red Deer River Post Journal, 1812–13, PAC HBC B 176/a/1, pp. 5–6
4 Unfortunately Tanner did not date his journal. However, he does mention certain events which enable one to establish approximate dates. Considering that just prior to this trip he mentioned that Alexander Henry the Younger had established his post on the Pembina River, and shortly thereafter he stated that the Lewis and Clark expedition had passed up the Missouri River, it is possible to date his visit to the Red Deer River District as having occurred sometime between 1801 and 1804. There is evidence to suggest that he was in the Red Deer River area in 1801. He apparently visited Daniel Harmon in that region 9 July 1801; see Harmon, *Sixteen Years in the Indian Country*, 49.
5 James, *A Narrative of the Captivity and Adventures of John Tanner*, 73–5
6 The Ojibwa in the area probably followed a similar cycle of movement. For example, according to the Dauphin District Report for 1819–20 the Ojibwa hunted along the Manitoba escarpment, but few of them ever remained in the

country around the north end of Lake Winnipegosis in the winter. The report also stated that no tribes lived in the lands to the north of this lake during this season. Dauphin District Report, 1820, PAC HBC B 51/e/1, pp. 17.

7 The Red Deer River Journal of 1812–13 indicated that the bands generally consisted of two nuclear families. These bands were constantly on the move. Red Deer River Journal, 1812, PAC HBC B 176/a/1, pp. 4ff

8 James, *A Narrative*, p. 75–76. Tanner said the 'whites' called the trees 'River Maples' and he added they were large trees, but widely scattered.

9 Red Deer River Post Journal, 1812, PAC HBC B 176/a/1, p. 10. Apparently some Métis were also tapping this resource. Most of the best points were occupied by parties who made from 20 to 30, 80-lb. kegs of sugar each year.

10 The Swampy Cree returned to Moose Lake in March before the sugar season began. Ibid., 5

11 Nipawi Post Journal, 1794–5, PAC HBC B 148/a/1, pp. 16–17

12 Ibid., 29–32

13 It should be recalled that Cocking had advised Hearne against building a post at Cumberland Lake because it was too far from the parkland area, making it impossible to haul in any large quantities of food during the winter. York Factory Journal, PAC HBC B 239/a/72, p. 8

14 Nipawi Post Journal, PAC HBC B 148/a/1, p. 32

15 As late as 1767 William Pink noted that the Saskatchewan Cree living in the vicinity of Prince Albert, Saskatchewan, were still building fishing camps on the tributaries of the Saskatchewan River. York Factory Journals, 1766–67, PAC HBC B 239/a/56, pp. 2–21

16 Later, in 1808–9 Alexander Henry the Younger reported from Fort Vermilion that the Strong Wood and Gens du Pied Assiniboine wintered between the lower Battle River and Redberry Lake, Saskatchewan. Coues, *New Light on the Early History of the Greater Northwest*, 2:500, 522–3

17 Ibid., 49. Earlier the Manchester House Journal of 1790–1 stated that the Cree maintained bison pounds in the same area. PAC HBC B 121/a/6, p. 14. In the autumn of 1808 Henry the Younger encountered a village of 100 Cree lodges camped in the vicinity of the present city of North Battleford, Saskatchewan. See, Coues, *New Light on the Early History of the Greater Northwest*, 2:500.

18 Morton, *The Journal of Duncan M'Gillivray*, 49, 76

19 Ibid., 49. This reference is of interest in that judging from the chief's name it would appear that he was an Ojibwa or Saulteaux. The band therefore apparently consisted of Cree and Ojibwa. Intermarriage between their two groups was common; they also married with Assiniboine.

20 Coues, *New Light on the Early History of the Greater Northwest*, 580

21 Ibid., 593

22 Carlton District Report, 1818–19, PAC HBC B 27/e/2, p. 2

23 PAC HBC B 27/e/4, p. 2. Meagre game supplies were cited as the reason.

24 Coues, *New Light on the Early History of the Greater Northwest*, 2:501

25 Gates, *Five Fur Traders*, 130. Not all of the Cree left, however, and at least twenty-six of them were still in the Nut Hills as of 17 December, *ibid.*, 140–1.

26 *Sixteen Years in the Indian Country*, 54. A year earlier while he was at Fort Alexandria he mentioned that all of the local Indians and most of his men had left the fort on 4 January. They headed for the grasslands where they intended to spend the winter living off of the bison herds. Ibid., 41.

27 Ibid., 55–7. The pattern of movement and economic activity outlined above for the Cree probably changed very little during the next twenty years. The Brandon District Report for 1822–3 stated that there were seventy-five lodges of Cree in the area who hunted in the Beaver and Touchwood Hills as well as in the 'Strong Woods' near the Nut Hills. These same Cree roamed between Carlton House and the lower Qu'Appelle River (Beaver Creek area), but conducted most of their trade at Fort Alexandria. Brandon District Report, 1822–3, PAC HBC B 22/e/2, p. 3

28 In 1804 Harmon visited 'Lac la Peche' on 22 February and he met some Assiniboine who were camped there. W. K. Lamb who edited Harmon's journal identified this location as the Fishing Lakes on the Qu'Appelle River (*Sixteen Years*, 72). However, John Warkentin is of the opinion that Harmon probably visited Fishing Lake, Saskatchewan, which is located farther to the north (personal communication, 16 February 1971). Considering that Harmon said that the lake was two-days journey out into the plains from Fort Alexandria, the latter assumption seems more likely. To travel from Fort Alexandria to the Fishing Lakes on the Qu'Appelle River they would have had to average almost fifty miles a day, which is very improbable.

29 Brandon District Report, 1822, PAC HBC B 22/e/2, p. 3

30 Ibid.

31 Ibid.

32 Ibid., 3–4. These two groups of Cree had a total of 55 lodges compared to over 450 for the Assiniboine.

33 The Ojibwa had only ten lodges in the district as of 1822, ibid., 4. In 1793 John MacDonnell, who was stationed near the confluence of the Assiniboine and Souris rivers, said that there was a band of Ojibwa who roamed between Fort Dauphin, Lake Manitoba, and the Souris River. He indicated that there was no regularity to their movements. They moved 'wherever fancy leads them,' John MacDonnell, 'The Red River,' 1:272

34 This may have been a consideration which lured Cree groups to the grasslands

at an earlier period. However, there is little evidence to support such a hypothesis.

35 For a detailed discussion of Ojibwa social organization in this area at the turn of the last century, see Hickerson, 'Journal of Charles Jean Baptiste Chaboillez,' 411–15.

36 The Dauphin District Report listed 572 Ojibwa, most of whom were living in the southern part of the department. The Fort Alexander Report tallied 136 and the Brandon Report ten lodges. If a ratio of seven people per lodge is applied to the latter figure a total of 778 is obtained. PAC HBC B 51/e/1, p. 15; PAC HBC B 4/e/1, p. 3; and PAC HBC B 22/e/2, p. 4, respectively

37 Henry, *Travels and Adventures in Canada*, 303. La Vérendrye met a village of them on the north side of Turtle Mountain in the winter of 1738. There were over one hundred lodges in the village. Burpee, *Journals and Letters of La Vérendrye*, 313. Other evidence suggests that the population of the southwestern shield and adjacent parklands may have been more than twice as large as that of the 1820s. For instance, the combined total of the Fort Alexander District in 1822 and the Lac la Pluie District in 1829 amounted to 591 or about 600. In contrast, in the 1730s La Vérendrye indicated that the Indians of these areas were sending out war parties against the Sioux which averaged between 300 and 600 men. The Fort Alexander and Dauphin reports of 1822 show that the total population of the Ojibwa was from two to five times larger than the total male population (not including boys under 20). Applying these ratios to La Vérendrye's figures would suggest that the population of the above departments in the 1730s would have been perhaps as much as 1200 to 3000. Fort Alexander District Report, 1822–3, PAC HBC B 4/e/1, p.2; Lac la Pluie District Report, 1822, pp. 6–8, PAC HBC B 105/e/9, p. 2; Burpee, *La Vérendrye*, 136, 145, and 178; and Fort Dauphin District Report, 1822, PAC HBC B 51/e/1, p. 15

38 It should be recalled that in the winter of 1737 La Vérendrye reported that there were two villages of Assiniboine located near the forks of the Red River. Burpee, *Journals and Letters of La Vérendrye*, 244

39 For a good discussion of the ecology of this buffer zone, see Hickerson, 'The Southwestern Chippewa,' 12–29. During peaceful conditions the Ojibwa were able to hunt in this portion of southern Manitoba since they held control over the lower Red and Assiniboine rivers.

40 Hickerson has studied their movements in response to these conditions in considerable detail; 'The Genesis of a Trading Post Band,' 289–330.

41 For a good discussion of the spread of Indian agriculture into southeastern Manitoba, see Moodie and Kaye, 'The Northern Limit of Indian Agriculture in North America,' 513–29.

10

The changing demographic picture after 1821

Tribal migrations continued unabated after 1821, as Indian groups moved in response to a number of stimuli. In eastern Alberta and adjacent Saskatchewan the general southward movement of Indian populations noted earlier was still under way, but the tempo of that movement quickened. The Assiniboine who had been centred in the middle Assiniboine and Qu'Appelle river valleys, as well as in the prairie portions of the Carlton District, began moving out of these areas and gravitated toward the international boundary. Several factors favoured this movement. American trading posts on the Missouri River were attracting the Indians, and the pull of these posts was magnified over time by the southward contraction of the bison ranges and the increased importance which the buffalo robe and hide trade had for the Assiniboine and Plains Cree after 1821 as will be discussed subsequently. Since hides and robes, particularly the latter, were bulky items, it was difficult to carry large quantities of them long distances over land. Consequently, as the bison retreated to the southward, the American posts were more attractive outlets for this produce since they were closest to the areas where the Indians hunted these animals in the middle and late nineteenth century.

Governor Simpson of the Hudson's Bay Company was quick to recognize the effects that this combination of circumstances were having on tribal locations and on the ability of the Americans to exert their influence on the Indians of the prairie provinces. In one of his 1831 reports to London, he commented on this problem. Regarding Assiniboine and Plains Cree he wrote:

These Indians rove about in all directions over the extended plains between the Assiniboine and Missouri; they give little or no attention to Fur hunting, but employ themselves chiefly in Buffalo Chase, and are more regular in their visits to the American Establishments on the Missouri than to us; this arises from Buffalo being more numerous in that quarter than in the vicinity of our Posts, and from their finding a market for their Skins or robes on the Spot instead of being at the trouble of dragging them overland a distance of several hundred miles.[1]

In a later dispatch filed in 1838, Simpson indicated that the company had lost much of the trade of the Assiniboine and Plains Cree and that the only way the trend could be reversed would be by building posts in southern Saskatchewan and Alberta, particularly in the Bow River region. However, he decided that even though it would be desirable to undermine the American influence by such an effort, the expenses were too great.[2]

Besides the environmental and economic factors, the decimation of the Assiniboine by smallpox in 1838 was another event which favoured a southward contraction of their territory. For reasons which will be discussed subsequently, the Assiniboine suffered greater losses than did their Cree neighbours, and the latter began moving into the former homelands of the Assiniboine in increasing numbers after 1838.

The effects that these controls had on the distribution of the Assiniboine could be seen as early as 1833. In that year, Prince Maximilian, a very observant German nobleman, visited the plains and reported that the tribe's territory lay between the Saskatchewan, lower Milk, and Assiniboine rivers – with most of them being found in the southerly portions of that area.[3] Some twenty years later, in 1856, E. Denig, an American trader stationed on the Missouri River, stated that the principal lands controlled by the Assiniboine were found in the country between the Cypress Hills and Souris River on the north, and the lower Milk and Missouri rivers on the south.[4] Supporting Denig's observations are a United States government report filed in 1857 and the Palliser Report of 1858. They indicate that in the late 1850s, roughly three-quarters of the Assiniboine population was found to the south of the international border. The remainder of the tribe lived mostly in the lands lying just to the north in southern Saskatchewan, principally in the vicinity of Moose Mountain.[5] Thus, toward the close of the pre-reservation period the Assiniboine had largely deserted their primary settlement areas of the early nineteenth century and had moved well beyond them into the open grasslands of southern Saskatchewan and adjacent Montana (Figure 42).

As has been noted above, the movements of the Cree after 1821 closely

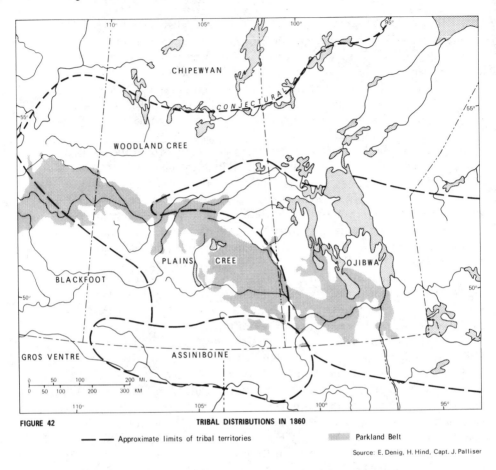

FIGURE 42   TRIBAL DISTRIBUTIONS IN 1860

— — — Approximate limits of tribal territories   ░░░░ Parkland Belt

Source: E. Denig, H. Hind, Capt. J. Palliser

paralleled those of the Assiniboine in much the same fashion as they had in earlier years. As the latter tribe abandoned most of the Saskatchewan region, the Cree replaced them as the principal inhabitants. Reflecting this development, the Palliser Report for 1863 showed that the Cree tribal territory extended from the Cypress Hills, Wood, and Moose mountains on the south, northeastward to the confluence of the Qu'Appelle and Assiniboine rivers, and northward to the boreal forest. To the northwest it included the Neutral Hills, Beaver Hills, and the lands immediately around Edmonton House. The distribution of the Cree within this vast tract of land has been summarized in Table 7 and mapped on Figure 43.

TABLE 7

Population distribution of the Western Cree in 1863 according to
Captain John Palliser*

Bands	No. of lodges
Plains Cree bands	
Moose Mountain	100
Moose Jaw	120
Coteau de Prairie	400
Eagle Hills	200
Moose Woods	200
Jackfish Lake	200
Vermilion River	300
Snake Portage and Lac la Biche	100
Beaver Hills	300
Total Plains Cree lodges	1920†
Total population: 11,520	
Thickwood (Woodland) Cree bands‡	
Carlton House	30
Fort Pitt	40
Edmonton House	15
Total Thickwood Cree lodges	85
Total Population: 425**	

  * Palliser, *The Journals*, 202
  † Palliser incorrectly tallied 1700 lodges
  ‡ Woodland Cree
** Family sizes of woodland groups were smaller than those of
    the grassland tribes. His figures show that there was roughly
    one less person per family.

By comparing the data in Table 7 to that of the previous period, the
magnitude of the change becomes apparent. It may be recalled that
Mackenzie's figures of 1789 indicated that only about one-third of the
Western Cree lived in the parkland-grassland region and he estimated
that they had only 110 lodges. As of 1820, the number had risen to 230,
according to the Hudson's Bay Company records, but most of them were
still located in close proximity to the forests. By 1860, Palliser listed 1920
lodges for the Plains Cree and only 85 for the Woodland Cree. If his
approximations for the latter group are correct, they would have accounted for less than 4 per cent of the total population of the Western

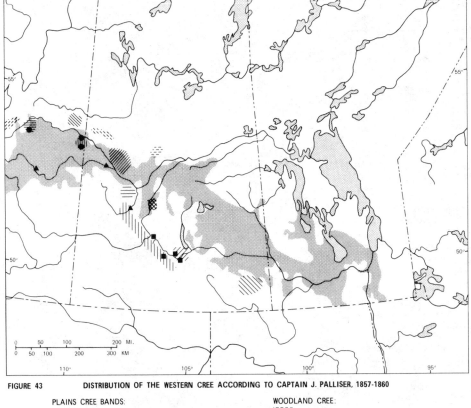

FIGURE 43   DISTRIBUTION OF THE WESTERN CREE ACCORDING TO CAPTAIN J. PALLISER, 1857-1860

PLAINS CREE BANDS:

≡ Beaver Hill Cree (300 lodges)

▨ Snake Portage & Lac la Biche Cree (100 lodges)

▥ Vermillion River Cree (300 lodges)

▨ Jack Fish Lake Cree (200 lodges)

≡ Eagle Hill Cree (200 lodges)

▥ Coteau des Prairies Cree (400 lodges)

▨ Moose Jaw Creek Cree (120 lodges)

▨ Moose Mtn. Cree (100 lodges)

▨ Moose Wood Cree (200 lodges)

WOODLAND CREE:

▨ Trading at Carlton House (30 lodges)

▨ Trading at Fort Pitt (40 lodges)

▨ Trading at Fort Edmonton (15 lodges)

LOCATIONS OF CREE CAMPS:

● Recorded in Winter

▲ Recorded in Summer

■ Recorded in Autumn

▨ PARKLAND BELT

Source: Capt. John Palliser, "EXPLORATIONS IN BRITISH NORTH AMERICA ", p. 200.

Cree at that time. Even if Palliser seriously underestimated their numbers, it is fairly certain nonetheless that they were the smaller of the two divisions by a wide margin, unlike the situation in the late eighteenth century.

The boundaries of the Ojibwa territory changed very little during the period from 1821 to 1860 and the tribe continued to be centred in the region lying to the east of the present western boundary of Manitoba. To the north, in the Saskatchewan River valley, and in the forests beyond, several small Ojibwa bands had moved well beyond the above country. Some were found as far to the northwest as the Lesser Slave Lake District (Figure 36). They and a number of Cree were found there as well. These groups had settled in the district largely as a result of the deliberate encouragement of the trading companies who valued them as trappers.[6] However, the Lesser Slave Lake Ojibwa comprised a small percentage of the total Indian population. The only sections of the Saskatchewan territory where the Ojibwa were an important group were in the forested Carrot, Red Deer, and Swan River valleys.

As the discussions of tribal migrations have suggested, the Assiniboine and Cree experienced quite different patterns of population growth after 1821.[7] The Assiniboine increased rapidly in numbers until 1838, when they were ravaged by a smallpox epidemic. Comparing the estimate of Alexander Henry the Younger of 850 lodges for the Plains Assiniboine in 1809 with E. Denig's calculation of 1200 lodges for the same group in 1838 just prior to the epidemic, it seems that the population of the tribe had increased by approximately 30 per cent in thirty years, assuming that the ratio of people per tipi had not changed significantly. According to Denig the outbreak of smallpox in 1838 reduced their numbers to fewer than 3000 people, living in some 400 lodges.[8] It would appear, therefore, that this catastrophe had carried off two-thirds of their population. Furthermore, in contrast to their experience after the 1781 epidemic, recovery was slow and they never completely regained their losses.[9]

The picture which emerges of Cree population growth during this period contrasts sharply with that of the Assiniboine. As the estimates of Alexander Henry the Younger and those of the Hudson's Bay Company district reports have shown, the Plains Cree were reckoned to have had between 200 and 300 lodges in the early 1820s. In 1833, Prince Maximilian estimated that the number of lodges totaled between 600 and 800, suggesting that their population was increasing much more rapidly than that of the Assiniboine. In addition, judging from the data which is available, the smallpox epidemic of 1838 did not have the same disastrous effect on the Cree as it did on their Assiniboine neighbours. For example, in 1853, Dr F. Hayden listed 1080 lodges for them, hinting that their population growth rate had remained quite high throughout most of the first six decades in the nineteenth century.[10] The smallpox epidemic which ravaged the Assiniboine thus apparently left the Cree relatively unscathed.

The contrasting experiences of the two tribes to the epidemic of 1837–8 appears to have been largely a result of point of entry of the disease into Western Canada, the paths of its diffusion, and the different measures which the various trading companies took to arrest the progress of the disease. As Figure 44 shows, the pattern of diffusion of the epidemic was quite similar to that of the outbreak of 1780–1 (Figure 35). Smallpox was first reported at the American trading posts on the Missouri River. It was at these posts, in particular at Fort Union, that the Assiniboine contracted the disease. Repeating past Indian reactions to this dreaded illness, they fled northward hoping to escape it. In this way, the Assiniboine quickly carried the disease northward into Saskatchewan and by November it had broken out among the Indians living in the vicinity of Carlton House.[11] Smallpox was also reported to be in the country around Edmonton House by the same time. According to John Rowand who was stationed there, the Blood Indians were the first to have contracted the disease and they appear to have been the principal carriers. As the epidemic ran its course, the Blood, Sarsi, Piegan, Blackfoot, and Assiniboine all suffered heavy losses – with up to three-quarters of their population being carried away, according to the Hudson's Bay Company traders.[12] John Rowand indicated that the Gros Ventre also caught the disease, but did not experience the same magnitude of loss because they had had the disease more recently than their neighbours.[13]

The Cree of Saskatchewan, on the other hand, were largely spared through the efforts of the Hudson's Bay Company men resident there – particularly those of William Todd, who was stationed at Fort Pelly. Todd appears to have been the first of the company men to have learned of the outbreak of smallpox. On 20 September, three Cree from the forks of the Qu'Appelle River arrived at the post and, according to Todd, 'they report that some bad disease has got into the American Fort in Consequence of which their gates are kept constantly Shut and no Indian Allowed to enter.'[14] Although he was not sure what the disease was, Todd suspected it was smallpox and began to take immediate action. The next day, 21 September, he wrote that he 'had all the Indians now here Enter'd in ... a full explanation with them respecting the reports brought yesterday of the disease at the American establishment which I pointed out to them was likely to be the Small Pox, and the danger they incurred if it once got among them[.] [I] proposed Vaccination as the only prevention to this ... They at once agreed, and I immediately Commenced and Vaccinated

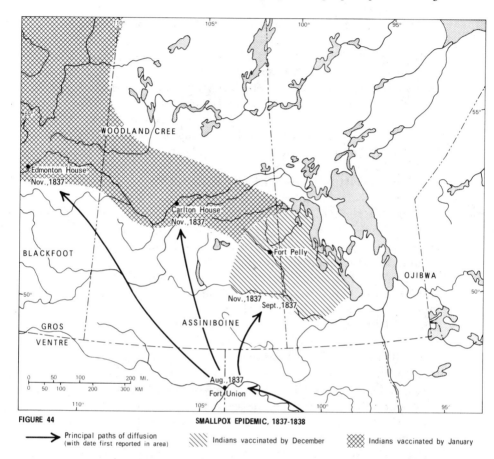

FIGURE 44   SMALLPOX EPIDEMIC, 1837-1838

→ Principal paths of diffusion (with date first reported in area)

\\\\ Indians vaccinated by December

XXXX Indians vaccinated by January

Sixty persons including Men Women and Children.'[15] Thus, before smallpox had been confirmed, Todd began what seems to have been the first massive vaccination campaign among the Indians of Western Canada in the hopes of arresting the progress of the epidemic.

The vaccine which Todd used had been provided earlier by the company and was of the newer cowpox variety which came into general use in Europe between 1790 and 1839.[16] The company directors had sent this vaccine to Canada in the hopes that the traders would make widespread use of it for both humanitarian and business reasons. But, in spite of encouragements from London, the traders had largely failed to do so, much to the distress of the governor and committee of the company, and few Indians had been vaccinated prior to the outbreak of smallpox in 1837.

Having initiated his vaccination program, Todd vaccinated all of the Indians who came into the post, even though it was not until late in December that he was sure that the reported epidemic was smallpox due to conflicting accounts which he received from the Indians. Confirmation came in a dispatch from Carlton House which was delivered by two company men on 20 December. All lingering doubt was dispelled on 23 December, when one of these two men, Pierre Le Rosque, came down with the disease and died from it on 5 January 1839.[17] With this evidence Todd redoubled his efforts. He had already taught several Indian leaders how to vaccinate their followers and sent them away with the supplies they needed to carry out the program. Many of these Indians were said to have been vigorous in their efforts to fulfil his instructions. In addition, on 28 December, he dispatched John Cummings northward to Shoal River and Swan Lake to vaccinate the Indians living there.

On 8 January he sent the surviving Carlton man back to the latter post along with two of his own men with vaccine and detailed instructions as to how it was to be administered. The vaccine was intended for use in the Carlton, Ile à la Crosse, and Edmonton districts. William Small at Carlton House had previously vaccinated his men, including the two whom he had dispatched to Fort Pelly in December, but the vaccine did not work and therefore he had asked for a fresh supply from William Todd.[18] Alexander McLeod, stationed at Fort Chipewyan had also asked for a supply on 30 December since his reserve was low and he suspected that it too was dormant like that of Carlton House. Similarly, R. Mackenzie Simon stationed at Ile à la Crosse was anxious to obtain fresh vaccine. He was particularly eager to receive the new vaccine because he feared that the close communications which were maintained between his district and that of Carlton House would facilitate the spread of the disease from the latter area.[19] The situation was equally desperate at Edmonton House. Rowand, who was in charge of the district, does not appear to have had any vaccine on hand when smallpox reached the area, nor any familiarity with vaccination procedures.[20] Therefore, William Todd's dispatch on 8 January was received with considerable relief in all three areas.

As a result of this extensive vaccination program many of the Plains Cree and nearly all of the Parkland and Woodland Indians living in south central Manitoba, Saskatchewan, and eastern Alberta were saved. Also, this vaccinated population set up a barrier which prevented any further spread of the disease to the north and east and during the course of the winter the epidemic died out (Figure 44). Regarding the unfortunate Assiniboine, on 25 January 1838, William Todd wrote:

men arrived from Beaver Creek by W. McKay's letter the Mortality among the Plains tribes from Small Pox has been very great, but principally confined to the Assiniboins who keep to the souther'd and in general traded with the Americans, about 200 tents have traded this year at Beaver Creek got vaccinated and have so far escaped and these are nearly all that remain of that once Numerous tribe.[21]

Although we might be tempted to conclude that Todd was perhaps exaggerating the effects of his efforts to control the disease, the contrasting population growth curves of the Assiniboine and Cree lends support to his claim. Furthermore, his estimation of the Assiniboine losses are corroborated by the pre- and post-epidemic approximations of their population given by Denig.[22]

As a consequence of the different experiences of the various tribes to the epidemic and the steady migration of Cree into the parkland-grassland area from the woodlands, the Cree became one of the most populous Indian groups living in the prairie provinces. For example, in 1863 Palliser estimated that the Plains Cree north of the United States border numbered about 11,500, whereas he believed that the population of the Assiniboine in Saskatchewan totaled only 1000. Another 4000 Assiniboine lived to the south of the border towards the Missouri River. To the west, Palliser estimated the population of the Blackfoot, Blood, Piegan, and Sarsi to number 600, 2800, 4400, and 1100 respectively.[23]

During the summer of 1869, yet another epidemic of smallpox broke out. As in the two previous instances, it was first contracted by the Assiniboine on the Missouri River who carried it northward. However, this time there was no vaccine on hand at the trading posts in Saskatchewan or Alberta. Apparently vaccine was to be found only in the Red River colony and the people there were vaccinated as soon as rumors of the disease reached the colony.[24]

Fortunately for the Indians of the Qu'Appelle regions, two Métis families arrived at Fort Qu'Appelle in the autumn and some of them had been vaccinated. Isaac Cowie, who was stationed at the post, and lacked a supply of cowpox vaccine decided to attempt to employ the older, no longer widely used preventive measure of inoculation.

I at once asked Mr. Breland [a Métis] to allow me to take the lymph from his grandchild's arm, and he gladly gave the permission.

I rode out to their camp with them ... and from a fine healthy child I secured, on bits of window glass, enough vaccine to protect everyone requiring it in the Fort, from whom the supply was increased sufficiently to vaccinate all the people about the lakes and the Indians visiting them that fall. With the fear of the former visitation before them, those who had been vaccinated at the fort took it out to the plains and spread it so thoroughly there among the Qu'Appelle and Touchwood Hills Indians that not one single case of smallpox was ever heard among them.[25]

Unfortunately, other Indians were not vaccinated and suffered heavily, particularly the Assiniboine, the various Blackfoot groups, and the Cree living along the North Saskatchewan. Thanks to Cowie's efforts, and vaccination and quarantine measures in Manitoba, the disease did not spread down the Saskatchewan into the Swan River district nor to the Red River.[26] Adding to the suffering of the Indians, widespread starvation followed the epidemic, carrying off many who had survived.[27] Thus, as the pre-reservation period was coming to a close, the Indians suffered yet another serious setback which was reflected in the 1871 population estimations for Manitoba and the Northwest Territories. According to the report of the Indian Branch, the Cree were said to have a population of about 7000, the Assiniboine of Saskatchewan 500, the Blackfoot 4000, the Blood 2000, the Piegan 3000, and the Sarsi only 200. The Woodland Cree were estimated at 425, the same total given earlier by Palliser.[28] It is unclear whether this was due to a lower mortality rate in the woodlands, or whether it simply reflected the fact that no new data was available. The latter explanation seems to be the most plausible since the figures are identical.

The period between 1821 and 1870 was one of rapidly changing demographic conditions. Until 1838 all of the Indian groups living to the west of the Red River, especially the Assiniboine, experienced rapid increases in their numbers. Because of its differential impact upon Indian populations, the smallpox epidemic of 1838 brought about considerable change in the relative numerical strength of the various tribal groups. In particular, the Cree suffered fewer losses, and therefore, emerged as one of the largest groups. Having been largely spared, their population continued to grow rapidly as a result of natural increases and a steady outward migration of Cree from the woodlands. By 1860, their population may have been as much as three to five times the size it had been in 1800. These differential losses and growth rates strongly influenced tribal migrations, especially in Saskatchewan where the Cree moved into areas largely vacated by Assiniboine.

NOTES

1 Report to the Governor and Committee in London, 26 August 1831, PAC HBC D/98, p. 23
2 Report to the Governor and Committee in London, 1838, PAC HBC D 4/106, p. 30
3 Thwaites, 'Maximilian, Prince of Weid, Travels in the Interior of North America, 1833–1834,' 13–14
4 *Five Indian Tribes*, xxvi–xxvii, 63
5 These reports were cited by Wissler in his population study of the northern plains Indians, 'Population Changes among the Northern Plains Indians,' 7. According to Captain John Palliser only 1000 Assiniboine were still living in the grasslands of Canada. Some of them traded at Fort Ellice during the winter. Palliser, *The Journals*, 201
6 Lesser Slave Lake District Report, 1823, PAC HBC B 115/e/1, p. 4. One of the most important Indian chiefs in the department was an Ojibwa. He was a 'Hudson's Bay Company Chief.' The Northwest Company had had a different chief. Cree were said to be the most numerous.
7 Little data is available for the Ojibwa during this period. Being a small group, they were often included by travellers in their estimations for the Assiniboine and Cree. Therefore, the following discussion will focus on the latter two tribes whose different experiences highlight the population trends which were underway at that time.
8 *Five Indian Tribes*, 72. A Mr Harriet, an employee of the Hudson's Bay Company, and Mr Rowand, chief factor of the Edmonton District, listed figures for the Strongwood and Plains Assiniboine in 1842 which totalled 380 lodges. These figures lend support to Denig's appraisal of the magnitude of the loss which the tribe had suffered. Hind, *Territories du Nord-Ouest, Rapports de Progres*, 18
9 Palliser, *The Journals*, 202, and Wissler, 'Population Changes,' 7
10 'Contributions to the Ethnology and Philology of the Indian Tribes of the Upper Missouri Valley,' 236–8. In all probability Hayden's figures were those of E. Denig. See, Denig, *Five Indian Tribes*, xxxv–xxxvii. In 1855 Denig estimated that the Cree had 1000 to 1100 lodges, *ibid.*, 109. Both Denig's figures and those of Hayden are much lower than Palliser's tally for 1863 of 1920. The discrepancy is difficult to account for. Considering his long association with the Indians of the region, those of Denig probably are more accurate.
11 John Rowand, Edmonton House, 28 December 1837, to Governor George Simpson, PAC HBC D 5/4, p. 360
12 Ibid.

13 Edmonton House, 5 January 1839, to Governor George Simpson, PAC HBC D 5/5, p. 89

14 Fort Pelly Post Journal, 1837–8, PAC HBC B 159/a/17, p. 2

15 Ibid.

16 John Rowand, Edmonton House, 28 December 1837, to Governor George Simpson, PAC HBC D 5/4, p. 360; and letter from Hudson's Bay House, London, 1 June 1838, to Governor George Simpson, PAC HBC D 5/5, p. 49. In this dispatch the company's directors indicated that they were sending new vaccine to all of the districts and the traders were informed that they must exert every effort to vaccinate all of the Indians in their areas.

17 For Pelly Post Journal, 1837–8, PAC HBC B 159/a/17, p. 11. According to John Rowand, Le Rosqeu's death had a demoralizing affect on the company's men since he had been vaccinated with the newer cowpox vaccine. This raised fears in their minds that vaccinations would not control the spread of the disease. John Rowand, Edmonton House, 28 December 1837, to Governor George Simpson, PAC HBC D 5/4, p. 360

18 Fort Pelly Post Journal, 1837–8, PAC HBC B 159/a/17, p. 12

19 Alexander McLeod, Fort Chipeweyan, 30 December 1837, to Governor George Simpson, PAC HBC D 5/4, p. 364, and Mackenzie Simon, Isle à la Crosse District, 10 January 1838, to Governor George Simpson, PAC HBC D 5/5 p. 5

20 Rowand indicated in his 28 December 1837 letter to Governor Simpson that it was very distressing not to have the medical assistance necessary to look after his own men or the Indians, PAC HBC D 5/4, p. 360

21 Fort Pelly Post Journal, 1837–8, PAC HBC B 159/a/17, p. 13

22 Five Indian Tribes, 68–72. Indeed, in Denig's account he credits the Hudson's Bay Company's vaccination program for having saved 200 of the 400 lodges of Assiniboine who survived the epidemic.

23 Detailed Reports, 200

24 Cowie, The Company of Adventurers, 381

25 Ibid., 382

26 Ibid.

27 Christie, Chief Factor, Edmonton House to Liet. Governor Archibald, 13 April 1781, Sessional Papers, 7, no. 22, p. 32

28 'Comparative Statement of the Population of the Indian Tribes and Bands Throughout Canada between the years 1870–71,' Sessional Papers, 7, no. 22, p. 60

11

Declining opportunities in a changing fur trade

After a protracted struggle for control of the fur trade, the two chief competitors, the Hudson's Bay Company and the North West Company, joined forces in 1821. This merger marked the end of an era of bitter rivalry and set in motion forces which were to have a profound effect on the lives of the Indians of southern Manitoba and Saskatchewan. Significantly, the merger gave the Hudson's Bay Company a new, if short-lived, monopoly on the fur trade throughout most of Western Canada, except the boundary region where American traders carried on a clandestine trade north of the border. Although the monopoly was undermined somewhat over time by the activities of private traders, usually Métis and company servants who quit from time to time to strike out on their own, this new opposition was limited in scale during the 1820s. Indeed, throughout the period between 1821 and 1870 the level of trade rivalries did not approach that of earlier years.

When George Simpson was installed as governor of the newly organized company and placed in charge of its operations in Canada, he planned to institute a series of reforms which were aimed at placing the fur trade on a more economical basis. In his report to the governor and committee in London dated 31 July 1822, Simpson outlined his intended plan of action:

In regard to the proposed reduction on the standard of Trade, no question exists that it would be much to the interest of the concern and beneficial to the Indians could it be effected, if at the same time the system of giving presents and treats was abolished, but it will be difficult and require a great length of time and much caution to bring such reform about. During the heat of opposition in some Districts, it was necessary to give Indians expensive presents in Clothing, Guns, etc., whether they made a hunt or not in order to attach them to either party ... This ruinous practice has been discontinued and nothing beyond Tobacco and Ammunition in some parts and a few trifles such as Firesteels, Needles, Vermillion, etc., in others have been given and occasionally a dress to a Chief or Indian of considerable influence ... Heavy Debts are ascertained to be injurious to the Trade and of little benefit to the Indians, it is therefore understood that no more shall be given than there is a reasonable prospect of being repaid.[1]

From this statement it is clear that Simpson hoped to make some basic changes in the trading system. However, in the parkland area trade practices remained largely unchanged and at best the company managed only to trim the excesses. For example, Isaac Cowie indicates that in southern Saskatchewan as late as the 1860s the Plains Indians, particularly the Cree, were still in the habit of sending one or two men into the posts to pick up trade goods in advance of the arrival of the trading parties. The usual presents sent out to them were tobacco, as before, as well as sugar and tea. When the band arrived at the post a feast was held at the conclusion of which the chief was given food and clothing and 'was presented with the semi annual gratuities – tea, tobacco, ammunition, etc. – which his written and carefully wrapped up certificate as a Company's chief specified.'[2] Following this exchange, the chief and his followers made their presents; then the company's traders gave in return 'Quantities of tea, tobacco, sugar, and perhaps some other rare expensive luxuries, such as flour, rice and raisins ... preliminary to the individual payment in full to each of those who had contributed to the "presents" strictly according to his proportion.'[3] Thus, gift-giving was still a central feature of the trade, but rather than make liberal presents of fancy clothing to many Indians, along with beads, bells, and other frills, as well as alcohol, the traders gave away smaller gifts – mostly of food stuffs.

Credit was still being extended to the Plains Assiniboine, Cree, and Ojibwa. However, the company had returned to its earlier practice of the pre-1763 period of limiting the credit given to individual Indians to the amount which the local traders could reasonably expect them to repay. Under this system Cowie indicated that successful traders were those who knew thoroughly the capabilities and reliability of all the Indians who lived in their district as well as the state of the country's resources. With a firm grasp of this information they could keep their accounts reasonably current.[4]

In the forested districts the company was able to institute more radical reforms and implement them more quickly because of the increasing economic dependency of the Woodland Indians and the lack of effective opposition throughout much of their territory. Under these conditions, the Indians had little choice but to go along with the changes which the Hudson's Bay Company introduced. In 1825 Governor Simpson reported to London that the frilly and expensive gifts given to band leaders in the past had largely been discontinued even though initially the Indians had strongly opposed this new policy. Also, he indicated that credit abuses had been brought under control and smaller advances were being given out.[5] As a humanitarian gesture, gifts of ammunition were being given to aged and infirm Indians. Simpson stated that the Indians who received them were thereby able to attach themselves to a good hunter who would then look after them in exchange for these supplies.[6]

Since Governor Simpson also regarded the practice of trading high-quality goods to the Indians as an unnecessary extravagence born out of competitive conditions, he further proposed that in the future cheaper goods be brought in. For example, he urged the Company to send cheaper trade blankets.[7] He believed that this was especially important for the Woodland Indian trade because deteriorating resource conditions in those areas were making it increasingly difficult for the Indians to obtain enough furs and produce to purchase the goods they needed. This problem was being exacerbated by the growing dependence of Woodland Cree and Ojibwa on the company for clothing. Regarding this subject, in an 1828 report to London Simpson wrote:

The consumption of woollens, I am concerned to say is increasing very much throughout the country among the natives, this is a very heavy and costly article for which they cannot afford to pay in many Districts where Furs are become scarce, and which might, in a great measure be dispensed with, as we find that the Plains Indians who use no other articles of Dress then such are made of Leather and Rabbit skins are as healthy as those who are entirely clothed in British manufactures; the increasing demand for this article from all parts of the country is the only general course of complaint I have against our commissioned Gentlemen [Company factors] and I trust they will not give further occasion to repeat it.[8]

Thus the governor hoped to end the long-standing company practice of attempting to encourage the Indians to use English clothing.[9] However, he was unsuccessful since these articles were no longer luxury items to the Indians, except those who inhabited the plains region.

In order to comply with new parliamentary regulations regarding the fur trade and as part of its policy to trim excesses and bring about more orderly conditions, the Hudson's Bay Company made a concerted effort to reduce the use of alcohol in trade.[10] In order to achieve this end Governor Simpson informed the company directors in London in 1822:

we have taken steps as will tend to wean the Indians from their insatiable thirst for Spirituous Liquors by passing a resolution that no more than half the quantity usually allowed be given as presents and that trade in Furs for that article (which was very limited) be altogether discontinued.[11]

In the parkland-grassland area this policy was implemented gradually. Simpson pointed out that until the company's dependency on the Plains Indians' provision supplies were reduced, he couldn't risk alienating them. Furthermore, he believed that, unless some indulgence was permitted, a sudden discontinuance of their supplies of brandy and rum might lead the militarily powerful Plains Tribes to attack company posts.[12] By the 1860s, in spite of the fact that 'free traders' were bringing rum to the Indians from the American posts south of the border, the Hudson's Bay Company had discontinued trading alcohol or giving it as gifts to tribal groups living in the grasslands.[13] According to Walter Traill, although the company lost some of the trade to the 'free traders' as a consequence it was nonetheless able to hold a large portion of it by virtue of its more favourable standards and greater array of other commodities.[14]

As with other reforms, the reduction of Indian consumption of spirits was brought about more quickly in the woodland region. As early as 1826, only four years after the temperance policy was introduced, Simpson reported 'we came to the determination of sending no more Liquors of any description to any Establishment North of Cumberland House.'[15] Thus, after a very brief transitional period the company attempted to impose a total ban in the more northerly forested lands.

In addition to his attempts to economize and amend trading operations, Simpson believed that many of the over-hunted woodland and parkland districts could be brought back into production and operated on a sustained yield basis. Reflecting this optimism, in his 1822 report to London he wrote, 'The country is without doubt in many parts exhausted in valuable Furs [,] yet not to such a low ebb as has been generally supposed and by extending the Trade in some parts and nursing others our prospects are by no means unfavourable.'[16]

One of his first efforts to 'nurse' the fur trade back – especially the beaver trade – consisted of encouraging and cajoling the Indians to stop the practice of taking skins out of season, that is, during the summer. Accordingly, in his report for 1822 he said 'the Indians have been informed that Skins out of Season will not be taken off their hands.'[17] In a similar vein he tried to encourage the Indians to stop taking cub beaver during the winter; but he doubted this effort would succeed since the Indians considered the meat of the young beaver to be a delicacy. And indeed, the attempts to discourage summer trapping of this animal failed for similar reasons. In many districts food had become so scarce that the Indians would kill and eat beaver whenever they ran across them. To prevent the Hudson's Bay Company traders from finding out, the Indians would not bring these pelts into the posts for trade. In fact, to avoid detection they often hid the furs or disposed of them in such a way that no one could find them.[18]

To reduce the effectiveness of Indian trapping operations and thereby give beaver populations a chance to rebound, Simpson believed the use of steel traps should be discontinued. In 1822 he wrote: 'The uses of Beaver Traps should have been prohibited long ago, they are the scourge of the Country and none will in the future be given out except for new Districts exposed to opposition and frontier establishments.'[19]

In addition to his efforts to end the practices of taking summer furs and cub beaver and using steel traps, Simpson made repeated efforts to persuade the Indians in various districts not to trap endangered species for periods of one or more years depending on local conditions. In order to achieve this aim the governor and the various district factors and traders employed a variety of devices. Recognizing the difficulties in obtaining Indian approval to local moratoriums on the trapping of particular animals, Simpson began to shift trading posts around within districts in accordance with fluctuations in fur resources. For example, in 1824 he closed Fort Dauphin and the Swan and Red Deer River posts in the Swan River District and opened Fort Pelly on the Upper Assiniboine River (Figure 45). He reasoned that the Indians would gravitate toward the latter post, giving other parts of the district a chance to recover.[20] Similar shifts were made in other departments. Generally these moves had a positive effect and in the Swan River and upper Red River areas, for instance, fur populations, especially beaver, were reported to be rebounding by 1826.[21]

Besides shifting post locations as local conditions warranted, the company attempted to swing the focus of Indian trapping activities from one fur animal species to another. In doing this the traders hoped to take advantage of the natural fluctuations of animal populations which took

place and of the fact that the variations of one species often com-
plemented rather than paralleled those of others. Therefore, heavy
hunting pressure could be brought to bear on one animal species while
others would be allowed to recruit their losses. This practice of hunting
different animals in alternating periods worked particularly well in
southern Manitoba and the adjacent portions of northern Ontario and
eastern Saskatchewan where muskrat were plentiful. As noted earlier, the
population of the latter animal varied widely depending on water-level
fluctuations. For example, in Western Canada the years 1822, 1823, and
1824 were dry while the period between 1825 and 1830 was wet. During
the wet phase the Hudson's Bay Company made every effort to get the
Indians to focus their attention on trapping muskrat as the numbers of
the latter increased. Meanwhile the Indians were encouraged to allow
beaver and marten to recover. According to Simpson this policy was
responsible for the drop in beaver and marten returns from the Cumberland, Swan River, and Red River departments in the late 1820s.[22] Beginning in 1830 the trend was reversed and these same areas showed an
increase in marten, beaver, and cat (lynx) returns while those of muskrat
dropped off drastically.

Most of the company's schemes depended upon the persuasiveness of
various district traders and factors and on the willingness of the latter to
go along with Simpson's long-term aim of putting the fur trade on a
sustained-yield basis. Yet, there was always the temptation to the local
traders to increase their fur intake on a short-term basis and therefore
'look good' in the company's eyes in terms of profits. Also, Indians who
lived in one district could trade their furs in another if individual traders
attempted to be too insistent on conservation measures. In order to deal
with these problems the company decided upon a more coercive plan of
action. In 1826 a quota system was introduced in the Northern Department. Under this scheme, the average beaver returns of each of the
fourteen districts of the department were determined for the three-year
period between 1823 and 1825. Using this as a base, each district was
allowed to take a percentage of that average. These values are shown in
Table 8. In the case of two districts, those of the lower Red River and Lac
la Pluie, beaver trapping quotas were not established since they could not
be enforced due to the close proximity of the American traders. In the
other districts the fur trade was reduced from between one-fifth to one-
half of what it had been. Simpson indicated that all of these quotas would
be rigidly enforced except that of the Saskatchewan District. There larger
intakes of beaver would be permitted since much of that trade came from

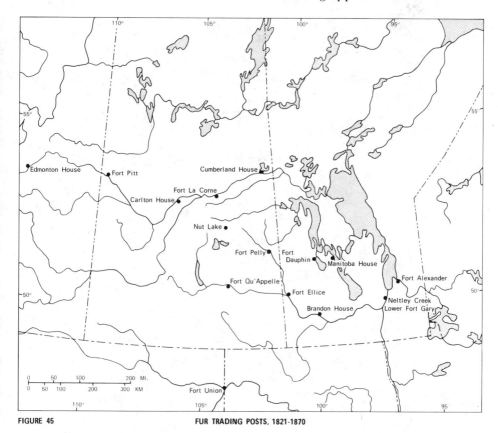

FIGURE 45   FUR TRADING POSTS, 1821-1870

the Pigean Indians who obtained it from trading and raiding south of the Canadian border.[23] In the case of the Saskatchewan District this was part of Simpson's plan to nurse the local country back. In a sense, he was using the resources of the American side of the border to cover the expense of his conservation effort. In subsequent years the quotas of the various districts were adjusted by the governor and the governing council for the Northern Department as conditions warranted.[24] In attempting to implement these various schemes the Hudson's Bay Company faced a number of serious obstacles. The Woodland Cree and Ojibwa attitudes towards conservation, territoriality, and trespassing, and the lack of any strong coercive political institutions among these groups were particularly troublesome. Regarding conservation, the Indians were unaccus-

TABLE 8
Fur quotas for 1826*

Beaver Assorted	Athabascan	Saskatchewan, Lesser Slave Lake, and Ft Assiniboine	English River	Cumberland	Swan River and upper Red River	Lower Red River	Winnipeg	Lac la Pluie	Norway House	Island Lake	Severn	Nelson River	Churchill	York Factory
Outfit 1823	7726	7800	1757	272	663	30	44	826	138	352	660	794	447	504
Outfit 1824	5479	6493	1201	303	644	37	123	735	7	187	368	1033	317	370
Outfit 1825	6186	6896	1078	397	433	80	76	501	26	152	211	702	342	285
Total returns in beaver for 3 years	19,391	21,189	4036	972	1740	147	243	2062	171	691	1239	2529	1106	1159
Average per year	6463	7063	1345	324	580	49	81	687	57	230	413	843	368	386
Less	1292†	1412†	673**	162**	145‡		27†		29**	115**	207**	422**	184**	193**
Quota not to be exceeded in Outfit 1826	5771	5651	672	162	435		54		28	115	206	421	184	193

* HBC D4/89, and Fleming, *Minutes of Council*
† Less approximately one-fifth of average
‡ Less approximately one-quarter of average
** Less approximately one-half of average

tomed to long-range planning and saving. Rather, they lived on a day-to-day basis and believed that if the animal spirits were given due respect there would always be enough game for the future.[25] If the traders managed to convince particular Indian bands that they should conserve their resources and that various species should not be hunted year after year when they were being endangered locally the neighbouring bands would often move in and trap the animals. This occurred because traditionally there was no well-developed sense of territoriality or trespass among these groups. Band territories were not sharply defined, but rather bands tended to return to the same general area year after year. However, neighbouring groups could encroach on any portions of a band's hunting range which was not being exploited in a given year. Likewise, unexploited resources in a territory were considered to be 'free resources' which any party could use.[26] Under these conditions game management was not possible because whenever a group agreed not to hunt beaver, muskrat, or some other animal for an extended period, bands living in the adjacent country had every right to move in and hunt them.

In an effort to deal with this problem Governor Simpson initiated a new company policy that was to profoundly affect the lives of the Indians. He proposed settling Indian families in well-defined territories on a permanent basis. He fully realized that this would involve changing a basic feature of the Indian life style – mobility – and that a family territory system was not well suited to all areas because of varying cultural and ecological conditions. Regarding these matters, in his 1828 report to the directors in London he wrote:

On the subject of nursing the country ... the plan suggested in ... my Dispatch from Moose [Factory] of allotting certain tracts of country to the different Bands can only be carried into full effect in extended Districts such as Albany, where the population is very thin; but in small districts frequented by Rein Deer and where the Fisheries are not numerous the Indians are under the necessity of going sometimes from one extremity thereof, to the other, in search of the means of living ... We are endeavouring to confine the natives throughout the country now by families, to separate and distinct hunting grounds, and in a few years, I hope it will become general, but it is a very difficult matter to change the habits of Indians although they may see the ultimate benefit thereof to themselves and families.[27]

As Simpson thus recognized, population densities, game conditions and the economic orientations of the various bands determined whether or not the new scheme would work.

Generally, as long as the Indians focused their subsistence activities on the hunting of migratory large-game animals a rigid family territory system was unworkable. However, as was discussed previously, by the 1820s these animals were becoming scarce in many tracts of wooded country, especially the lands east of Lake Winnipeg and the Winnipeg River. As a consequence, the Indians were forced either to abandon these areas and move to more favourable regions such as the parkland-grassland territory, as many did, or to use small game and fish resources more intensively. The latter resources were more fixed and could be successfully exploited by less mobile Indian populations. This transition from large game to small game and fish-oriented subsistence economies became widespread by the middle of the nineteenth century and facilitated the adoption of the family territory system in many forested districts – especially in the more northerly departments which were not within the effective range of American competition or the Selkirk colony.[28]

Indeed, without a monopoly none of the company's conservation schemes were feasible since there was no means of enforcing them. This was recognized at the outset, and as noted earlier no attempts were made to set beaver quotas in the Red River and Lac la Pluie Districts due to the proximities of the American posts. Likewise, the ban against the trading of steel traps to the Indians had to be lifted in the northern Ontario area in 1848 because the Indians were obtaining them from American traders.[29] The Hudson's Bay Company faced similar problems in the Cumberland Lake and Swan River departments. For example, in 1827 Simpson reported that it would be necessary to re-open Fort Dauphin which had been closed in 1824 even though he felt the district should be rested another three years. He said this action was necessitated by the fact that the Indians, Freemen, and Settlers (Selkirk colonists) were hunting the land anyway and taking their returns to the 'Petty traders' at the Red River settlements.[30] Because of the district's proximity to the colony this illegal trade was difficult to control and led Simpson to the conclusion that any future attempts to manage the game resources of the district would be futile. Therefore, he proposed to operate Dauphin House only until such time as it became unprofitable to do so. He then planned to close it permanently.

Although most of the above-mentioned attempts at economy and game management more strongly affected the Woodland Indians, especially those living in the areas where the Hudson's Bay Company held a virtual monopoly, the re-organization of the fur trade after 1821 also had important implications for the lives of the parkland-grassland tribes. Of particular importance to these groups, Simpson's efforts to streamline trading operations led him to eliminate redundant posts which were a product of competition. He also closed the costly overland canoe route to Montreal. These moves had the effect of considerably reducing the manpower requirements of the fur trade. Many men were therefore released from company service. It has been estimated that the fur-trade labour force was therefore cut by as much as two-thirds.[31]

The men who were released from service were mostly of Indian-European ancestry and they began to congregate in the Red River valley. Many of these people, particularly those of French-speaking background, developed a strong sense of self-identity and regarded themselves as different from either the Indian or the white groups resident in the region. They came to be known as the Métis or Freemen. As early as 1821 some 500 of them had gathered in the vicinity of the Pembina River post. The colonial authorities, fearful that this group would come under the influence of the Americans if they remained there, persuaded the Métis to move northward in 1823 and they resettled primarily in two locations, the parish of St Boniface on the east side of the Red River opposite its confluence with the Assiniboine River, and to the westward up the Assiniboine in the region of the White Horse Plains.[32] The size of the group grew rapidly thereafter due to its high natural rate of increase and the steady influx of new Métis settlers which was being maintained by the continuing retirement of men from the company. In addition, many Métis who had been employed by the Nor'Westers found service in the Hudson's Bay Company, their old rival, distasteful, and considerable numbers of them quit after a short period of time. Others tried their hand at farming after leaving the fur trade, but it was a way of life which was more tedious. Consequently, large numbers of them abandoned their farmsteads and took up the more nomadic life style which became characteristic of the Métis.

Reflecting these trends, the Métis, who totaled only 500 persons in 1821, increased in numbers to nearly 1300 in 1831 and 2600 in 1843. By 1856 the population had climbed to 3250, while in 1870 it exceeded 12,000. Besides these Red River Métis, there was another Métis settlement in the area of the present city of Portage la Prairie, Manitoba. However, it was much smaller than the colony to the east, having no more than 120 residents in 1856.[33]

The emergence of this rather large group had important consequences for the Parkland and Grassland Indians living in Manitoba and Saskatchwan. Since many of the Métis had served at the parkland provision posts of the North West Company and had married Assiniboine and Plains Cree women while stationed there, they were quite familiar with the Plains Indian way of life. Indeed, they used it as a model to pattern many aspects of their own culture. The meat of the bison was their favourite food and in the summer they organized the famous Red River buffalo hunts. The hunts were similar to those of the Indians in most respects, with the exception that the Métis used the two-wheeled Red River cart rather than the travois to transport their produce. Each cart could carry up to 900 pounds and enabled the Métis to transport very large quantities of meat over long distances with relative ease.[34]

Soon after their inception around 1820 these hunts became a central feature of the Métis way of life and they provided the group with its principal source of income. As a result they rapidly increased in scale. In 1820, 540 carts were dispatched from the colony; ten years later the number had risen to 820 and by 1840 to 1210.[35] In terms of transportation capacity, the Métis could have brought back 486,000 pounds of provisions in 1820; 738,000 pounds in 1830 and 1,089,000 in 1840. They disposed of most of their rather large surplus by selling it to the Hudson's Bay Company and to the Selkirk colonists who began settling along the Red River below the forks in 1812. The latter outlet was small, however, and most of the excess went to the company. Thus, the Métis emerged as serious competitors with the prairie Indians for the fur-trade provision market.

In addition to the Métis buffalo hunters, the Indian provisioners in the eastern parklands had to contend with the colonial farmers; however, this rivalry was a modest one at best. It was not until the late 1820s that agriculture, in conjunction with the returns from the Red River buffalo hunts, was able to feed the colony's population adequately. Thereafter, a small surplus was available for trade and consisted largely of flour. For example, in 1825 the colony supplied the Hudson's Bay Company with 200 hundredweight of this product. In 1833 it furnished 1200 hundredweight, and in 1845, 750 hundredweight. Other commodities were also traded, such as butter, pork, ham, beef, cheese, eggs, and some vegetables, but only in rather small quantities.[36] Over time, the company's orders for these commodities increased slowly (see Table 9). In brief, the agricultural surpluses which were sold to the Hudson's Bay Company before 1870 were not particularly large, but nonetheless they did further reduce the amounts of food that the company would have been required to purchase from the Indians. Indeed, the deterioration of the competitive position of the Indian in the provision market was further aggravated by the lower volume of demand which was being generated by the fur trade in the 1820s and 1830s. This decline was the result of the reduced scale of operations after 1821, the associated reductions in manpower, the shorter supply routes, and Simpson's economy measures. The magnitude of change can be roughly indicated by comparing the Hudson's Bay Company's request for provisions in the 1820s and 1830s with those of one of its predecessors, the North West Company. In 1813, the latter company alone required 644 bags of pemmican to conduct its operations in Western Canada. In contrast, in the 1820s and 1830s the new combined company's need fluctuated between 500 to slightly more than 700 bags a year.[37] Therefore, initially the newer company, which was engrossing nearly all of the trade, generated provision demand which was roughly of the same magnitude as one of the older firms.

Since it took the Métis a few years to establish themselves as provisioners, and even longer for the colonists to produce a sizable surplus, the Plains Cree and Assiniboine did not feel the effects of a declining market for foodstuffs until the 1830s. As noted earlier, it was partly for this reason that it was difficult for the Hudson's Bay Company to be too insistent that the Plains Assiniboine and Cree and their neighbours accept the new conditions for trade which it was trying to establish after 1821, since these Indians knew the company was still heavily dependent upon them for its food supplies. Commenting on this problem in 1823, Simpson wrote:

The Plain Tribes ... continue as insolent and independent if not more so than ever; they conceive that we are dependent on them for the means of subsistence and consequently assume a high tone, but the most effectual way of bringing them to their senses would be to withdraw the Establishments / particularly those of the Saskatchewan / for two or three years which ... would enable us to deal with them on fair and reasonable terms ... This however cannot be affected until Red River settlement has the means of furnishing us with a considerable stock of Provisions for our Transport business.[38]

Thus, Simpson conceded that the Indians' perception of the company's dependence upon them was accurate, but he hoped to change the situation as quickly as possible. Although he was over-optimistic in his belief that the colony's agricultural output would quickly alleviate the situation, the returns of the Métis hunts were to serve the same end. Indeed, by the 1840s they were bringing in more meat and pemmican than the company required.[39]

TABLE 9

Hudson's Bay Company provision orders for the Northern Department*

	1830	1840	1850	1860	1870
To be supplied by the Saskatchewan Dept.:					
Beef, smoked (cwt.)	–	–	–	–	–
Grease, common (cwt.)	–	–	80	111	127
Grease, soft (kegs)	–	–	16	7	–
Dried meat (100 lb. bales)	–	150	50	100	80
Pemmican, common (90 lb. bags)	–	570	600	700	1,390
Pemmican, fine (45 lb. bags)	–	80	60	58	24
Tongues, buffalo	–	500	500	200	430 (or cured hams)
Pemmican, fine (90 lb. bags)	–	–	–	10	–
To be supplied by the Swan River Department:					
Beef, smoked (cwt.)	–	–	5	–	–
Grease, common (cwt.)	–	–	–	–	–
Grease, soft (kegs)	–	–	–	–	–
Dried meat (100 lb. bales)	–	–	16	10	10
Pemmican, common (90 lb. bags)	–	–	50	200	100
Pemmican, fine (45 lb. bags)	–	–	15	–	–
Tongues, buffalo	–	–	200	–	–
Salt (bushels)	–	30	52	100	100

TABLE 9 (*continued*)
Hudson's Bay Company provision orders for the Northern Department*

	1830	1840	1850	1860	1870
To be supplied by Red River:					
Barley (bushels)	300	30	45	60	70
Corned beef (cwt.)	-	12	6	40	40
Biscuit (cwt.)	-	30	30	45	46½
Butter (firkens†)	-	40	40	46	50 + 2 salted
Butter (½ firkens†)	-	10	10	10	16
Butter (Maccarons)	-	6	8	-	6
Cheese (lbs.)	-	80	300	360	230
Eggs, preserved (kegs)	-	-	12	10	16
Flour, 1st grade (cwt.)	500	650	300	10	50
Flour 1st & 2nd grade (cwt.)	-	-	900	1,700	1,420+ 10 coarse
Hams	-	70	50	40	56
Hogs lard (100 lbs.)	-	-	4	5	3
Dried onions (bushels)	-	3	4	2	-
Potatoes	-	40 (kegs)	24 (bu.)	20 (bu.)	20 (bu.)
Pemmican, common (90 lb. bags)	-	400	650	600	750
Pemmican, fine (45 lb. bags)	-	-	-	-	-
Grease, common (cwt.)	-	-	-	-	-
Dried meat (100 lb. bales)	-	50	100	-	-
Tongues, Buffalo	-	-	-	-	-
Salted pork (cwt.)	-	45	60	80	-

* Minutes of the Council for the Northern Department, 1840–70, PAC HBC B 239/k/1–3
† A firken was equal to a quarter barrel

In succeeding decades the provision market began to change again, however, as game-animal populations continued to decline in forest regions. Accordingly, the pemmican orders of the company increased (see Table 7), but the departments, Saskatchewan for example, were often unable to meet these orders, as the bison ranges contracted in a southerly and southwesterly direction. Compensating somewhat for the reduced provision trade of the 1821–40 period was a growing market for buffalo robes. The demand for these commodities developed largely as a result of the expansion of American fur trade up the Missouri River during the first two decades of the nineteenth century. Prior to that time the Hudson's Bay Company had shown little interest in buffalo robes since they were bulky and therefore costly to transport. The account books for Brandon House, for instance, show that only fifteen robes were traded in 1811, thirty in 1813, and eight in 1814. None were bartered in 1815.[40] At Carlton House, even smaller numbers were being traded. None were listed in 1811 or 1812, only four in 1813, none in 1814, and twenty in 1815.[41] Apparently the company had had little success in its initial attempts to market these commodities in England and the Governing Committee in London ordered Simpson to stop sending them. In his report to London dated 15 August 1823, Simpson said that he would comply with these instructions. However, he indicated that he had sent some hides and robes eastward to Canada and the United States where a market was developing. He dispatched them in canoes with company men who planned to retire in the east.[42]

The American traders on the Missouri River also began to market robes in the Eastern North America market, but on a much larger scale. Between 1815 and 1830 the annual trade of this article has been estimated to have fluctuated between 26,000 to 200,000 robes.[43] Granting that these estimates may be inflated, they nevertheless do indicate that the magnitude of traffic was much greater in that quarter. The principal reason for this difference relates to the cheaper transportation route which was available to the Americans via the Missouri and Mississippi rivers.

The Hudson's Bay Company, on the other hand, was hampered in its attempts to reach the eastern market by its costly overland route. As the Nor'Westers and the French who preceded them had learned, this route was unsatisfactory for the transportation of heavy items like robes due to the expenses which were incurred in transit. Indeed, the Hudson's Bay Company found it was even impractical to ship less bulky furs. For example, during the 1820s there was a sizable market for muskrat in eastern North America and Governor Simpson hoped to take advantage of it. However, the cost of wages, canoes, and equipment which would be required to transport them to Montreal were prohibitive and accordingly, on 5 June 1824, Simpson wrote the directors in London informing them that he could:

scarcely muster the Crews of Six Canoes on any terms and the few who might be prevailed upon to undertake the voyage would exact higher wages than could be offered ... this with the expense of Canoes and Tackle, extra men to bring those Canoes from Lac la Pluie to the place of embarkation, Freight [charges] from Sault Ste. Marie and other contingent expenses would run the charges up to nearly the amount of Gros proceeds. I therefore beg leave to recommend, that if Musquash [muskrat], Robes and leather be admitted to entry on bond in England the whole be sent thither and such quantity thereof as would not be required for the home Market, re-shipped from thence to Canada or the States.[44]

Thus, Simpson had come to the conclusion that it was more economical to ship goods to Canada and the eastern United States via England by ship.

Facing these transportation difficulties, the Hudson's Bay Company was unable to compete on the same footing with the American fur traders for the robe and hide trade of the Plains Indians. As Simpson pointed out:

The Americans ... can afford to give a better price for those Skins than we can, transport being no expense to them as they have merely to pile them up in large flat bottomed Batteaux which require only two men to steer them down current to St. Louis ... in 25 days, whereas our inland navigation is so much obstructed by rapids & falls that small craft sufficiently light to be carried across the portages can only be used, a mode of transport which would cost more than the skins could fetch at Market.[45]

In spite of improvements in its transportation capabilities facilitated by the introduction of York boats, batteaux, and Red River carts, Isaac Cowie stated that as late as the 1860s the American traders could still ship goods more cheaply than the Hudson's Bay Company because they used steam boats on the Missouri River.[46] Therefore, the attractiveness of the Missouri River posts to the Indians which was related to their closer proximity to the bison hunting area was reinforced by the fact that the Indians also obtained the best prices for their hides and robes at these establishments. Consequently, the Americans provided an outlet for a product which might otherwise not have been available – at least not on the same scale.

As time passed, the above pattern changed only slightly. The Hudson's

Bay Company did become more involved in the robe trade, but never to the same extent as the Americans. For example, in 1869 Fort Edmonton shipped 9090 buffalo robes. Fort Carlton traded 1099 robes in 1865, only 58 in 1866, 228 in 1867, and 520 in 1868. At Fort Pitt, the figures were 783 in 1865, 1434 in 1866, 948 in 1867, and 232 in 1868.[47] One important new development did take place, however, which provided the eastern parkland Indians with access to the southern market. In 1844, the Métis initiated the cart trade between Fort Gary on the lower Red River and St Paul over a route which became famous as the Red River Trail. Buffalo robes were among the many items which they carried to the latter city. In 1856, over 7500 of them were taken southward.[48] Although it was probably important to the Indians of southern Manitoba, the cart trade apparently had little effect on the tribes living further to the west. Instead of dealing with Métis middlemen, most of these groups, such as the Assiniboine, dealt directly with the Americans located on the Missouri River, particularly at Fort Union which was situated near the confluence of the Missouri and Yellowstone rivers.

After 1870, the nature of the buffalo trade changed again and the interest shifted from robes to hides in response to the growing demand for leather which was being generated by the tanneries in the eastern United States and Canada. This new alternative assured the Grassland-Parkland Indians of a continued outlet for the products of their hunts when the robe trade began tapering off after the 1860s. Yet, because of the different character of this trade, it also meant that the Indians faced increasingly severe competition from white hunters. Whereas formerly the robes had to be taken during the winter season and took a considerable amount of know-how to prepare, hides were secured in the summer and required little skill to make them ready for trade. As a result, large numbers of non-Indian groups became involved.

The increased hunting pressures brought about by the appearance of the Métis, the demand for robes, and later for hides played a major role in bringing about the final destruction of the northern bison herds in the 1870s and 1800s. However, long before that time these pressures began to have a telling effect on the numbers and range limits of this animal. The Métis hunts rapidly depleted the relatively meager bison resources in southeastern Manitoba, and by the late 1820s Métis hunters were beginning to range as far westward as the vicinity of the Cheyenne River in North Dakota. The herds in southern Manitoba had not been totally annihilated, however, and they were often spotted in the southwestern portions of the province as late as the 1850s and early 1860s. For instance, in 1852 they were reported to be numerous in the vicinity of the present town of Carberry, Manitoba, and nine years later a large herd was seen grazing on the site of the present city of Brandon, Manitoba.[49] The last herd to be reported in the Souris River country was sighted in 1867, and the last wild bison to be killed in that area was taken in 1883.[50] From the above it is therefore clear that long before their final disappearance in the eastern parklands and prairies in the 1880s the principal bison range had contracted to the territory lying farther to the southwest beyond the Cypress Hills.

A similar contraction of the northern range of the animal was well under way by the 1850s. As early as 1852 pemmican and dried meat were becoming scarce in the lands bordering on the Saskatchewan River, especially downstream from Fort Edmonton.[51] By the late 1870s a few herds were to be found in the prairies north of the Cypress Hills and Wood Mountain areas. By the 1880s a few bison were being encountered occasionally in the Saskatchewan territory, but they had long since ceased to be a significant resource.[52]

The period from 1821 to 1870 was one of declining opportunities for the Indians in the fur trade. The Woodland Indians were the first to feel the effects of these changes. Declining resources and a growing economic dependency placed them in a weak position vis-à-vis the traders and they were forced to accept most of the economic reforms which the company initiated. Within the fur trade they functioned mostly as trappers although some found employment in the transport brigades. The Parkland-Grassland Indians, on the other hand, were able to resist these changes somewhat longer because of the company's continued dependence upon them for food for a short period after 1821, and because of the proximity of American trading houses. The latter posts became increasingly important over time as the Indian's role as provisioner was undermined by the Métis. However, by the 1870s the independence of the Plains Indians was also being threatened as other groups began to compete with them in the hunting of bison and the sales of hides. Ultimately, this hunting pressure nearly exterminated the bison and undermined the economic basis of the Plains Indian way of life. They were thus reduced to the same state of economic dependency as their woodland relatives had begun to experience some fifty years earlier.

NOTES

1 York Factory, 31 July 1822, to the Governor and Committee in London, PAC HBC D 4/85, p. 16

2 Cowie, *The Company of Adventurers*, 276. As Cowie pointed out, the chiefs

received an 'outfit' also. According to Cowie they wore it for a few days and then distributed the garments to their followers. The only symbols of office which they retained were a long-stemmed pipe of peace and a 'big lowland Scotch blue bonnet' similar to those worn by curlers.

3 Ibid., 276

4 Ibid., 272

5 Governor George Simpson, York Factory, 1 September 1825, to the Governor and Committee in London, PAC HBC D 4/88, p. 92

6 Ibid., 92

7 York Factory, 1 August 1823, to the Governor and Committee in London, PAC HBC D 4/86, p. 20

8 York Factory, 10 July 1828, Governor and Committee in London, PAC HBC D 4/92, p. 7

9 In the late eighteenth century the factors were instructed to encourage the Indians to wear English cloth. Rich, *Hudson's Bay Copy Booke of Letters Outward, 1688–1696*, 61

10 In 1821 Parliament passed, 'An Act for regulating the Fur Trade and establishing a Criminal and Civil Jurisdiction within certain parts of North America.' In the same year the newly amalgamated Hudson's Bay Company was given an exclusive monopoly to the trade of the areas covered in the act for a period of twenty-one years. Before being granted this monopoly, the company had to agree to abide by and enforce the regulations set forth in the act. In particular, it was obliged to take steps which would reduce or ultimately eliminate the sale or distribution of alcohol to the Indians. Thus, besides attempting to bring about order for the sake of trade, the company was also under parliamentary pressure to put an end to the abusive use of liquor in its transactions with the Indians. A. Morton, *A History of the Canadian West*, 628–9

11 York Factory, 31 July 1822, to the Governor and Committee in London, PAC HBC D 4/85, p. 16

12 Ibid., 16

13 Cowie, *The Company of Adventurers*, 206–7

14 *In Rupert's Land*, 152–3

15 York Factory, 20 August 1826, to the Governor and Committee in London, PAC HBC D 4/89, p. 17. Spirits continued to be sent into that region for consumption by company servants and officers. However, after 1837 this allowance was cut off. As a compensation, the company substituted tea, chocolate, and sugar. Minutes, Council for the Northern Department, 1835–49, PAC HBC B 239/K/2, pp. 85–225

16 York Factory, 16 July 1822, to the Governor and Committee in London, PAC HBC D 4/85, p. 2

17 Ibid., 17

18 Ibid., 17, and Governor George Simpson, York Factory, 1 September 1826, PAC HBC D 4/89, p. 16

19 York Factory, 31 July 1822, to the Governor and Committee in London, PAC HBC D 4/85, p. 17

20 Fort Garry, 5 June 1824, to the Governor and Committee in London, PAC HBC D 4/87, p. 11–12

21 Governor George Simpson, York Factory, 20 August 1826, to the Governor and Committee in London, PAC HBC D 4/89, p. 29

22 York Factory, Annual Reports to the Governor and Committee in London between 1827 and 1830, PAC HBC D 4/90–7

23 York Factory, 20 August 1826, to the Governor and Committee in London, PAC HBC D 4/89, p. 26

24 The Northern Department comprised the fourteen districts shown on Table 6. The Company governed these districts in accordance with the Parliamentary Act of 1821 through the Council for the Northern Department.

25 Glover, *David Thompson's Narrative*, 75–6

26 E.S. Rogers has termed this the 'hunting range system,' in 'The Hunting Group–Hunting Territory Complex among the Mistassini Indians,' 82. C. Bishop has pointed out that prior to 1828 there is little evidence to suggest that the Indians living in the Albany Fort hinterlands had any concept of trespass. Rather, it appears to have developed later in the nineteenth century in response to the need to implement conservation measures. Bishop, 'The Emergence of Hunting Territories,' 3–5, 10–13.

27 York Factory, 10 July 1828, to the Governor and Committee in London, PAC HBC D 4/92, p. 5–6

28 Bishop, 'The Emergence of Hunting Territories,' 7–13

29 Ibid., 5

30 York Factory, 25 July 1827, to the Governor and Committee in London, PAC HBC D 4/90, 28–9

31 Innis, *The Fur Trade in Canada*, 288

32 Morton, *Manitoba*, 62

33 The census for 1831 listed a total population for the Red River Valley of 2390 and 450 families. Thus, each family averaged slightly more than five persons. There were 262 Catholic families (mostly Métis) suggesting that the Métis population would have been about 1300. The same procedure was used with subsequent censuses. See *Census of Canada 1665 to 1871*, 4: 105 (1831), 141(1843), and 242–3(1856).

34 The Red River cart had been introduced to the region by the early nineteenth century. According to W.L. Morton it was of Scottish origin; however, similar

carts were in use in Quebec and it may therefore have been of French origin. Morton, *Manitoba*, 79. For an excellent account of the Métis buffalo hunts, see Ross, *The Red River Settlement*, 255–67.

35 Ross, *The Red River Settlement*, 246, and Pritchet, 'Some Red River Fur Trade Activities,' 406

36 Innis, *The Fur Trade*, 303

37 Ibid., 301–2

38 York Factory, 1 August 1823, to the Governor and Committee in London, PAC HBC D 4/86, p. 20

39 Ross, *The Red River Settlement*, 273. Only the fat market remained unsaturated.

40 Brandon House Account Books, 1810, 1812, and 1813, PAC HBC B 22/d/1–4

41 Carlton House Account Books, 1810–13 and 1815, PAC HBC B 27/d/1–6

42 York Factory, 15 August 1822, to Governor and Committee in London, PAC HBC D 4/85, p. 35

43 Burlingame, 'The Buffalo in Trade and Commerce,' 266

44 York Factory, 5 June 1824, to the Governor and Committee in London, PAC HBC D 4/87, p. 16

45 Governor George Simpson, York Factory, 18 July 1831, to the Governor and Committee in London, PAC HBC D 4/98, p. 23

46 Cowie, *The Company of Adventurers*, 437. Steamboats had been introduced on the Missouri River in 1831. Burlingame, 'The Buffalo in Trade,' 275

47 For example, in 1869 Fort Edmonton shipped 9090 buffalo robes. Edmonton Account Book, 1869, PAC HBC D 60/d/175. At Fort Carlton 1099 were traded in 1865, 58 in 1866, 228 in 1867, and 520 in 1868. At Fort Pitt the figures were 783 in 1865, 1434 in 1866, 948 in 1867, and 232 in 1868. *Ibid.*, PAC HBC B 60/d/172

48 Burlingame, 'The Buffalo in Trade,' 280 and Innis, *The Fur Trade*, 330

49 Roe, *The North American Buffalo*, 393–5

50 Ibid., 373

51 Innis, *The Fur Trade*, 302

52 For the records of the last encounters see Roe, *The North American Buffalo*, 468–8

12

End of a way of life

As resources were depleted throughout the West, and as the Hudson's Bay Company's policies and practices were changed, Woodland and Grassland Indians alike were forced to make economic adjustments. These adjustments brought about new patterns of activity and interaction. As shown earlier, in southeastern Manitoba the annual large-scale migrations of Indian populations from the woodlands to the parklands had largely come to an end by the early nineteenth century. After 1821, such movements took place only occasionally when the bison herds approached relatively close to the Red River colony. This happened, for example, during the winter of 1823–4, and Simpson recorded that a large proportion of the Woodland Indians living in the Winnipeg District, mostly Ojibwa, spent the major portion of the winter in the parklands hunting these animals.[1] However, in time these winter hunts became very infrequent as the range limits of the animal were pushed westward due to the increasingly heavy hunting pressure exerted on the bison by the Métis.

For the Indians of southeastern Manitoba the disappearance of the bison from the parkland region posed serious problems, since moose and deer had virtually been exterminated from the forest country to the east of Lake Winnipeg and the Winnipeg River, and the fisheries were said to be unreliable in many portions of that territory.[2] Consequently, survival during the winter was becoming increasingly difficult for the Indians as the safety valve which the parklands had offered them was no longer available. It was partly for this reason that the Red River colony began to attract a steady flow of Indians. There they could obtain food and shelter when in need. Initially Governor Simpson attempted to discourage this movement, since many of the Indian immigrants were what he and others considered to be 'hangers on' who had little use for work, but rather begged for food and clothing, or as Alexander Ross expressed it, 'began to edge themselves in; not indeed to labour themselves, but to partake, if possible in the fruits of our toil.'[3] Also, Simpson feared that if these migrations were not checked the woodland regions might be depopulated too rapidly, depriving the company of Indian labour as trappers and hunters. In an effort to halt this trend, Simpson attached the post of Netley Creek to the Winnipeg District and planned to maintain Fort Alexander (also known as Bas de la Rivière) at the mouth of the Winnipeg River for the same purpose. He reasoned that these two posts could supply the Indians with the things they required, thereby eliminating their excuse for travelling to the colony.[4]

In spite of these actions Indians continued to drift into the settlement. Besides being a place where they could obtain charity, the colony provided them with seasonal farm employment. Since there was a large Métis population living along the Red and lower Assiniboine rivers, many of the Indians living in the Winnipeg, Swan River, and Cumberland districts had relatives in the settlement for whom they could work during the spring, summer, and autumn when labour demands were at a peak. Thus, they provided an important service for the colony. Simpson did recognize the value of this labour and he hoped that by this process the Indians would be gradually 'civilized'; that is, would learn to become farmers themselves.[5] Alexander Ross, among others, shared his optimism concerning the prospect. Indeed, he claimed that the first Indian to settle permanently in the colony and to take up agriculture had done so in this manner. Ross said that he was a Swampy Cree from Oxford House who originally came to visit a daughter and stepson living along the Red River, and the stepson reportedly persuaded him to stay and settle down.[6]

Between 1821 and 1832 a number of Indians had taken up residence in the colony, but most were not farmers in any real sense. In the early 1830s the Reverend William Cochran, of the Church Missionary Society, organized the first Indian agricultural settlement just to the north of lower Fort Garry and tried to persuade all of the Indians living in the colony to move there. Some Indians and many Métis responded to his call. However, this missionary effort, as well as those of other churches, had limited initial success. A number of Indians and Métis were taught European agricultural methods, but few of them developed a taste for a sedentary life style. Rather, all too frequently they abandoned their farms for the chase after the farms were nearly established. Ross reported they justified this action saying 'It is easier ... to hunt than to dig. A bow and arrow ... are lighter than a spade.'[7] In effect, the Indians were willing to cooperate with the missionaries when they were in need of food and clothing which the ministers and priests provided for them. On the other hand, when alternative opportunities presented themselves most of the Indians took them.

As time passed it became increasingly difficult for the Indians in southern Manitoba to make a living in the fur trade as hunters, trappers, canoe men, boat men or cart drivers, and they were forced to rely increasingly on agriculture – either as part-time farmers, or as hired hands on the farms of settlers. By the time of Confederation large numbers of Indians were making a part of their livelihoods in these ways. Recognizing this fact, in 1871 W.M. Simpson, the Indian Commissioner reported:

Although many years will elapse before they can be regarded as a settled population, settled in the sense of following agricultural pursuits, the Indians have already shown a disposition to provide against the vicissitudes of the chase by cultivating small patches of corn and potatoes. Moreover, in the province of Manitoba, where labour is scarce, Indians give great assistance in gathering in the crops. At Portage La Prairie, both Chippewas [Ojibwa] and Sioux, were largely employed in the grain field, and in other parishes I saw many farmers whose employes were nearly all Indians.[8]

To the west, in Saskatchewan and eastern Alberta, the same changes were to take place but at a slower rate since the final destruction of the bison herds came much later. Thus, the Indians were less receptive to the efforts of the missionaries. Furthermore, since agricultural settlement came later to this area, part-time farm employment was not available. Reflecting these different conditions, the older patterns of seasonal movements and interactions of Woodland and Grassland Indians persisted until the middle of the nineteenth century, some thirty to fifty years later than was the case in Manitoba. To illustrate, the journal record of Fort Pitt (Figure 45) for 1830–1 shows that bison herds were moving back and forth across the North Saskatchewan River with the changes of the season. They generally crossed the north side of the river in January and returned southwards in late May or June.[9]

Regarding Indian movements in the vicinity of the post, Patrick Small, who kept the journal record, indicated that in May of 1830 large numbers of Cree and Blackfoot were gathering in the grasslands to the south of the fort. Their camps were said to number over 200 lodges.[10] Few large groups came in to trade then or for the rest of the summer. However, beginning in September and October large trading parties began visiting the post to barter their stocks of dried meat, tallow, and pemmican. The largest of these parties were those of the Assiniboine and Cree with some of the former totalling over 150 men and their families, while one of the latter consisted of 130 lodges. When conducting this fall provision trade Small stated that these bands normally spent a day or two in a nearby forest where they obtained their annual supply of tent poles.[11]

Upon completion of their autumn trade nearly all of the Assiniboine scattered to the parklands. The Cree groups appear to have separated: some headed northward to trap furs in the late autumn and early winter, while others moved toward the south to establish their winter bison pounds. With respect to the latter, a Hudson's Bay Company employee who travelled overland from Fort Carlton to Fort Pitt during the month of February 1831 informed Small that there were eight Cree pounds situated between the two posts on the north side of the river. Presumably most of them were located in the general vicinity of Jackfish Lake, Saskatchewan, since he had received a report earlier, on 25 December, which indicated that the Assiniboine and 'lower Cree' were operating eight such pounds there at that time.[12] In addition to these, the Beaver Hill Cree had constructed pounds in the vicinity of the Beaver Hills between the North Saskatchewan and Battle Rivers.[13]

According to Small's 1830 account, the Cree who travelled north to trap furs in the forests faced severe hardships in their attempts to find adequate subsistence. Some of these bands returned to Fort Pitt as early as the second week in December complaining that they had been starving since they left the parklands in autumn. Furthermore, they had been unable to take any furs. Nearly a year later the same movement was repeated and Small reported that the first Cree to abandon the woodlands arrived on 13 December, starving.[14] Thus, groups living in the bordering forests were yet in the habit of resorting to the parklands for food during the lean winter months. However, the length of time which they were able to spend in the forests appeared to have become progressively shorter as the game resources of the latter environment continued to wane.

Similar conditions were reported in the parklands to the southeast some twenty years later. For instance, the keeper of the journal at Egg Lake House, a small outpost of the Swan River district which was located to the north of the Quill Lakes, Saskatchewan, recorded that all of the

Indians camped in the area around the post and in the nearby woods were starving in the fall of 1853. In fact, he stated that some of them had already died from a shortage of food. Toward the end of November he claimed that this shortage would soon drive all of the Indians to the plains. He attempted to delay departures of some of the families by sending them food from his stores, but in spite of this effort most of them deserted the forests because his relief was insufficient to alleviate their suffering.[15] After passing a month or more in the parklands some of these Indians started returning to conduct their late winter fur hunts. This movement began in the third and fourth weeks of February.[16]

Besides showing the persistence of older patterns of subsistence, the Egg Lake House journal suggests that some important changes were under way by the middle of the nineteenth century. As has been noted above, the trader at the House tried to assist the Woodland Indians in their attempts to obtain the food which they required to remain in the forests long enough to conclude their trapping operations. This was done not only for the rather obvious economic reasons, but also for humanitarian considerations. The journal makes it clear that the trader was deeply concerned about the plight of the local Indians.

At Fort Pelly, one of the principal Hudson's Bay Company posts in the Swan River District (Figure 45), economic considerations appear to have been the leading motivation behind the traders' practice of feeding the Indian bands in the department. This fort was situated near the parkland-forest boundary in the upper Assiniboine River valley area. Consequently, most of the furs which were taken in trade came from the Ojibwa bands living in the woodlands to the north and east. Game animal populations had been depleted in these territories long before and recovery was very slow. Moderate fur resources still remained in many sections, however, but to tap them it was necessary to support the more reliable Indian hunters. One of these was an Indian called 'The Rattlesnake.' On 16 November 1853, he came to the post to trade his furs and he was given 'gratis' ammunition, meat, and barley. According to the journal he was given these gifts because 'it is a poor place for Moose where they [his band] are tenting, but still a fair Fur Country.'[17] Two days later an Indian boy arrived from a band camped on the Red Deer River; he hoped to obtain provisions to take back to his relatives who he said were starving.[18]

Granting that the food supplies of the Woodland Indians were not nearly as plentiful as those of the Parkland Indians, there is some evidence to suggest that the condition of the former groups was not as desperate as such journal entries indicate. For instance, the Fort Pelly journal of 1853 shows that in the last two weeks in December the 'Rattlesnake's' and a 'Mr. Cote's' bands carried on a considerable amount of trade at the post. Among the commodities which they brought in during this period were six bear skins and eighteen moose skins. Since it was winter and food preservation was not therefore a problem, it could be assumed that the meat of these animals would have been sufficient to sustain them for that short span of time. Yet, they were said to be starving and they asked the traders to provide them with food.[19] Similarly, on 3 January 1854 all of the Indians camping around the Guard House, a small outpost of Fort Pelly located in the Red Deer River valley, were reported to have departed for the plains to secure provisions. They promised to return in late winter to resume their trapping operations. Although game was thus presumably scarce in the country around the post, the December returns from the Guard House listed nineteen moose skins and nine bear skins.[20]

These apparent discrepancies between the descriptions of the situation of the Woodland Indians which are found in the post journals and the data which is available in account books are difficult to explain. The evidence indicates that food preferences were probably largely responsible. Written records show that in the borderland regions bison was often exploited to the virtual exclusion of other game, even among recent immigrants into the area such as the Swampy Cree and Ojibwa. When Daniel Harmon was stationed near Bird Mountain (the present Thunder Mountain, Saskatchewan), just to the north of the bend in the Swan River during the winter of 1801–2, he reported that he and his men were reduced to eating dried meat and chokecherries due to the mildness of the season. These weather conditions had permitted the bison to remain in the open plains where the Cree and Ojibwa had gone to hunt them. However, he added that moose and red deer were abundant nearby. The Indian movement to the grasslands in this instance was clearly based on choice not necessity. They were in pursuit of 'their beloved food – buffaloe meat.'[21]

The lack of interest shown for hunting moose is somewhat surprising since the meat of this animal was highly esteemed by almost all Indian groups. The meat of red deer or wapiti was another matter. Throughout the journal accounts it is repeatedly pointed out that this animal was taken only when other resources failed. Samuel Hearne was one of the first traders to take note of this fact. He wrote: 'those deer are seldom an object of chace with the Indians bordering on Basquiau [Saskatchewan River], except when moose and other game fail.'[22] According to Hearne the difficulties associated with the consumption of red-deer meat related to the fact that the tallow of this animal (the external fat) was hard, and when it was eaten, even if relatively hot, it chilled quickly leaving a very disagreeable scale of fat coating the teeth and roof of the mouth.[23] For trade purposes the animal was of little value since its flesh, like that of most deer, was not well suited for preservation in casks with salt. Furthermore, it was the most difficult of all deer meat to preserve by drying. Unless it was cut into thin slices and dried quickly, it spoiled.[24] Similarly, there was little demand for red-deer hides because they lacked the strength and durability of other deer skins.[25]

The apparent failure to consume bear meat in any quantity in the parklands in the middle of the nineteenth century may have been the result of a clash of economic necessity with older cultural practices. As the more valuable furs such as beaver and marten declined in abundance, the Indians were forced to exploit other resources in order to obtain commodities which could be exchanged at the trading posts for the European goods they had grown dependent upon. Moose and bear skins were among these items. However, the use of bear for this purpose rendered it useless to the Indian as a food source since it interfered with the traditional method of cooking it. In the late eighteenth century some Hudson's Bay Company men attempted to encourage the Indians to bring in bear robes, but their efforts were unfruitful. When explaining this failure Hearne wrote that the Cree:

kill great numbers of those Bears [black] at all seasons of the year; but no encouragement can prevent them from singeing almost every one that is in good condition: so that the few skins they do save and bring to the market, are only of those which are so poor that their flesh is not worth eating. In fact, the skinning of a Bear spoils meat thereof, as much as it would do to skin a young porker, or a roasting pig.[26]

In this way, as conditions changed and the Indians were forced to market these skins through economic necessity, the bear may have declined in importance as a source of food.

In order to obtain the supplies of dried buffalo meat, fat, and pemmican which they required, the Indians living adjacent to the parkland-forest border found it necessary to travel greater distances during the latter half of the nineteenth century as the bison range contracted. For example, the Fort Pelly and Egg Lake journals of 1853–4 and the Fort à la Corne journals of 1851–2, 1863–4, and 1864–5 indicate that the Touchwood Hills area was the northernmost point in central Saskatchewan where bison continued to be relatively plentiful in winter after mid-century.[27] By the late 1860s, they were abundant only in the area to the south of the Qu'Appelle River.[28] Therefore, it was becoming impractical for many of the above bands to trap furs in the late autumn and early winter months and hunt bison during the middle of the winter also. Partly for this reason the annual congregations of Woodland and Plain Indians in the parklands of Saskatchewan during the winter came to an end as they had earlier farther eastwards.

The practice described above of the Hudson's Bay Company traders of providing the Woodland-Parkland Indians with as much of their provision requirements as was feasible hastened these changes. It was in the best interest of the company to meet this demand since otherwise these Indians would have spent greater portions of their winter trapping time travelling to and from the bison ranges. However, it also meant that the company's ability to obtain and transport larger quantities of dried meat, pemmican, and grease were being taxed. For instance, during the winter of 1868–9, Walter Traill indicates that at Riding Mountain House, a small but important woodland outpost of Fort Ellice, between three and four thousand pounds of pemmican were traded to the Indians. If this supply had not been available, the local Indians would have abandoned the region during the winter and the company would have been deprived of a valuable return of mink, marten, and fisher pelts.[29]

The Hudson's Bay Company was able to meet these needs by making rapid adjustments of the functions and locations of its parkland-grassland posts as game conditions warranted, and by developing a good system of overland transportation that permitted them to move considerable supplies of provisions during the winter or summer. For example, in southern Saskatchewan Fort Ellice served as a key bison hunting post until mid-century. However, as Brandon House had become marginal to the bison hunting country in the 1830s, so too did Fort Ellice by the late 1860s. Beginning in the 1850s it started receiving a large proportion of its pemmican from the Touchwood Hills. With the southward retreat of the bison, the post in the Touchwood Hills declined in importance to be replaced by Fort Qu'Appelle in the early 1860s. In addition, the so-called 'flying posts' became increasingly significant as sources of pemmican for Fort Ellice. These posts were small encampments which were set up during the winter as close to the bison herds as access to woods would permit and thus, were shifted from year to year. In the 1860s, the 'flying posts' of Fort Ellice were often located in the Turtle and Moose Mountains.[30]

In order to move the supplies of meat and fat which were being obtained by the company to the places where they were needed, a variety of modes of transportation were used. During the summer, trains of Red River carts brought in large quantities of meat, fat, and pemmican from the grasslands, while in the winter, dog sled trains were used. The increased need to use the latter further taxed the company's provision supply problems, however, because the dogs had to be fed also. In order to conserve its valued supplies of pemmican, the traders attempted to obtain fish for dog food wherever possible. Thus, at Fort Pelly an Indian was hired to fish for this purpose. Likewise, at Riding Mountain House, in the early 1860s an Indian supplied Walter Traill with large quantities of jack fish for his dogs.[31]

By making these adjustments and improvements in overland transportation, the company was able to alleviate seasonal and local food shortages to the extent that fur-trapping bands living in the parklands and adjacent forests could remain there year-round. However, the changes also made the Indians dependent on the company not only for clothing, as had been the case for nearly fifty years by 1870, but also for food – and not just pemmican, but so-called 'store food' as well, such as flour and biscuits. In effect, to a large extent the woodland Indians had virtually become company employees. They trapped for the company and were provided with nearly all of their requirements at the company store on credit.

In contrast, the Plains Assiniboine, Cree, and Ojibwa of Western Canada were able to continue their nomadic and somewhat more independent life style for a short while longer until the bison were exterminated. However, by the 1860s buffalo were becoming scarce and these three tribes were being forced to increasingly encroach upon Blackfoot territory to hunt. The trader Issac Cowie said that this was serving to intensify the long standing hostilities between these various Indian groups.[32] In southern Saskatchewan the summer bison hunt of 1870 was a total failure and a harbinger of things to come. The herds were said to be largely scattered and withdrawn to a region where the Assiniboine, Cree, and Ojibwa dared not venture, for example, the Blackfoot territory.[33] During the ensuing winter, starvation was widespread and Indians and traders alike suffered. Men in the Qu'Appelle District had to resort to eating gophers obtained by pouring water down their holes and setting snares at the openings. The summer of 1871 proved to be equally lean in southern Saskatchewan.

With the rapidly approaching disappearance of the bison, the Indians were in a desperate situation. During the preceding century, the decline of game had driven large numbers of Cree and Ojibwa to the grassland areas, and once again the same problem was arising. However, in this instance there were few alternatives open to them. The fur trade could support only limited numbers of Indians as trappers – even fewer as the bison diminished and furs became scarcer. Clearly, they could not return to the forest in large numbers, as they had previously migrated to the plains. Furthermore, for those groups who resided in the grasslands for any length of time, the adjustments which would have been required to make such a move would have been difficult to achieve. Whereas Woodland-Parkland Indians had rather generalized economies and could effectively exploit any of the three habitant zones of the region with relative ease, this was not true of the Plains Indians. By the middle of the nineteenth century they had developed highly specialized cultures whose subsistence depended almost entirely on the bison. Consequently, they lost the skills needed for stalking other game animals.

Issac Cowie, among others, made this point very clear in 1871–2. The rapid decline of the bison in southern Saskatchewan forced the Indians there to turn to other game animals. One of the richest game areas of that territory was found in the Cypress Hills (see Figure 2). According to Cowie, the Cypress Hills had been a neutral ground between the Assiniboine-Cree-Ojibwa and the Blackfoot groups. Since none of them held control of the hills, the area was never intensively hunted and therefore red deer and grizzly bear were numerous. During the winter of 1871–2 Cowie and several other company men as well as a large party of Métis hunters wintered in the Cypress Hills to hunt these animals. The presence of these men encouraged a small number of Assiniboine to join them, even though the Blackfoot menaced the group for much of the time and in the end killed many of the Assiniboine. In their endeavours to hunt in the woods, Cowie indicated that the Assiniboine had great difficulty. He reported:

Quite a number of those hunting in the wooded ravines of the hills were shot accidentally by their fellows mistaking men, wearing red buffalo calfskin jackets for red deer. I heard of five deaths due to that mistake and the fact that the plain hunters were unskilled in woodcraft. In fact, I may mention that a prairie Indian often lost himself in the woods.[34]

These problems which the Plains Indians faced when attempting to hunt game in wooded country had been mentioned previously by other traders. In fact, in addition to inter-tribal trade it may have been one of the factors that favoured peaceful co-residence of Woodland and Grassland groups in the parklands in earlier years. When bison herds failed to move into the parkland belts during the periodic mild winters, the Plains Indians often depended on the Woodland Indians to hunt other game such as moose and deer.[35] Thus, in the late nineteenth century, most of the Plains Cree, Assiniboine, and Ojibwa would have found it difficult to readjust to a woodland hunting and trapping economy if the option had been available to them, even though many of their ancestors had made the transition from woodland- to grassland-oriented economies with relative ease only a century before.

Once the neutrality of the Cypress Hills had been violated, heavy hunting pressure was brought to bear on the game animals living there. Cowie's party of Métis killed 750 grizzly bears and 1500 red deer in their first winter.[36] As the number of Métis rapidly increased in Saskatchewan following the Riel Rebellion, they played an increasingly decisive role in the destruction of game in the wooded sections of the plains while at the same time put added pressure on the bison herds.[37]

By the early 1870s, many of the Indians of southern Saskatchewan and the adjacent sections of Alberta were coming to the realization, albeit reluctantly, that the country would not support their traditional way of life much longer. On 13 April 1871, a delegation of Plains Cree chiefs from the Edmonton and Carlton House areas arrived at Edmonton House to have a council with W.J. Christie, chief factor of the District. The object of their visit was to ascertain what the intentions of the Canadian government were with respect to their territory. According to Christie the Indians had become concerned about the stories they had heard of the motives behind the government's decision to send troops to Red River. He explained to the Cree that these troops had been sent to keep peace in the Red River area. Furthermore, he assured them that the government had made no requests for their lands nor had anyone sold them. The Indians were concerned about that matter as well since they had heard that the Northwest Territories had been transferred from the Hudson's Bay Company to the Dominion of Canada and did not understand the meaning of the transfer.[38]

After Christie had clarified these matters to the satisfaction of the assembled Cree chiefs, their leading spokesman, Chief Sweet Grass, asked him to transcribe and submit a petition on behalf of the Cree to His Excellency Governor Archibald at Fort Garry. In his petition, Chief Sweet Grass said:

We heard our lands were sold and we did not like it; we don't want to sell our lands; it is our property, and no one has a right to sell them.

Our country is getting ruined of fur bearing animals, hitherto our sole support, and now we are poor and want help – we want you to pity us. We want cattle, tools, agricultural implements, and assistance in everything when we come to settle – our country is no longer able to support us.[39]

By the mid-1870s this view appears to have been widespread among the Plains Assiniboine, Cree, and Ojibwa, as well as their Woodland relatives, and although some bands were still reluctant to settle down and enter into a treaty with the government, they were in a minority and were unwilling or unable to offer strong, effective opposition. Therefore, between the summer of 1871 and 1876, all Indian claims were extinguished in the grassland, parkland, and bordering woodland areas of the prairie provinces by Treaties 1 through 7 (Figure 46).

Thus, in Western Canada, the period of Indian occupance came to an end in a relatively peaceful manner, and the extensive bloodshed which had characterized this transitional phase to the southwards in the United States never occurred. Although other factors no doubt were partly responsible for this peaceful change, economics certainly played a key role. For nearly 200 years the fur trade had dominated the economic life of the West. Over time the character of this trade changed, as did the roles which the Indians played in it. Yet, even though their roles changed, they were central characters in the system and without them the trade could not have been successfully prosecuted. But, in spite of the fact that necessity for cooperation prevented any deliberate attempts to destroy the Indians and their cultures by hostile actions, their traditional life ways were transformed nonetheless. The fur trade favoured economic specialization. While conditions permitted, some groups emerged as trade specialists or middlemen, some became skilled trappers, while others devoted all of their attention to the hunting of large game animals in order to supply the provision needs generated by the fur companies. Ultimately, the resource bases upon which these specialized economies developed were destroyed due to over-exploitation. Significantly for Western Canada, this occurred before extensive European settlement began. Therefore, out of economic necessity, rather than intensive political and military pressure, the Indians agreed to settle on reserves with the promise that the government would look after their welfare and help them make yet another adjustment to changing economic conditions.

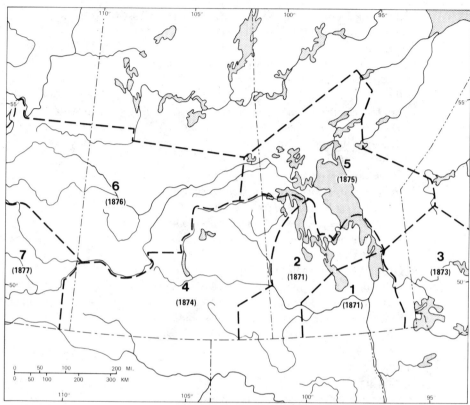

FIGURE 46   INDIAN LAND CESSIONS, 1871-1877

— — BOUNDARIES OF TREATY AREAS

TREATY NUMBERS
1 Stone Fort Treaty (Ojibwa and Swampy Cree)*
2 Manitoba Post Treaty (Ojibwa and Swampy Cree)
3 North-West Angle Treaty (Ojibwa)

4 Qu'Appelle Treaty (Cree and Ojibwa)
5 Winnipeg Treaty (Swampy Cree and Ojibwa)
6 Forts Carlton and Pitt Treaties (Cree)
7 Blackfeet Treaty (Blackfoot)

*Principal Signatories

NOTES

1 York Factory, 10 August 1824, to Governor and Committee in London, PAC HBC D 4/87, p. 48

2 Ibid., 48. Simpson believed that the Winnipeg district would therefore soon be abandoned by the Indians.

3 *The Red River Settlement*, 275

4 Governor George Simpson, York Factory, 10 August 1824, to the Governor and Committee in London, PAC HBC D 4/87, p. 44

5 Governor George Simpson, York Factory, 10 August 1832, to the Governor and Committee in London, PAC HBC D 4/99, p. 41

6 *The Red River*, 276–7

7 Ibid., 280–1. For an in depth discussion of the agricultural missions see, Pannekoek, 'Protestant Agricultural Missions in the Canadian West to 1870.'

8 To the Secretary of State for the Provinces, 3 November 1871, included in Report of the Indian Branch, *Sessional Papers*, 7, no. 22 (1872), 31

9 PAC HBC B 165/a/1, pp. 4 and 22

10 Large camps would have been common at that time of the year among plains Indian groups since it was the sun dance season.

11 Fort Pitt Post Journal, 1830–1, PAC HBC B 165/a/1, pp. 3–12

12 Ibid., 19 and 24. A few Ojibwa were also found in the vicinity of the lake.

13 These pounds apparently were usually established in October, 1831–2, PAC HBC B 165/d/2, p. 5

14 Fort Pitt Post Journal, 1831–2, PAC HBC B 165/a/2, p. 8

15 Egg Lake Journal, 1853–4, PAC HBC B 62/a/1, pp. 1–6

16 Marten and muskrat appear to have been the principal fur-bearing animals which were being taken by the Indians, ibid., 10–11

17 Fort Pelly Post Journal, 1853–4, PAC HBC B 159/a/18, 19–20

18 Ibid., 20

19 Ibid., 23–6

20 Ibid., 25

21 *Sixteen Years in the Indian Country*, 53–4

22 *A Journey*, 231

23 Ibid., 337. It has been reported that the tallow of this deer is harder than that of any other North American deer and has a texture similar to that of beeswax. Temperatures of up to ninety degrees have little effect on it. See, Caton, *The Antelope*, 407

24 James Isham, for example, noted that it did not take salt. Rich, *James Isham's Observations on Hudson's Bay*, 116. For a more extensive discussion of the problems of salting and drying red deer meat see, Caton, *The Antelope*, 407.

25 Caton, *The Antelope*, 411–12. Samiel Hearne said that the one useful property of these skins was that they remained soft after washing and were thus similar to 'shamoy leather.' Hearne, *A. Journey*, 231

26 Hearne, *A Journey*, 238. He also pointed out that bear was a good source of food only from the month of July to the middle of winter. In late winter bears were very lean and their early spring diet consisted largely of insects which were said

to give the meat of the animal an objectionable taste. However, their consumption of berries during the summer improved the flavour considerably.

27 Fort à la Corne carried on some trade with the Plains Indians. Also, a few men from the post were stationed at the 'edge of the woods' during the winter; however, the Plains Indians and the post hunters had little success hunting big game and brought in only small quantities of meat. Fort à la Corne Post Journal, 1851–2, and 1864–5, PAC HBC B 2/a/1 and 2/a/4

28 Atwood, *In Rupert's Land*, 57, 101

29 Ibid., 143

30 Cowie, *The Company of Adventurers*, 186–91

31 Fort Pelly Post Journals, PAC HBC B 159/a/18, p. 13, and Atwood, *In Rupert's Land*, 134

32 *The Company of Adventurers*, 305–6

33 Ibid., 415

34 Ibid., 437

35 For example, bison were scarce around Fort Pitt during the winter of 1830–1 and Patrick Small reported, 'the Blackfoot are obliged to run where the Crees are for ... a little moose and Red Deer flesh to eat, the Blackfeet being very poor wood animal hunters,' PAC HBC B 165/a/1, p. 19

36 Cowie, *The Company of Adventurers*, 436

37 Ibid., 458. According to Cowie, there was a considerable amount of hostility amongst the Plains Assiniboine, Cree and Ojibwa towards the Métis because of the role which the latter were playing in pushing the bison ranges farther to the westward; ibid., 303

38 'Extract of a Despatch – W.J. Christie, Esq., Chief Factor to Lieut. Gov. Archibald, bearing date, Edmonton House, 13th April, 1871,' in Report of Indian Branch, *Sessional Papers*, 7, no. 22 (1872), 32

39 Ibid., 33–4

Select bibliography

SECONDARY SOURCES

ADAMS, ARTHUR T., ed. *The Explorations of Pierre Esprit Radisson.* Minneapolis: Ross and Haines, 1961
Atlas of Alberta, edited by J. Klawe. Toronto, University of Toronto Press, 1969
Atlas of Canada. Ottawa: Department of Mines and Technical Surveys, Geographical Branch, 1957
BURLINGAME, M.C. 'The Buffalo in Trade and Commerce.' *North Dakota Historical Quarterly* 3, no. 4 (1929), 262–91
BURPEE, L.J. 'Highways of the Fur Trade.' *Transactions, Royal Society of Canada.* Series 3, vol. 8 (1914), Section 2, 183–92
– ed. 'An Adventurer From Hudson Bay: Being the Journal of a Journey Performed by Matthew Cocking, Second Factor at York Fort in Order to Take a View of the Inland Country, and to Promote the Hudson's Bay Company's Interest, Whose Trade is Diminishing by the Canadians Yearly Intercepting Natives on Their Way to the Settlements, 1772–1773.' *Transactions, Royal Society of Canada.* Series 3, vol. 2 (1908), Section 2, 91–121
– 'Journal of a Journey Performed by Anthony Hendry: to Explore the Country Inland, and to Endeavour to Increase the Hudson's Bay Company's Trade, A.D., 1754–1755.' *Transactions, Royal Society of Canada.* Series 3, vol. 1 (1907), Section 2, 307–61
– *Journals and Letters of Pierre Gaultier de Varennes de La Vérendrye and His Sons.* Toronto: Champlain Society, 1927

CATCHPOLE, A.J.W., D.W. Moodie, and B. Kaye. 'Content Analysis: A Method for the Identification of Dates of First Freezing and First Breaking From Descriptive Accounts.' *Professional Geographer* 22, no. 5 (1970), 252–7

CATLIN, GEORGE. *North American Indians*. 2 vols. Edinburgh: J. Grant, 1903

CATON, JOHN D. *The Antelope and Deer of America*. New York, 1877

Census of Canada 1665 to 1871, vol. 4. Ottawa: Dominion Bureau of Statistics, 1876

CHAMBLISS, CHARLES. 'The Botany and History of *zizania Aquatica L.*,' *Smithsonian Institution Annual Report* (1940). 369–82

CHARLEVOIX, REV. P.F., SJ. *History and Description of New France*, 6 vols,: edited by John G. Shea. New York, 1868

CHITTENDEN, HIRAM M. *The American Fur Trade in the Far West*. Stanford: Academic Reprints, 1954

COUES, E., ed. *New Light on the Early History of the Greater Northwest: The Manuscript Journals of Alexander Henry, Fur Trader of the Northwest Company, and of David Thompson, Official Geographer and Explorer of the Same Company*, reprinted edition. Minneapolis: Ross and Haines, 1965

COWIE, ISSAC. *The Company of Adventurers*. Winnipeg: William Briggs, 1913

CROUSE, N.M. *Contributions of the Canadian Jesuits to the Geographic Knowledge of New France*. Ithaca. NY, 1924

DAVIES, G.F.K., ed. *Letters from Hudson Bay, 1703–40*. London: Hudson's Bay Record Society, 1965

DENIG, E., *Five Indian Tribes of the Upper Missouri*. edited by J.C. Ewers. Norman: University of Okalahoma Press, 1961

DOBBS, ARTHUR. *An Account of the Countries Adjoining to Hudson's Bay in the Northwest Part of America*. London, 1744

DOUGHTY, ARTHUR G., and CHESTER MARTIN. *The Kelsey Papers*. Ottawa: Public Archives of Canada and the Public Record Office of Northern Ireland, 1929

DOUGLAS, R. and J.N. WALLACE, eds. *Twenty Years of York Factory, 1694–1714*. Ottawa, 1926

DRIVER, HAROLD. *Indians of North America*. Chicago: University of Chicago Press, 1961

EVANS, G.E. 'Prehistoric Blackduck–Historic Assiniboine: A Reassessment,' *Plains Anthropologist*, 6 (1961), 271–5

EWERS, JOHN C. 'The Horse in Blackfoot Indian Culture, With Comparative Material From Other Western Tribes.' Bureau of American Ethnology, Bulletin 159, 1955

– *Indian Life on the Upper Missouri*. Norman: University of Oklahoma Press, 1968

– *The Blackfeet.* Norman: University of Oklahoma Press, 1968
FLEMING, R. HARVE, ed. *Minutes of Council, Northern Department of Rupert's Land, 1821.* Toronto: Champlain Society. 1940
FRANKLIN, (SIR) JOHN. *Narrative of a Journey to the Shores of the Polar Sea in the Years 1819–20–21, and 22,* reprinted edition. Edmonton: Hurtig, 1969
GATES, CHARLES M. *Five Fur Traders of the Northwest.* Saint Paul: Minnesota Historical Society, 1965
GLOVER, RICHARD, ed. *David Thompson's Narrative 1784–1812.* Toronto: Champlain Society, 1962
HALL, E. RAYMOND, and KEITH KELSON. *The Mammals of North America.* 2 vols. New York: Ronald Press, 1959
HANSON, CHARLES E., JR. *The Northwest Gun.* Lincoln: Nebraska State Historical Society, 1955
HARMON, DANIEL WILLIAMS. *Sixteen Years in the Indian Country,* edited by W. Lamb. Toronto: Macmillan, 1937
HAYDEN, F. 'Contributions to the Ethnology and Philology of the Indian Tribes of the Upper Missouri Valley.' *Transactions of the American Philosophical Society* 12, no. 2, NS (1862)
HEARNE, SAMUEL. *A Journey From Prince of Wales' Fort in Hudson's Bay to the Northern Ocean in the Years 1769, 1770, 1771 and 1772,* edited by R. Glover. Toronto, 1958
HEIDENREICH, C.G. *Huronia.* Toronto: McClelland and Stewart, 1973
– 'The Historical Geography of Huronia In the 1st Half of the 17th Century.' PH D Dissertation, McMaster University, 1970
HENNEPIN, LOUIS. *A New Discovery of a Vast Country in America 1679–1681,* edited by R.G. Thwaites. Chicago: A.C. McLurg, 1903
HENRY, ALEXANDER. *Travels and Adventures in Canada and the Indian Territories Between the Years 1760 and 1776,* reprinted edition, edited by James Bain. Edmonton: M.G. Hurtig, 1969
HICKERSON, HAROLD. 'Genesis of a Trading Post Band: The Pembina Chippewa,' *Ethnohistory* 3, no. 4 (1956), 289–345
– 'The Southwestern Chippewa: An Ethnohistorical Study.' *American Anthropological Association, Memoir* 92 (1962)
– ed. 'Journal of Charles Jean Baptiste Chaboillez, 1797–1798,' *Ethnohistory* 9 (1962), 265–316
– 'Journal of Charles Jean Baptiste Chaboillez, 1797–1798 (concluded), *Ethnohistory* 9 (1962), 363–427
HIND, H.Y. *Territories du Nord-Ouest, Rapports de Progres.* London, 1859
HLADY, WALTER, ed. *Ten Thousand Years: Archaelogy in Manitoba.* Winnipeg: Manitoba Historical Society, 1970

- 'Indian Migrations in Manitoba and the West.' *Papers of the Manitoba Historical and Scientific Society*, Series III, vol. 17 (1960), 25–53

HORNADAY, WILLIAM T. 'The Extermination of the American Bison, With a Sketch of Its Discovery and Life History,' *Smithsonian Institution Annual Report* (1887), Part II, 367–548

HYDE, GEORGE. *Red Cloud's Folk*. Norman: University of Oklahoma Press, 1937

INNIS, HAROLD A. *The Fur Trade in Canada*. Toronto: University of Toronto Press, 1956

JENKS, ALBERT E. 'The Wild Rice Gatherers of the Upper Lakes,' *Annual Report of the Bureau of American Ethnology*, pt. 2 (1901), 1013–1137

JENNESS, DIAMOND. *The Indians of Canada*. Ottawa: National Museum of Canda, 1932

JEREMIE, N. 'Relation du Detroit et de le Baye de Hudson,' in *Recueil de Voyages au Nord, Contenant divers Memoires tres Utiles au Commerce et la Navitation*, compiled by Jean-Frederic Bernard. Amsterdam, 1724, vol. 5, 396–435

KEATING, W.H. *Narrative of an Expedition to the Source of St. Peter's River, Lake Winnepeek, Lake of the Woods, &c*. Minneapolis: Ross and Haines, 1959

LA FRANCE, JOSEPH. 'Narrative,' in Report, Houses of Parliament, *Report from the Committee Appointed to enquire into the State and Condition of the Countries adjoining to Hudson's Bay and of the Trade Carried on there*, London, 1749, app. no. 11

LOWIE, ROBERT. 'The Assiniboine,' *Anthropological Papers of the American Museum of Natural History*, 4 (1909), 1–270

- *Indians of the Plains*. New York: McGraw-Hill, 1954

LUKENS, PAUL, JR. 'The Tailrace Bay Site Fauna,' in *Life, Land and Water*, edited by W.J. Mayer-Oakes. Winnipeg: University of Manitoba Press, 1967, 313–22

MACDONNELL, JOHN. 'The Red River,' in *Les Bourgeois de la Compagnie du Nord-Ouest*, vol. 1, edited by L.R. Masson. New York: Antiquarian Press, 1960

MACKENZIE, ALEXANDER. *Voyages From Montreal Through the Continent of North America to the Frozen and Pacific Oceans in 1789 and 1793 With an Account of the Rise and State of the Fur Trade*, reprinted edition. Hurtig, Edmonton, 1971

MACNEISH, R.S. 'An Introduction to the Archaeology of Southeastern Manitoba,' National Museum of Canada, Bulletin 157, Ottawa, 1958

- 'The Stott Mound and Village Near Brandon, Manitoba,' Annual Report, National Museum of Canada, 1952–3, Bulletin 132, 1954, 20–65

MANDELBAUM, DAVID. 'The Plains Cree,' *Anthropological Papers of the American Museum of Natural History*, 37 (1940), 155–316

MARGRY, PIERRE. *Découvertes et Etablissements des Français dans le Sud de l'Amerique Septentrionale, 1614–1734: Memoirs et Documents Originaux*, vol. 6. Paris: D. Jouast, 1886

MASSON, L.R. *Les Bourgeois de la Campagnie du Nord-Ouest*, 2 vols. New York: Antiquarian Press, 1960

MAXIMILIAN, PRINCE OF WEID. 'Travels in the Interior of North America, 1833–1834,' in *Early Western Travels*, edited by Ruben G. Thwaites, vols. 22–5. Cleveland: A. Clark, 1926,

MAYER–OAKES, W.J. *Archeological Investigations in the Grand Rapids, Manitoba, Reservoir, 1961–1962*. Winnipeg: University of Manitoba Press, 1970

– 'Prehistoric Human Populations of the Glacial Lake Agassiz Region,' in *Life, Land and Water*, edited by W.J. Mayer-Oakes. Winnipeg: University of Manitoba Press, 1967

MCKERN, W.C. 'The Mid-Western Taxonomic Method as an Aid to Archaeological Culture Study,' *American Antiquity*, 4 (1939), 301–13

MERK, F., ed. *Fur Trade and Empire* [Sir George Simpson's Journals for 1824–1825]. Cambridge, Massachusetts: Harvard University Press, 1931

MERRIMAN, R.O. 'The Bison and the Fur Trade,' *Bulletin of the Departments of History and Political and Economic Science in Queen's University*, Kingston, Ontario, no. 53, September, 1926, 1–19

MOODIE, D.W., and BARRY KAYE. 'The Northern Limit of Indian Agriculture in North America,' *Geographical Review*, 59 (1969), 513–29

MORTON, A.S. *A History of the Canadian West to 1870–1871*, second edition. Toronto: University of Toronto Press, 1973

– ed. *The Journal of Duncan M'Gillivray*. Toronto, 1929

MORTON, W.L. *Manitoba: A History*. Toronto: University of Toronto Press, 1957

O'CALLAGHAN, E.B., ed. *Documents Relative to the Colonial History of the State of New York: Procured in Holland, England and France*. Vol. 9, (Paris Documents, 1631–1744). Albany, 1856

PALLISER, JOHN. *The Journals, Detailed Reports, and Observations Relative to the Exploration, by Captain John Palliser, of That Portion of British North America, Which in Latitude, Lies Between the British Boundary Line and the Height of Land or Watershed of the Northern or Frozen Ocean During the Years 1857, 1858, 1859, and 1860*. London: G.E. Eyre and W. Spottiswoode, 1863

PANNEKOEK, FRITZ. 'Protestant Agricultural Missions in the Canadian West to 1870.' M.A. thesis, University of Alberta, 1970

PRITCHETT, J.P. 'Some Red River Fur Trade Activities,' *Minnesota Historical Bulletin*, 5 (1924), 401–23

RAY, ARTHUR J. 'Early French Mapping of the Western Interior of Canada: A view From the Bay,' *Canadian Cartographer* (1972), no. 2, 89–98

– 'Indian Adaptations to the Forest-Grassland Boundary of Manitoba and Saskatchewan, 1650–1821: Some Implications for Interregional Migration,' *Canadian Geographer*, 16, no. 2, 103–118

– 'Indian Exploitation of the Forest-Grassland Transition Zone in Western Canada, 1650–1860: A Geographical View of Two Centuries of Change,' PH D Dissertation, University of Wisconsin, 1971

Report From the Committee Appointed to Enquire Into the State and Condition of the Countries Adjoining to Hudson's Bay and of the Trade Carried on There. London, 1749

RICH, E.E. *Cumberland and Hudson House Journals, 1775–1782*, 2 vols. London: Hudson's Bay Record Society, 1951–2

– *The Fur Trade and the Northwest to 1857*. Toronto: McClelland and Stewart. 1967

– *The History of Hudson's Bay Company 1670–1870*. 2 vols. London: Hudson's Bay Record Society, 1958–9

–'Trade Habits and Economic Motivation among the Indians of North America,' *Canadian Journal of Economics and Political Science*, 27 (1960), 35–53

– ed. *Hudson's Bay Company Letters Outwards*. London 1957

– ed. *James Isham's Observations and Notes, 1743–1749*. London: Hudson's Bay Record Society, 1949

– ed. *Hudson's Bay Copy Book of Letters Commissions Instructions Outward, 1688–96*. London: Hudson's Bay Record Society

RICHARDS, J.H., and K.I. FUNG, eds. *Atlas of Saskatchewan*. Saskatoon: University of Saskatchewan, 1969

RODNICK, DAVID. 'Political Structure among the Assiniboine Indians.' *American Anthropologist*, NS, 39 (1937), 408–16

ROE, FRANK GILBERT. *The Indian and the Horse*. Norman: University of Oklahoma Press, 1955

– *The North American Buffalo*. Toronto: University of Toronto Press, 1951

ROGERS, E.S. 'Band Organization among the Indians of Eastern sub-Arctic Canada,' in 'Contributions to Anthropology: Band Societies,' National Museum of Canda, Bulletin 228 (1969), 21–55

– 'The Hunting Group–Hunting Territory Complex among the Mistas-

sini Indians,' National Museum of Canada, Bulletin no. 195, Ottawa, 1963
- 'Subsistence Areas of the Cree-Ojibwa of the eastern Sub-Arctic: A Preliminary Study,' Contributions to Ethnology, v, National Museum of Canada, Bulletin 204, (1967), 59–90
ROSS, ALEXANDER. *The Red River Settlement.* Edmonton: Hurtig, 1972
RUGGLES, RICHARD I. 'The Historical Geography and Cartography of the Canadian West, 1678–1795.' PH D dissertation, University of London, 1958
RUSSELL, CARL P. *Guns on the Early Frontiers.* Berkeley: University of California Press, 1957
Sessional Papers, Report of the Indian Branch, 7, no. 22, Ottawa, 1782
SETON, E.T. *Life Histories of Northern Mammals: An Account of the Mammals of Manitoba*, New York: Charles Scribner's Sons, 1909
TANNER, JOHN. *Narrative of the Captivity and Adventures of John Tanner During Thirty Years Residence Among the Indians in the Interior of North America*, edited by Edwin James. Minneapolis: Ross and Haines, 1956
THWAITES, R.G., ed. *The Jesuit Relations and Allied Documents*, reprinted edition. New York: Greenwood Press, 1959
TRAILL, WALTER. *In Rupert's Land: Memoirs of Walter Traill*, edited by Mae Atwood. Toronto: McClelland and Stewart, 1970
TYRRELL, J.B., ed. *Journals of Samuel Hearne and Philip Turnor Between the Years 1774 and 1792.* Toronto: Champlain Society, 1934
- ed. *Documents Relating to the Early History of Hudson Bay*, reprinted edition. New York: Greenwood Press, 1968
UMFREVILLE, EDWARD. *The Present State of Hudson's Bay*, London, 1790
- *The Present State of Hudson's Bay*, edited by W.S. Wallace. Toronto, 1954
VICKERS, CHRIS. 'Burial Traits of the Headwaters Lakes Aspect in Manitoba,' *American Antiquity*, 12 (1947), 109–14
- 'The Historic Approach and the Headwaters Lakes Aspect,' *Plains Archeological Conference Newsletter*, 1 (1948), 8–11
VOORHIS, ERNEST. *Canadian Historic Forts and Trading Posts.* Winnipeg, 1932
WALLACE, W.S., ed. *Documents Relating to the North West Company.* Toronto: Champlain Society, 1934
WARKENTIN, JOHN, and RICHARD I. RUGGLES. *Historical Atlas of Manitoba: A Selection of Facsimile Maps, Plans and Sketches From 1612 to 1969.* Winnipeg: Manitoba Historical Society, 1970
WATTS, F.B. 'The Natural Vegetation of the Southern Great Plains of Canada,' *Geographical Bulletin*, 14 (1960), 25–43

WHITE, T.E. 'A Method of Calculating the Dietary Percentage of Various Food Animals Utilized by Aboriginal Peoples,' *American Antiquity*, 4 (1953), 396–8

WILFORD, L.A. 'A Tentative Classification of the Protohistoric Cultures of Minnesota,' *American Antiquity* 6 (1941), 231–249

WILLIAMS, GLYNDWR, ed. *Andrew Graham's Observations on Hudson's Bay, 1767–1791*. London: The Hudson's Bay Record Society, 1969

WISSLER, CLARK. 'Ethnohistorical Problems of the Missouri-Saskatchewan Area,' *American Anthropologist*, 10 (1908), 197–207

– 'The Influence of the Horse on the Development of Plains Culture,' *American Anthropologist*, 16, no. 1 (1914), 1–25

– 'Population Changes among the Northern Plains Indians,' *Yale University Publications in Anthropology*, vol. 18 (1936), 3–18

WRIGHT, J.V. 'The Michipicoten Site, Ontario.' National Museum of Canada. Bulletin 224. Ottawa, 1968.

– 'The Pic River Site.' National Museum of Canada, Bulletin 206. Ottawa, 1966.

– 'Cree Culture History in the Southern Indian Lake Region,' Contributions to Anthropology VII: Archeology Paper 1, National Museum of Canada Bulletin 232. Ottawa, 1968

ARCHIVAL SOURCES

Those sources which are located in the Public Archives of Canada have been indicated by the abbreviation PAC. Hudson's Bay Company Records have been indicated by the abbreviation HBC.

Archival sources other than Hudson's Bay Company records

CORONELLI, P. *Partie Occidentale du Canada ou de la Nouvelle France, 1688*, PAC, Map Division

FIDLER, PETER. *Journal Kept at Red River 22 July 1814–16 July 1815*, Selkirk Papers, vol. 69, nos. 18,430–18,536, Public Archives of Manitoba

HENRY, ALEXANDER. *Map of the North West Parts of America, 1775*, PAC, Map Division

JAILLOT, H. *Le Canada ou Partie de la Nouvelle France, 1696*, PAC, Map Division

LA FRANCE, JOSEPH. *New Map of Part of North America, 1739-1742*, PAC, Map Division

MACDONNELL, JOHN. Journal of 1793–5, Masson Collection, PAC Manuscript Group 19, C 2, no. 5

Journals of company employees

Graham's Observations, 1768, PAC HBC B E 2/4–6
ISHAM, JAMES. Isham's Observations and Notes, 1743–9, PAC HBC B E 2/1–6
PINK, WILLIAM. 'Willm Pink Journal in Land From the 15th of June in 1766 & 7,' in York Factory Journals, PAC HBC B 239/a/56
SIMPSON, GEORGE. Letters Inward, 1837–41, PAC HBC D 5/4–5/6
SIMPSON, GEORGE. Letters Outward, 1822–38, PAC HBC D 4/85–4/106
SMITH, JOSEPH. 'A Journal of the Most Remarkable Observations and Occurrences on a Journey in Land Performed by Joseph Smith and Joseph Waggoner Who Departed From York Fort August the 23rd, 1756 and Returned June the 25th, 1757,' in York Factory Post Journal, 1756–7, PAC HBC B 239/a/43
– 'A Journal Made While on an Inland Voyage, 1757–1758,' PAC HBC B 239/a/45
– 'Remarks of a Journey Inland Commencing July ye 3rd, 1763 and Ending June ye 16th, 1764,' in York Factory Post Journal, 1763–4, PAC HBC B 239/a/52
TOMISON, WILLIAM. 'An Abstract From a Journal of Journey Inland to the Great Lake, Performed by William Tomison From Severn House on Severn River to Endeavour to Promote the Hon'ble Hudson's Bay Company's Trade,' in Graham's Observations, PAC HBC E 2/4, 1768
– 'Observations of a Journey Inland to the Great Lake Performed by William Tomison Steward at Severn House Mr. Andrew Graham Master From June 16th, 1767 to June 30th, 1768,' PAC HBC B 198/a/10

Post records, District reports, and Minutes of Council

Ash Fall Journal, 1798–9, PAC HBC B 7/a/1
Brandon House Account Books, 1810–11 to 1813–14 and 1821–2, PAC HBC B 22/d/1–4 and 6
Brandon House District Reports, 1819, 1822, and 1828, PAC HBC B 22/e/1–3
Brandon House Post Journals, 1793–4 and 1794–5, PAC HBC B 22/a/1 and 2
Buckingham House Post Journals, 1792–3 and 1796–7, PAC HBC B 24/a/1 and 4

Carlton House [Assiniboine River] Post Journal, 1795–6, PAC HBC B 28/a/1
Carlton House [Saskatchewan River] Account Books, 1810–11 to
   1814–15 and 1820–1, PAC HBC B 27/d/1–7
Carlton House [Saskatchewan River] District Reports, 1815, 1818, 1820,
   and 1826, PAC HBC B 27/e/1–4
Carlton House [Saskatchewan River] Post Journals, 1795–6 to 1838–9,
   PAC HBC B 27/a/1–23
Cumberland House Account Books, 1810–11 to 1813–14, PAC HBC B
   49/d/1–4
Cumberland House District Reports, 1815, 1819, 1823, and 1825, PAC
   HBC B 49/e/1–5
Cumberland House Post Journals, 1784–5 to 1796–7, PAC HBC B
   49/a/15–27
Egg Lake Post Journal, 1853–4, PAC HBC B 62/a/1
Fort à la Corne Post Journals, 1851–2 and 1863–4, PAC HBC B 2/a/1 and 4
Fort Albany Account Books, 1699–1700 to 1789–90, PAC HBC B
   3/d/11–100
Fort Albany Post Journal, 1780–1, PAC HBC B 3/a/77b
Fort Alexander Report on District, 1822–3, PAC HBC B 4/e/1
Fort Assiniboine Account Books, 1826–7 and 1832–3, PAC HBC B 8/d/1
   and 2
Fort Assiniboine District Report, 1824–5, PAC HBC B 8/e/1
Fort Assiniboine Post Journals, 1828–9 and 1830–1, PAC HBC B 8/a/1 and 2
Fort Dauphin District Report, 1820–1, PAC HBC B 51/e/1
Fort Edmonton Account Books, 1865–6 to 1868–9, PAC HBC B 60/d/172–5
Fort Edmonton District Reports, 1815, 1819, 1822–4 and 1862, PAC HBC B
   60/e/1–9
Fort Edmonton Post Journals 1795–9, PAC HBC B 60/a/1–4
Fort Ellice Post Journals, 1794–5, 1812–13, 1822–3, 1858–9, and 1862–3,
   PAC HBC B 63/a/1–6
Fort Nipawi Post Journal, 1794–5, PAC HBC B 148/a/1
Fort Pelly Account Books, 1821–2 and 1825–6, PAC HBC B 159/d/1a and 3a
Fort Pelly District Reports [Swan River], 1818–19, 1819–20, and 1828–9,
   PAC HBC B 159/e/1–3
Fort Pelly Post Journals, 1837–8 and 1853–4, PAC HBC B 159/a/17 and 18
Fort Pitt Post Journals, 1830–1 and 1831–2, PAC HBC B 165/a/1 and 2
Fort Vermillion [Saskatchewan River] Account Book, 1814–15, PAC HBC B
   225/d/1
Ile à la Crosse District Report, 1822–3, PAC HBC B 89/e/1
Indian Lake District Report, 1820, PAC HBC B 91/e/1

Knee Lake Journal, 1815–16, PAC HBC B 101/a/ 1

Lac la Biche Journals, 1799–1800 and 1819–20, PAC HBC B 104/a/ 1 and 2

Lac la Pluie District Reports, 1822–3 to 1826–7 and 1828–9, PAC HBC B 105/e/ 2–7 and 9

Lesser Slave Lake District Reports, 1819 and 1822, PAC HBC B 115/e/ 1 and 4

Manchester House Post Journals, 1789–90 and 1790–1, PAC HBC B 121/a/ 5 and 6

Manitoba Lake–Big Point District Report, 1818–19, PAC HBC B 122/e/ 1

Minutes, Council of Northern Department, 1830–70, PAC HBC. B 239/k/ 1–3

North West Company Invoice of Fort des Prairies Outfit, 1821, PAC HBC F 4/48

North West Company Minute Book, 1807–14, PAC HBC F 3/ 1

North West Company Scheme for the Northwest Outfit 1794, PAC HBC F 3/ 1

Portage de l'Isle, 1793–5, PAC HBC B 166/a/ 1–3

Red Deer River Post Journal, 1812–3, PAC HBC B 176/a/ 1

Shell River Post Journal, 1794–5, PAC HBC B 199/a/ 1

Somerset House [Swan River] Post Journal, 1794–5, PAC HBC B 203/a/ 1

South Branch House Post Journals, 1786–7 to 1793–4, PAC HBC B 205/a/ 1–8

York Factory Account Books, 1688–9 to 1782–3, PAC HBC B 239/d/ 1–72

York Factory Correspondence Books, 1722–3 to 1786–7, PAC HBC B 239/b/ 3–48

York Factory Post Journals, 1715 to 1774–5, PAC HBC B 239/a/ 1–61

Index

Acculturation, *see* economic dependency

Agriculture: adoption by Indians 218–19; in Red River 206–7

Albany River (Eitayikytchidyanus) 6–9

Alcohol, trade of 85–7, 142–6, 148–9, 154–5; in gift-exchanges 142; trade restricted 197–8, 214 n10 and 15

Alimbegouek Indians, *see* Cree

Allouez, Father 9

Ammunition, trade of 87, 148, 155; *see also* gunpowder and shot

Archecadrene Indians, *see* Gros Ventre

Archithinue Indians, *see* Blackfoot

Assiniboine Indians (Assiniboils, Assinipoualak, Senipoett, Sinnepoet, Stone)

divisions of: Canoe 95; Eagle 157; Eagle Eyed 16–18, 26 n39; Eagle Hill 95–6; Foot 94–6; Gens du Pied 161, 179 n16; Grand River 171; Little Girl 94–5; Mountain Poet 25 n22; Paddling 94–5; Plains (Southern Senipoett) 17, 20, 53; Pw Sym a

Wock 157; Rabbit 95; Red River 95; Rocky 95–6; Swampy Ground 171; Those Who Have Water for Themselves Only 95–6; Woodland (Northern Senipoett, Strongwood) 17, 19–20, 53, 98, 179 n16

location of: in the seventeenth century 4–13; (1700–63) 12–23, 25 n35, 42–3; (1763–1821) 94–8, 101; (after 1821) 183–4

migrations of 19, 21, 94, 104, 182

population of 105–6, 111, 113, 114–15 n30, 187, 192, 193 n5 and 8

and smallpox 183, 191

separate from Sioux 3–6, 24 n9

allied with: Cree 12, 18; Ojibwa 18

at war with: Beaver Indians 21; Blackfoot 21, 104; Chipewyan 19–21; Sioux 5–6, 14–15, 104; Mandan 104; Muscotay 21; Sarsi 21

as trappers 12–13, 132–3; as middlemen 13, 59, 61, 68–70, 87–91, 126; as provision suppliers 131–5 trade: at York Factory 12–13, 20, 53, 57, 60–1; with Blackfoot 90; with Mandan 37–8, 40, 88–9

Assinipoualacus River, *see* Pigeon River

Assinipoualak Indians, *see* Assiniboine

Ashkee Indians, *see* Gros Ventre

Axes, trade of 81, 83, 87–8, 90, 92 n8, 145–7, 151; *see also* metal goods

Band leaders: traditional authority of 137; efforts to increase status of 137–40

Bas de la Rivière 128

Beads: trade of 80, 85, 87, 148–9, 156; *see also* luxury goods

Bear meat: preparation of 223; consumption of 230–1 n26

Beaver: as food 27, 199; exhaustion of 117–18; trapping moratoriums proposed 118, 199–200; quotas introduced 200–2; returns of 200, 202

Beaver Indians 21

Bison 28, 35, 42, 135; annual cycle of 33; seasonal migrations of 31–2; ranges of 177–8, 223–5

Blackduck focus, ethnic identity of 3, 23 n2; characteristics of 32–5

Blackfoot Indians (Archithinue, Earchithinue) 70–1 n9; location of 20, 22, 101, 104, 184; population of 191; at war with Assiniboine and Cree 21, 104, 226; trade at York Factory 55, 59–60; trade with Assiniboine and Cree 90, 156

Blankets: trade of 79–81, 87, 92 n7, 146–9, 154–6

Blood Indians, location of 20, 71 n16, 104; population of 191–2; trade at

York Factory 55, 59–61; at Fort George 140–1

Brandon House 147–54

Brandy, trade of, *see* alcohol

Brazil tobacco, trade of, *see* tobacco

Buffalo, hide and robe trade 182, 210–12, 216

Canoes 60, 157–9, 162; built for trading companies 134–5

Captain's outfit 139–40, 196, 163 n8, 213–14

Caribou, woodland 27–8, 48 n1, 121–2, 217

Carlton House 147–54

Chiefs, Indian, *see* band leaders

Chipewyan Indians (Northern Indians): location of 20, 98, 101, 184; at war with Assiniboine and Cree 19–21, 98; trade at York Factory 59; at Fort Churchill 59

Churchill River (Michinipi River) 53, 70 n1

Circees, *see* Sarsi

Cloth, trade of 79–80, 82, 87, 146–8, 151, 154–6, 164 n28

Cocking, Mathew 44–5

Comparative standard, *see* standards of trade

Competition, intensity of 51–3, 125–6, 195; effects on culture change 144–5; on resource base 117–19

Conservation program of Hudson's Bay Company 199–204; Indian reactions to 201–2

Consumer demand: of Indians 68–9, 141–2; *see also* trade goods

Credit: use of 137–8; Indian abuse of 138, tightened 196–7

Cree Indians (Christinaux, Cristinaux,

Kilistinon, Southern Indians)
divisions of: Alimbegouek (Nipigon)
12; Beaver Hill 185-6; Carlton
House 185-6; Coteau de Prairie
185-6; Cote's Band 222; Eagle
Hill 185-6; Edmonton House
185-6; Fort Pitt 185-6; Grand
Soteau's band 171, 179 n19; Jackfish
Lake 185-6; Michinipi (Misshenipee, Misshenepih) 20, 53; Moose
Jaw 185-6; Moose Mountain
185-6; Moose Woods 185-6;
Plains Cree 99-101, 184-6; Rattlesnake's band 221-2; Snake Portage--
Lac la Biche 185-6; Sturgeon 17,
20, 40-3, 49 n31; Swampy 35-6,
85; Vermilion River 185-6; Woodland 99, 171-2, 184-6
location of: in the seventeenth
century 4, 11-13; (1700-63) 16-23;
(1763-1821) 98-101; (after 1821)
184-6
migrations of 19, 22-3, 94, 98,
102-4, 182-3
population of 109-13, 187, 191-2,
193 n8 and 10
allied with: Assiniboine 5, 12, 18;
Ojibwa 18
at war with, Chipewyan 19-21, 98;
Sioux 14, 104; Gros Ventre 98
serve as, trappers 12-13, 102;
middlemen 13, 59, 61-70, 90-1,
126; provisioners 102, 134
trade: at York Factory 13, 53, 55,
60-1; with Blackfoot 90-1; with
Ottawa 12
Cristinaux Indians, see Cree
Crow Indians 56-7, 71 n12
Cumberland House 126, 128, 148-53
Cypress Hills, a neutral ground 226; a

game refuge 226, hunting pressures
in 227

Deer, see caribou
de Noyon, Jacques 11
Dog 161, 165 n54, 225
Double standard, see standards
of trade
Droughts, effects on fur-bearing
animals 120-1
Druilettes, Father Gabriel 6-7
du Creux, Father François 6-9
du Lhut (Duluth), Daniel Greysolon:
meets Assiniboine on Lake
Superior 11; builds post on Lake
Nipigon 11, 51-2
Duluth, see du Lhut

Eagle-Eyed Indians, see Assiniboine
Eagle Indians, see Assiniboine
Earchithinue Indians, see Blackfoot
Economic dependency, of parkland-
grassland Indians 147-57; of wood-
land-parkland Indians 147-57, 164
n31, 225
Eitayikytchidyanus River, see Albany
River

Factor's standard, see standards of
trade
Files, trade of 81, 84; see also metal
goods
Firearms, trade of 19-21, 22-3, 25
n30, 73-8, 87-8, 146, 151, 156; de-
gree of dependence upon 19-21,
73-8
Fisher 27
Flour, gifts of 196, trade of 206-9
Flying posts 224
Focus, definition of 23 n1

Food preferences 199, 222–3

Food resources: spatial variations of 27–30; temporal variations 29–32; shortages in the woodlands 121–3, 126–8, 217–21; *see also* fur trade, provision market of

Fort à la Corne, Assiniboine and Cree trade at 90–1

Fort Bourbon, *see* York Factory

Fort Paskoyac, Assiniboine and Cree trade at 91

Fort Union 212

'Free resources' 203

French: blocked from Hudson Bay 51; expand inland 11, 14–16, 51–3; effect on York Factory trade 90–1, 92 n3 and 9

Fur resources: of woodlands 27; of grasslands 28; of parklands 28; exhaustion of 118–21, 198–204, 123 n5

Fur trade, changing ecological base of 126; provision market of 126–32, 206–9, 216 n39, 224–5

Game resources 27–9; exhaustion of 121–3, 172, 217–21

Gift-exchange ceremonies, traditional function of 65–8; changing role of 137–9; value of 141, 163 n8, 196–7

Grand Soteau's Band, *see* Cree

Gros Ventre Indians (Archecadrenes, Ashee, Ashkee) 21, 70, n5, 158–9; location of 12, 104, 170; trade at York Factory 55; at war with Assiniboine and Cree 98

Gunpowder, trade of 74, 78–9, 87–8, 146, 148, 152

Guns, *see* firearms

Hatchets, *see* axes

Henday, Anthony 89–91

Hennepin, Father Louis 11

Hidatsa Indians (Mountain) 55–7

Home Guard, *see* Cree, Swampy

Horses 49 n26, 59–60, 88, 90, 156–62

Ice chisels, trade of 81, 84, 87, 92 n8, 147, 152, 154; *see also* metal goods

Imperial plan of 1763 125, 135 n2

Inoculation, *see* smallpox

Issati Indians, *see* Sioux

Jérémie, Nicholas 19

Kelsey, Henry 12, 39–40

Keskatchewan Indians 20, 57

Kettles, trade of 81–5, 87–91, 145, 152, 156, 163 n19

Kiliston Indians, *see* Cree

Kilistonum River, *see* Nipigon River

Knives, trade of 81, 84, 87–90, 148, 152, 155–6; *see also* metal goods

Lac Alimibegyeci, *see* Lake Nipigon

Lac des Assiniboils, *see* Lake of the Woods

Lac des Cristinaux, *see* Rainy Lake

Lac la Peche (Fish Lake, Saskatchewan) 173, 180 n28

Lac Tecamamiouen, *see* Rainy Lake

Lake Michinipi, *see* Reindeer Lake

Lake Nipigon (Alemipigon, Alembegyeci) 6–9, 11

Lake of the Assiniboine, *see* Lake of the Woods

Lake of the Woods, identified as Lake of the Assiniboine 11–12, 16, 25 n35

Lake Superior, account of the geography of 8–10

Land tenure among Indians 203, 215 n26

La Vérendrye: builds posts 52–3; describes economies of Assiniboine and Cree 36–9; discusses nature of Assiniboine-Mandan trade 87–9; peace-making efforts of 18

Liquor, *see* alcohol

Luxury goods, trade of 85, 87, 146

Lynx 118, 200

MacBride site 3

Made Beaver currency 61–2

Mandan Indians (Mountain): trade at York Factory 55–7, 60, 89; trade with Assiniboine 87–9

Manitoba focus, *see* Blackduck focus

Marten 27, 117–18, 200, 224

Measles 106–8, 110

Metal goods: trade of 81–5, 90, 148, 155; *see also* specific goods

Métis: population of 205, 215 n33; Red River hunts of 206; as provisioners 206; Indian attitude toward 231 n37

Michinipi Indians, *see* Cree

Middlemen: emergence of 59–61; trading practices of 69, 91, 144; bypassed 102, 104, 126

Mink 27, 224

Misshenipee Indians, *see* Cree

Missouri River, posts on 211

Moose 121–3, 124 n21, 168, 217

Mountain Indians, *see* Hidatsa, Mandan

Mountain Poet Indians, *see* Assiniboine

Mule deer 28

Muscotay Indians, *see* Blackfoot

Muskrat 27, 30–1, 118, 121, 200

Nelson River 13

Nipigon River 6–9

Northern Indians, *see* Chipewyan

Northern Sinepoett Indians, *see* Assiniboine

Norway House 128

North West Company 125–6; and York Factory trade 126, 135 n3; merges with HBC 195

Official Standard of Trade, *see* standards of trade

Ogoki River 7, 9

Ojibwa Indians

location of (1700–63) 18–23; (1763–1821) 101–3; (after 1821) 180 n33, 184, 187

population of 110–13, 181 n36, 193 n7

allied with Assiniboine and Cree 18; at war with Sioux 104; trade at York Factory 61; horticulture 177; social organization of 175

Ottawa Indians 167

Otter 27

Overplus 58, 65

Piegan Indians: population of 191–2; trade at Fort George 140–1

Pigeon River Indians (Assinipoualacus) 6–8, 10

Pink, William 43–4

Poett Indians, *see* Sioux

Population: southern Manitoba 163 n24, 175–6, 181 n36 and 37; differential growth rates 191–2; *see also* specific groups

Pounds, bison 169, 171–2, 179, 220

Pronghorn antelope 28

Provision market, *see* fur trade

Rainy Lake (Lac des Cristinaux, Lac Tecamamiouen) 11, 18, 128–9
Raisins, gifts of 196
Red deer 28, 49 n30, 122–3, 222–3, 230 n23
Red River carts 215, 216 n34
Red River colony, 217–18
Red River hunts, see Métis
Red River: tribal buffer zone 18, 177; game refuge 177
Reindeer Lake 50, 70 n1
Rice 196
Rum, see alcohol

Sarcee Indians, see Sarsi
Sarsi Indians (Sarcee, Shussuanna, Shusuanna, Su Hannah, Susuhannah, Sussou): population of 191–2; at war with Assiniboine 21; trade at York Factory 57–9; at Fort George 140–1
Seasonal cycles of activity and migration: in southern Manitoba 35–9, 46–7, 167, 174–8, 180 n27, 217; in Saskatchewan River valley 166–8, 170–2, 178, 179 n15 and 17; in western Manitoba, central Saskatchewan, and Alberta 39–48, 167–70, 172–74, 219–25
Second-hand trade 87; see also middlemen
Selkirk focus: associated with Cree 3; distribution of 3–4; characteristics of 32–5
Senipoett Indians, see Assiniboine
Shot, trade of 76–9, 87–8, 146, 153; see also ammunition
Shusuanna Indians, see Sarsi
Simpson, Governor George 195–203
Sioux Indians (Poetts), allied with the French 14; at war with Assiniboine-Cree-Ojibwa 5–6, 14–15, 104
Slave Indians 104
Smallpox (1780–1) 105–6, 110; (1838) 183, 187–91; (1869) 191–2; Indian reaction to 105–6; and wildlife 119–20; vaccination and inoculation 188–92, 194 n22
Smith, Joseph 40–3
Southern Indians, see Cree
Southern Sinepoett Indians, see Assiniboine
Standards of trade, comparative standard 62; double (factor's) standard 63; official standard 62, 66–7; Indian attitudes toward 62–4
Stone Indians, see Assiniboine
Store food 225
Strange Indians 57
Sturgeon Indians, see Cree
Sugar 196
Sugar-making 168, 179 n8 and 9
Su Hannah Indians, see Sarsi
Susuhannah Indians, see Sarsi
Sweet Grass, Chief 227

Tailrace Bay site 3
Tea 196
The Pas 45
Tobacco: types traded 143–4; quantities 85–7, 153; importance of 87, 91, 142–4, 148, 155; given as gifts 142, 146, 196
Trade goods
  types demanded by: Assiniboine 85–7, 155; Cree 87, 93 n20, 155–6; Ojibwa 87, 155–6; Parkland-Grassland Indians 85–91, 146–55; Woodland Indians 85–7, 146–8
  relative costs of 66–7, 141, 143–5

Traps 147
Treaties 228
Tulerimia 31

Upland Indians 20, 53

Waggoner, Joseph 40–3
Wapiti, *see* red deer
War Road River 18

Warkesews, *see* red deer
Waskesews 41, 49 n30
Whooping cough 106–8
Wild rice 27, 29, 30, 31, 129, 135 n9

xy Company 126

York Factory 51–62